MUSKIE
OF
MAINE

MUSKIE OF MAINE

David Nevin

Random House
New York

Library of Congress Cataloging in Publication Data

Nevin, David, 1927–
 Muskie of Maine.

 1. Muskie, Edmund S., 1914–   I. Title.
E840.8.M85N4   973.924'0924 [B]   72-159361
ISBN 0-394-48086-3

Selections from Duane Lockard, New England State Politics (copyright © 1959 by Princeton University Press): pp. 79 and 105. Reprinted by permission of Princeton University Press.
Grateful acknowledgment is extended to Schroder Music Co. for permission to reprint lines from "Little Boxes," words and music by Malvina Reynolds, copyright © 1962 by Schroder Music Co. (ASCAP), used by permission.

Manufactured in the United States of America by The Book Press, Brattleboro, Vt.

9 8 7 6 5 4 3 2

First Printing

For my father
Colonel Stanley McLeod Nevin, U.S. Army,
1897–1971

All of us are sorting out our values. We are in one of the great periods of ferment in our country's history, one of the great potentially creative periods, out of which could emerge an entirely different relationship between Americans, between Americans and their government, between Americans and other human beings in other parts of the world. These new relationships, whether new institutions can be formed to house them and new policies generated to reflect them, depends on how Americans deal with this current period of ferment and creativity.

EDMUND S. MUSKIE, Los Angeles, 1970

. . . the outcome of many changes being fought over may someday be summed as historian Allan Nevins described two earlier passages of national turbulence: "Roosevelt's so-called revolution, though unprecedentedly broad and swift, was like Jefferson's "revolution"; it was simply a combination of numerous practical changes, the main test of which was whether or not it worked." As with the citizens of those periods, a central question for the seventies is whether we can and will assimilate a "revolution" without feeling threatened and insecure. The culture and politics and peace of the country will depend heavily on how that is resolved and on whether the resulting public mood is one of buoyancy or an enervating fear that things are coming unstuck.

FREDERICK G. DUTTON, *Sources of Changing Power*, 1971

CONTENTS

MUSKIE
OF
MAINE

1

The
Candidate I

When Edmund Sixtus Muskie was nominated for the Vice Presidency of the United States in 1968, the reaction to him was pleasant and entirely uncritical. He was unknown. His name had meaning only to political sophisticates and people from Maine. He ran for an office that may be only a heartbeat from the real thing but to which most people have given no more importance than have its various occupants. He was a captive of a situation for which he was not responsible and which he could not change. People vote for Presidents, not Vice Presidents, so nothing really serious could develop, and they settled back to enjoy a new face and a personality they found warm and attractive.

One might imagine that campaigns are organized months in advance with the party machinery poised to serve whomever the convention chooses. Neither is true. All is disorganization and in the sense that "machinery" implies structure and continuity, there is no such thing. After a late Democratic convention in which there long had been the possibility but never the certainty that he would be chosen, Muskie found there was no staff, no schedule, no plans, no policies and no themes for his campaign. He called together a few associates, and while he went off to Maine to get ready they constructed an instant campaign. They forged a schedule; assembled an impromptu staff and a small corps of advance men; evolved systems for the complex matter of moving a hundred people (including press) around the country —feeding, bedding and getting them back to the plane on time; developed a communications system; established liaison with Vice President Hubert H. Humphrey's Presidential campaign; and rented a Boeing 727 jet aircraft, which they called *The Downeast Yankee*. On the campaign's first day Muskie flew to San Antonio and spoke before the Alamo, not because it was a good place to begin, though it was, but because a priest of Polish extraction, Father Erwin A. Juraschek, had called him in Maine to invite him.

It was haphazard and frantic, but Muskie enjoyed himself because wherever he went people seemed to respond to him. This was the first time he had campaigned for himself outside of Maine, he told one audience, and he found it very heartening. At first when the plane stopped and he came out the door he could hear people asking, "Which one is he?" But Muskie was catching on: soon when the tall figure appeared there were ragged little cheers and then he would grin with pleasure and wave. People responding to his calm, steady, pleasant way and his tart Maine humor had no way of knowing that it was also a time of real tension for Muskie. He was feeling his way, testing his ability to function nationally as he had in Maine, and his comfortable rapport with the crowds was interspersed with flashes of anger and hours of gloomy meditation spent staring from the window of *The Downeast Yankee*.

The odd and rather bemused excitement that he began to generate in the country probably started on September 25, 1968, at Washington, Pa., when Muskie suddenly invited a student heckler to the platform and gave him ten minutes to speak. It appeared a matter of impulse and caught everyone by surprise, though in fact it was a tactic that Muskie had thought out carefully. He had even offered it to Humphrey, who then was being bullyragged by angry students from coast to coast. Typically, Humphrey liked the idea but had done nothing with it. A few days later at a street rally in Washington, Pa., Muskie encountered mild heckling and said equally that he would try to speak "if you'll give me the chance." Someone shouted, "You have a chance. We don't!" Muskie paused, smiled with a look of inspiration and told them to choose a spokesman and send him up. The student, a long-haired, bespectacled young man named Rick Brody of Washington & Jefferson College (where the faculty remembers him with disapproving frowns: "He wasn't representative of *our* students") made a creditable but not dynamic speech. Muskie, now completely engaged, made one of his best speeches, and his best is very good. By chance it fell on a quiet newsday, and newspapers and television played it heavily.

Muskie was delighted with the attention, which he always enjoys, but what really caught his interest was the fact that both sides of the controversy approved warmly. Young people who felt cut out of that unhappy campaign saw that Muskie had given them a chance to be heard. People who disapproved of the young, however, found little of value in what Brody said and concluded that the effect had been to expose the emptiness of the young. See, older people told Muskie all over America, I knew they didn't really have anything to say. The fact of the matter actually is a bit more subtle than that, however, and relates to the difficulty the two sides have in understanding each other. Brody's speech cut instinctively to the heart of what disturbs the people of the new culture—the feeling that a political system which does not place first importance on human values cannot really represent human beings. The people of the old culture, who blandly accept that conclusion without in the least perceiving the agonized premise from which it grows, heard nothing to inspire or dismay them in what Brody said and thus dismissed him.

As the campaign continued, Muskie grew steadily in the friendly if not very concerned estimation of the American people, who saw in him some of the quiet freshness that Eugene McCarthy first brought to that political year. Muskie suggested directness and homespun integrity and apolitical candor. He was a relief. At a time when polls showed Humphrey lagging far behind Richard M. Nixon, a poll by Louis Harris put Muskie seventeen points ahead of Spiro Agnew. By the end of the campaign the smart thing to say was that the Democrats should have reversed their ticket, though this merely reflected the campaign's emptiness. Muskie had not really become popular in his own right; he was still essentially an unknown profiting by contrast. Humphrey took generous pleasure in Muskie's appeal, called attention to him constantly, and as the campaign closed insisted that Muskie join him in Los Angeles for the final telethon. Muskie, who can be very stubborn, resisted the idea. He was going home to Maine, where he belonged, for the rally in the armory at Lewiston where he always finishes a campaign. He did not finally agree until Larry O'Brien, then managing Humphrey's campaign, called him directly and, half pleading and half demanding, cast it in terms of duty. Muskie moved the Lewiston rally up a day, gave a long, gentle, friendly speech, slept a few hours, flew to Los Angeles, joined the telethon (across the networks, Nixon was alone), and then returned to his plane and flew all night so that, as always, he could vote when the polls opened in Maine and then wait out the returns surrounded by old friends and familiar reedy accents as a tide of cold air seeped in from the north in warning of winter to come. He sat most of that night in a dove-gray suit with a carnation in his buttonhole silently watching the chance that always had been narrow slip away to nothing, and the next morning, face puffy but serene, he stood in the sunshine with a little group of supporters and told a handful of reporters how he felt. "I've always found that the turns life takes work out quite well," he said. If the road goes in one direction, there's no point in crying for the other —you take the curves as they come. Someone shouted, "Muskie for President!" and Muskie grinned and went off to play golf.

There was no way to know then if the interest he had generated would sustain itself, but by the time he returned to Washington, signs were pouring in—letters, offers to help, invitations to speak. The first speech he gave was in Dallas and the first question he was asked upon arrival was, "Who will be the Democratic nominee in 1972?" The new campaign began as soon as the old one ended. This was most unusual and the reason for it probably lies in the interim quality that Nixon brought to his campaign and continued in his Presidency. It was as if people understood in some instinctive way that new directions were coming and chose a standby figure while they sorted out what those new directions might be.

This interest that should still have been dormant translated itself into real demand. He had not even decided that he wanted to run for the Presidency, let alone that he had a chance. In calmer times he might have engaged in a simple testing of his relationship with the American people, a pleasant exploration of its possibilities. Instead he was drawn into a pace so swift that it resembled a campaign but had none of a formal campaign's advantages. It was a difficult and uncomfortable time for Muskie, who values the thoughtful, steady, reasonable approach. In 1969, while maintaining a full Senate role (he answered 90 percent of the roll-call votes that year) he also was running on what became a national treadmill, hurtling around the country in response to demand rather than to reason, to invitations rather than to his own schedule. He was always tired, usually late—and it was so frustratingly *unplanned*.

Even more important, however, was the effect of this pace on his passion for thoroughness. Thoroughness in dealing with the substance of government had been basic to Muskie's success as governor of Maine and in the Senate, and it suited his nature as well. Of course when he moved to the national level, he took these attitudes with him. He wanted every speech and position researched and analyzed. When he criticized he wanted an alternative policy thought out, developed and ready to offer. But Muskie still had no political resources beyond his Senate staff and the income from speaking fees, since he would not accept campaign contributions until he had a campaign. At the national level his demands for substantive thoroughness placed greater burdens on himself and his staff than they could meet. More than any other thing, more than the pace, the confusion, the chronic exhaustion, Muskie was frustrated in this period because he was running on instinct when his nature, his habit and the force of his career had been to act only on positions developed with great care.

This quality of acute discomfort rarely showed in public, because crowds, audiences and political action are tonic for him and immediately improve his mood.

It really was a matter of growth. He was still a senator, prospecting in the fields of leadership; when he became a leader, considerably later, he operated much more comfortably on instinct and on the broad application of principle. And as he followed the demand, accepting invitations, arriving, speaking, answering questions and flying on again, simply playing out his string to see what would happen, his style and personality were taking root in the American mind. The pleasant image of 1968 was taking on flesh. There were no sudden bursts. Muskie just grew on a lot of people. He was still candid and fresh, a big man who came through as solid and strong. He was thoughtful, intelligent and seemed to know what he was talking about, not extreme but always on the side of decency. You could trust him, many people felt intuitively, he was comfortable and worthwhile and inspired your confidence, and if he wasn't highly exciting, still he was attractive and cool. He simply kept moving, being himself, doing what there was to be done, and his image gradually took hold.

In the meantime, however, Muskie's expanding relationship with the people was hardly noticed by the national press, the party professionals and the politically aware, who had already awarded the 1972 nomination to Edward M. Kennedy despite the anguished signals of reluctance he sent out so regularly. In 1968, after the second assassination of a brother, Kennedy had said the year was not right for him. He said that again in early 1969 and was still saying it in mid-1971. The embers of Presidential ambition are always subject to rekindling, but considering the trauma and pain that he and his family have suffered, considering the dangers and the weight of family responsibility, considering his youth and the awesome odds involved in not two but three brothers being struck of Presidential material, the desire to wait that he expressed seemed as thoroughly reasonable as it was thoroughly ignored. The situation changed only after the accident at Chappaquiddick Island in the summer of 1969. Kennedy formally removed himself from contention and for a while people had to take him at his word.

Kennedy was out, McCarthy was going on retreat, Humphrey had not yet resurrected himself, McGovern was hardly moving, and Muskie emerged as the clear front runner, a position he has held ever since. There was some consternation among the press and party professionals, who confidently announced that Muskie was ahead only in the absence of a real candidate, but in the meantime Muskie was moving into a commanding position with a broad mass of the American people. Statistically the force of that movement is best seen in measurement against a sitting President. In May 1969, before Chappaquiddick, the Louis Harris poll gave Muskie 33 preference points against President Nixon's 51 points. By October of that year Muskie was up to 35, and by November the President was down to 49. In May 1970 Muskie had 38 points, the President 42. By September 1970, long before the national telecast on Election Eve that drove Muskie well ahead for months, he and President Nixon ranked 43–43.

This consistent rise in the polls is the more significant because he was on his own. Muskie had no national standing to carry him; he was unknown before 1968. At that time, for instance, as major national figures, Humphrey dated from the Democratic National Convention of 1948, and Nixon from the Hiss case in 1949; and Kennedy was heir to the Camelot legacy. Though newer, George Wallace and McCarthy rode narrow but very cohesive minorities, as had Barry Goldwater in 1964. Not only was Muskie painfully new on the national scene, his only accomplishment had been to lose a campaign for a secondary office.

Furthermore, it was a long time before Muskie began doing very purposeful things to enhance his position. It was more than six months after Chappaquiddick and fifteen months after the 1968 election before he committed himself in his own mind to try for the prize, and longer still before he set his campaign in motion. As this rise in the national polls took place, Muskie continued to move about the country being himself, answering questions with open candor, making quietly sensible speeches and gradually impressing an ever-widening range of people. He was what he was, the same man to whom they had been drawn in 1968; he simply was growing.

By late 1971 Muskie had moved far beyond being the quiet man making his political rounds and investigating his opportunities. He had emerged as a full-force candidate running hard for the nomination. Though every campaign is crisis-prone and Muskie's was no exception, by this time he had a sound political operation and a restructured staff, and was keeping a punishing schedule that at least tried to use his time to full value. The exploratory figure of 1969 had become a commanding political personality.

As this change took place, however, the uncritical and even innocent reception given Muskie at the beginning faded away. Almost as soon as he began moving on the real prize, there appeared a strain of criticism that has persisted ever since. Thus a surprising division has arisen in the view in which Muskie is held. In time it has become a genuine dichotomy of reaction to a man who is himself complicated and difficult to understand. It is important because while it has had little effect on his standing in the polls, it has produced a deeply disturbing intellectual response to his candidacy. This dichotomy of view is most easily seen as a split between two distinct groups. On the one hand there is the broad mass of people whose approval of Muskie has held him consistently high in the polls; on the other, a group of people who can be called the politically aware.

The term "politically aware" is useful for describing a group that will recognize itself readily enough and yet is too loose to bear more specific definition. It is that group of people who are concerned with politics and politicians on a daily basis, who study issues and follow careers and keep count of men's positions, who feel consistently involved and generally reponsible for the way our public life is conducted. They are above average in awareness, often in education and sometimes in income. They include people of every occupation and begin with those who simply read good newspapers carefully and keep themselves informed. Their more active and vocal side draws heavily on the academic and intellectual world, on politically awakened students, on a segment of the legal industry, on much of the national press and on the communications industry with its mélange of advertising, entertainment and information revolving around its passion for personalities. Though they exist in every community in America (sometimes as embattled outposts), the politically aware tend to center on the coasts, from Washington to Boston, from Los Angeles to San Francisco. They do not hold the country's financial power or control its commerce, but they do help shape its opinions. Those we describe are liberals (a conservative counterpart lies across the spectrum), and they include a radical fringe that extend out to the modern version of anarchy. Generally, however, they are sensible liberals committed to change within the system because no better system appears to exist, and they struggle to retain their faith that American politics actually can respond to change in time to deal with it.

One cannot even assess their numbers accurately, let alone their influence, which is obviously far out of proportion to their numbers. In New Hampshire and in succeeding primaries in 1968, McCarthy's young followers demonstrated the enormous capacities of the politically aware when they organize and focus their energies. Their effect on the Democratic Party as a whole in 1968 is further evidence of their power when aroused. More specifically, they provide what Joseph L. Rauh, Jr., calls "the intensity factor in politics." Writing in an Americans for Democratic Action publication, he added, "The liberals do the work in the Democratic Party, and if they're not steamed up . . . Democratic candidates just don't make it." He believes it was the liberals' refusal to work rather than their refusal to vote that defeated Humphrey in 1968.

As for their broader influence, the argument for the effect of just one group, the intellectuals, suggests the pattern for the whole. Intellectuals generate many of the ideas, theories, analyses, attitudes and much of the research or source material that fuel the political activists and fill the intellectual and political journals and the editorial and opposite-editorial pages of the better newspapers. This in turn influences leaders of all kinds (including those of business and politics) all over the country, the press, the communications industry as a whole and people everywhere who are in the habit or the business of talking to other people about things beyond their daily affairs. The ultimate extension of this force probably lies in the televised comments of the activist entertainer, whose opinion on the state of the nation is guaranteed acceptance by the number of people who saw his latest film. The importance of all this is not so much the direct effect it might have on the housewife in Dayton as the momentum it can give ideas or political figures. And for a political figure, momentum can be nearly everything. It is often a cruel roundelay: momentum implies excitement, excitement means crowds, crowds mean coverage, coverage leads to financial backing, and financial backing makes possible the things necessary to maintain momentum. Enough momentum, of course, can lead right into the Presidential nomination.

And these people, the politically aware, complain about Muskie. They suspect he is soft on the great issues and sometimes, they wonder if his positions are purposely spongy and ill-defined in order to cover the broadest spectrum and thus offend the fewest people. They question his commitment to issues they consider paramount. All this frustrates Muskie, who, in fact, is solid on the issues that concern the politically aware. Sometimes when questioners squeezed him, Muskie would snap, "I don't think you go in sixteen years from small-town lawyer to contender for the Presidential nomination by lacking courage and refusing to take chances, by refusing to deal with issues." Eventually, however, he stopped making the retort, for while it was accurate, it did not help because it did not deal with the real problem. People continued to ask, "Why doesn't he speak out on this, Why doesn't he act on that, Why doesn't he do something about this? And he, flushing, would say, Goddammit, I *did* speak out on this or that. Ah, they would say, then why didn't I hear it?

That is the question, all right, and the answers to it go to the heart of Muskie's problem. For what is really being sought is not just propriety on the issues and stances invariably on the side of right, but a visceral sense of commitment, a pull of leadership that surges in the gut. The politically aware want, in other words, what everyone else wants: leadership that touches a follower's blood and assures him that the man who leads has a sense for the way.

So it is not enough to be right on the issues and right in attitudes. It is not for the followers to seek out leadership but for the leader to impose it upon them. Muskie has not managed to do so with this important group, but neither has he fully failed. On its surface the dichotomy appears simply to lie between the mass of the people who support Muskie and the politically aware, but its extension is even more important: it exists still more acutely *within the group of the politically aware itself.* If these people did not also feel the pull that Muskie exerts, they would not bother to question him; the sense of his leadership has not missed them completely, for it is what brings them to their examination, which in turn sets up their complaints.

The problem falls generally between the matter of simply perceiving a political figure and the act of examining him. The mass of the people perceive the man; they make an intuitive judgment that may not be thought out but is as genuine and often as sound as an intellectual judgment. Though the politically aware

are moved by these same perceptions, made in the same fashion, they take the further and in effect opposite step of subjecting the man to examinations which produce judgments that are rational instead of perceptual. It is the difference between those who examine politicians with their hearts and those who do so with their minds, and the ambivalence of the politically aware is that they do both.

It is a serious matter. It is personally disturbing to Muskie, who believes the criticism unjustified, and in political terms it is potentially dangerous. It exposes him to an undercurrent of hostility from people whose "opinion-making power is formidable," as one of its members, Susan Sheehan, described it in the *New York Times Magazine,* and from whom he deserves better on the simple basis of what he stands for. But this response also is Muskie's own fault, for it is a logical outgrowth of his nature. It is not a mistake or a simple misunderstanding on the part of the politically aware. Each of its seemingly opposite sides springs naturally from what Muskie is and its resolution lies in fully understanding his complexity, which few people do beyond his family and staff. In a political year that is likely to be more volatile than ever, therefore, it is important to see how each side of this dichotomy of view has developed.

Muskie's growth from tentative candidate to commanding political personality in three years was gradual, steady and not at all easy. The discomfort he plainly felt in this period came much more from the pain of growth than from the criticism he heard. It is an oddity of his nature, one that we will explore at length, that his growth tends to be in response to the situation before him rather than to internal thrusts of ambition. From the beginning of his career he has risen as necessary to expand within the situation, and at the same time the parameters of the situation have tended to contain his growth. Before 1968 his arena was the U.S. Senate and he grew within its boundaries. After 1968, for the first time in his life, his arena was national and thus unlimited. This is the most difficult and perilous and the least charted of all arenas.

There are no guides or standards. Each man's national leadership is his own, never transferable, impossible to imitate, succeeding or failing according to what he is and to the temper of the times. One simply feels one's way, testing the ground, reaching out somewhat blindly to people whose numbers have become so great that no man could hope to see or touch or directly influence them all—and awaiting their response.

American politics provides no leadership structure for the opposition and even less for out-of-office figures who might aspire to leadership. The President is a leader by definition, even if he doesn't lead; the White House as platform constitutes leadership, and there is no other real national platform. As to the Senate, though at the present time most Democratic Presidential aspirants are among its members, and though the Senate is rich in prestige, it is made up of a hundred separate power centers which form fragile and temporary alliances keyed to particular issues and which recognize no leadership but that of the Senate itself. Any senator may answer a President, but few would delegate to one of their fellows that honor and the focus of national attention that would follow.

Muskie has moved about the country offering himself on the one hand and reaching for people on the other in a contest between the force of his nature and the force of his growth. The leadership struggle pitted his essential need for exposure against his unwillingness to thrust himself forward in rude self-seeking, which is inconsistent with his nature and therefore probably would be unproductive as well. One of Muskie's key qualities is his desire for a valid platform from which to speak. It is not the Maine way to seize the floor and undertake to impose your views on your fellows. When they want your advice they are likely to ask for it. Throughout his career Muskie has been at his best when he felt that his right to the ground on which he stood was clear to everyone. When he does try to seize attention he is not sure is his due he often looks uncomfortable, which in a political situation is easily mistaken for phoniness. That is one reason Muskie is at his strongest while campaigning and at his weakest while trying to make a political impression between campaigns.

The leadership style which Muskie has developed turns on finding ways to persuade masses of people to view their own interests in the largest possible frame, to see that their interests are related to and ultimately dependent upon everyone else's interests. What sounds simplistic really is simple truth: people so persuaded and shown a way to make things work are lifted toward their best instead of driven toward their worst. But it is a narrow difference between being sufficiently noticeable to attract, and thus lead, and so noticeable as to tire and thus alienate a mass of people. And for a man who prizes the propriety of a valid platform, the trackless plains of national leadership were uncomfortable until his very success and his standing in the polls became in effect a solid platform.

He has considerable political skills, based on ability and years of experience in a difficult school. Maine was an arch Republican state when Muskie began and Republicans still outnumber Democrats. In such a setting a Democrat must be skillful to survive. He is effective in one-to-one political contact. He is an excellent extemporaneous speaker and he comes undiluted through television, that difficult medium that has wrecked so many political careers.

His more important assets, however, are less tangible. He seems to have sense for the feelings and attitudes of a mass of the American people. He has uncommon faith in common people, a quality politicians are more likely to claim than to feel. This may derive from his background in New England town-meeting government styles and the idealism his immigrant father expressed so clearly, but it also comes from his own experience. For much of his political life in Republican Maine, Muskie could not depend upon his party's strength, but had to go to the people, directly, in fair and open ways. They gave him a hearing and the political lesson he thus learned never failed him. It is at the root of his political style.

When Muskie goes to the people, however, he takes with him

a particular capacity for making them understand. Intellectually, it is a matter of penetrating to the core of human experience where things are simple and real. In human terms it is the capacity for showing people the bearing of abstract things on their own lives. Muskie, ever the practical fellow, once described it as "finding the handle to make the reality clear to everyone." And he added, "Reality, you know, is by no means necessarily clear just because it's real. It's usually hidden and the key to making people understand is to find ways to show them the reality in simple and direct terms."

Perhaps Muskie's real achievement in this period after the 1968 election is simply that he remained himself. Considering the pressures of Presidential politics and life in the public eye, this is a feat of strength. Most men are warped by these pressures; ambition and the tantalizing approach to power undermine their native balance and good sense. A man must be strong even to compete in this arena, but even the strong tend to bend bit by bit, here and there, until they no longer are nor even know what their instincts tell them to be—and then they are only what they and their associates hope will succeed.

Muskie has held to what he is. The basic man is still visible. He has been inundated by urgent advice, the more so because a superficial reading of his quiet ways can make him seem a man without real direction. This inspires the naïve to undertake to show him the way. Usually he listens politely to this advice, a curious hardening in his eyes which you only recognize after having watched many people instruct him, and then goes on as before, holding to an inner sense of what is right for him.

Occasionally Muskie strays from this inner sense. When Mississippi state police killed two black students at Jackson State College in the spring of 1970, Muskie hired a jet airliner and took a hundred people to Jackson to see the bullet holes and attend the funeral of one of the victims. It was a splendid gesture. Its motivation was fully consistent with Muskie's feelings and his record, but its flamboyance was unlike him. It disturbed people in Maine, who saw it as self-serving. Muskie says he has no regrets, and in terms of publicly expressing outrage, undoubtedly that is true. But it also is true that he did nothing to continue the move, initiated no investigations of that or the parallel incident at Kent State College in Ohio, and in fact, did nothing else of such conspicuous nature, so that the flight stands out across the years as an unusual flash of color. The flamboyant gesture simply is not Muskie's way.

The point is not that Muskie has remained unchanged but that he has followed a fairly consistent internal standard in making change. He had to grow to survive in the national arena, and in time one could hear this growth in his tone. Until 1968, Muskie's approach to politics had a problem-solving note, marked by the common sense and practical air so prized in Maine. Plans and programs are still key elements of leadership—the problems remain, like ogres that must be faced, and people do not really lose sight of this—but programs alone are not the leadership that people seek in a violent decade when change is overcoming not just practices and institutions but the very relations that men are to have with one another.

Muskie continued to propose programs to deal with problems, but there also crept into his attitudes and his speeches an increasingly evangelical note. It had always been there, straining around the cool edge of practicality, but on the national stage it came into the open, sometimes with high emotional impact, so that he would pause and grin and admit that it might be better suited for the pulpit than the platform. One night in West Virginia in the fall of 1971 he heard a young man sing "The Battle Hymn of the Republic" and was caught by the line, "The truth is marching on." A few nights later in Chattanooga, extemporaneous and in fine voice, Muskie described the doubts that many Americans feel, and sailed on, "What do they want? What do they ask for? They ask for the truth. They want their leaders to speak the truth. They want their government to represent the truth and to fight for it. They want to know the truth about each other. They want to know the truth about our collective wisdom and our collective shortcomings. Americans, I think, want a politics of truth. . . . the truth is that there are millions of Americans today who . . . believe there is no promise in their future. The truth is that Americans, born in this great tradition of humanism, still yield to prejudice and practice discrimination against other Americans. The truth is, having developed patterns and ways of living which reflect these shortcomings and weaknesses, we find it burdensome and difficult and all too often unacceptable to do the uncomfortable things that we must do to right the wrongs of our society. The truth is that although most Americans like to believe that they are decent, and most of them are, nevertheless they find it easy to persuade themselves that there's too much risk, too much danger, in trusting other Americans who are different . . ."

His famed national telecast on Election Eve, 1970, though eloquent and restrained in delivery, was essentially evangelical. It dealt with hard issues only in that it directly chastised President Nixon for the divisive campaign he had waged that year. It was a healing speech, designed to lift people from anger and fear, and was made more effective by contrast with the raw nature of the President's speech which preceded it on all three television channels. It had a huge effect on the country and on Muskie's political affairs, for it was the impossible opportunity. It made him the spokesman for the opposition, a Cinderella-like position brought into existence only momentarily by, ironically, the violence of the Republican campaign. For those fifteen minutes Muskie had a valid platform and an opportunity to exert leadership on a mass of people. It is one of the real marks of his professionalism that he made it all look easy. The speech obviously caught the national mood, for the strength of the response startled even Muskie. He shot well ahead of President Nixon in the polls and stayed there for several months. An audience of just under thirty million people saw the telecast, but most interesting of all were the tests that showed that many people who had missed it had come to believe that in fact they had seen it. It was so widely discussed that they formed mental pictures clear enough to substitute for the real picture.

This incident says a great deal about how the supporting side of the divided view of Muskie has grown. The mass of the people, those who perceive politicians rather than examine them, are not very interested in politics, spend little time thinking about it and usually react to it with boredom, suspicion and irritation. As we have seen, they respond less to a candidate's position on issues than to the man himself, to their estimation of his nature, his character and whether they trust him. The next set of criteria, already well down the scale of significance, is how well they think he can do the job in question, though by this they are less likely to consider background and experience than the impression he gives of ability, intelligence, judgment, self-control. These are all intuitive calculations and, for most voters, issues run a very poor third in their assessments.

A few issues override, of course. The war in Vietnam may have been such an issue—though there is real argument on the point—and it could be again. A failing economy and streets surrendered to muggers certainly are such issues. Occasionally a clumsy candidate will allow a mass of voters to perceive him as wrong on such a question as muggers and then he is finished. But since no candidate *favors* muggers, we are returned immediately to how the voter perceives the candidate and that is judgmental and intuitive and thus man-oriented rather than issue-oriented. In the actuality of real issues, the problems are so complex and therefore so susceptible to straddling that they are quickly vitiated as judgment factors for all but students of public affairs, and most people are thrust right back on their own perceptions.

People who perceive politics and politicians rely on a whole series of glimpses, hints, impulses, fragments of information and impressions. They have hunches and senses about a man. Gradually they decide that they trust him and like him or that they don't, and they rarely know when they arrived at the decision. Occasionally a stray remark or a false step on a position that counts can unhorse a man, but that usually is true only if it confirms or crystallizes a judgment toward which people were moving already. George Romney's famous comment in 1967 that he had supported the war in Vietnam because U.S. officials there had given him "the greatest brainwashing that anybody can get . . ."

was innocuous enough; Romney's real problem was that despite his fine appearance and his record in Michigan, people perceived him as a lightweight. His remark appeared to confirm the judgment, and people as a whole stopped taking him seriously. On the other hand, even such a critical thing as the incident at Chappaquiddick did not destroy Edward M. Kennedy; at most, people simply suspended judgment for a time. The point is that they did and do take Kennedy seriously.

That does not mean, however, that people think much about Kennedy, Muskie or any other politician except when elections force decisions upon them. While preference polls reflect the relative standing of politicians accurately enough, they imply a somewhat false sense of public interest. To show Muskie neck and neck with the President, 43–43, with George Wallace holding his 10 or 11 adherents and the remainder undecided, suggests a whole electorate grimly attentive to the matter, whereas in fact, day in and day out not five in a hundred give thought to any of them. This quality tends to favor Muskie, since he finds it difficult to keep himself in the public limelight between legitimate political situations. The politically aware, who think often of politics and politicians, find it disturbing for a putative leader to drop out of sight, but the mass of the voters hardly notice it. Their interest simply idles until the next time something forces Muskie or some other political leader into their awareness and thus adds something new to the body of their intuition.

These are the people whose approval has propelled Muskie forward. In essence, they seem to feel that Muskie is to be trusted —but this takes a parallel sense: trusted both to do the right thing and to be able to get it done. They find him honest, decent, fair—a solid man, together, whole, who does not seem tailored or ideologically bound or haring after villains they know in their hearts are counterfeit. He speaks in their language and understands their impulses and so they feel easy with him. He appeals to their best instincts, to their hopes instead of to their fears, which is less attractive per se than because he does so in believable ways. There is a quality of restraint and judgment in Muskie, a solidly practical and accomplishing sense, that forces people to take him seriously.

Whatever is coming in America, there are only basic attitudes to deal with it. Liberal government has often failed but no real alternatives have appeared. The new culture sees a new paradigm to come, something that may be less a matter of form of government than of new attitudes toward living together, and that will be a happy day. But in the meantime, today's liberal rhetoric shows a disturbing split between those whose impulse is toward visionary change and those who are interested in making things work. The visionary approach is stimulating, while talk of making things work suggests yielding to old hacks who fear reform will be their finish. But the fact is we do still have to get from here to there.

Sometimes the pressure *of* change seems greater even than the pressure *for* change. Amidst talk of radical improvements which should be made, we daily respond as a matter of course to shattering alterations in living forced on us by change, alterations so vast that they are at once obvious and impenetrable. Such a grossly obvious example as the mass movement to the suburbs illustrates: everyone understands generally what has happened and generally the problems that follow, but few of us have the insight to connect the deteriorating quality of life and our increasing psychic strain to our inability to deal wisely or even at all with this incredible migration. Furthermore, this works both sides of the chasms in society; it is the same alienation that the new culture celebrates as houses "all made of ticky tacky . . . boxes on the hillside," and the old celebrates on Martini Avenue.

It really is a twofold question—how to force change to improve the quality of life for those the society has left behind, and at the same time how to deal with change which in itself is terrifying to a mass of the American people. And because there are no real answers anywhere but only generalities for the transition period from here to there, there is broad comfort in a man who makes both idealism and realism believable.

And yet, it is just such statements as this—unprovable,

ambiguous, generalized—that irritate the politically aware. Muskie exerts the same appeal on politically aware liberals that he does on the broader mass, but when they embark on objective testing, the intangible images of emotional perception fade away and they are brought right back to issues. And Muskie's problem is that an issue-rooted examination focuses on his weaknesses and obscures his assets.

Issue-oriented complaints about Muskie begin with the war in Vietnam. His position, when he finally took it, was clear, argued with vigor and consistent with the general liberal Democratic view that the war was a mistake from which the United States should extract itself as quickly as possible. He supported both McGovern-Hatfield resolutions to end the war and introduced a similar one of his own. We will examine Muskie and the Vietnam question in more detail, but the important point here is that the time for decision was in 1967 or earlier and Muskie did not arrive at his position until late 1969.

He appears to have been somewhat against the war from the beginning. In 1965 he was a member of the second Mansfield mission that warned President Johnson against an open-ended commitment in Vietnam. In early 1968 Muskie wrote Johnson privately, urging him to stop the bombing of North Vietnam, which then was the issue on which opposition to the war turned. Yet at the Democratic National Convention in 1968, Muskie led the debate *for* the administration plank on Vietnam before the platform committee. The difference between the majority or administration plank and the minority or peace plank may have been technically narrow, but in fact it stood as the watershed between repudiating the war or persevering in it until the enemy could be forced to strike a bargain. It was a clear dividing line and Muskie stood on the wrong side. He did not publicly change sides until October 15, 1969, the first Vietnam Moratorium Day, and he let slip an opportunity to make his declaration at noon on the green at Yale University where coverage would have been heavy, and chose instead to speak at night at his alma mater, Bates College, at Lewiston, Maine. The timing happened to be too late for national news roundups, and the speech was noticed generally only in Maine. It was very late to have come to decision. Furthermore there was the nagging and never fully answered question of why he spoke for a plank that in effect endorsed the continued bombing of North Vietnam when months earlier he had been sufficiently against it to write the President twice on the subject.

The whole question of Vietnam has become a source of great anguish for Muskie. The attitudes that guided his actions and conditioned his judgment grew naturally from what he was at the time, but on balance his stand on Vietnam was clearly his greatest misjudgment. Vietnam had become a moral issue, a point he now accepts, and he had continued to treat it as a political issue. This was an occasion when his propensity for getting things done and making things work betrayed him because it obscured his sense of right and wrong. Muskie appears to agree generally with this judgment today: he says now that he considers his past position on the war a mistake and wishes that he had done otherwise. The subject is not one on which many Americans have cause to feel self-righteous, but nevertheless one expects more of a national leader. The fact that he was not a national leader, and had no pretensions to national leadership in 1967 when the decision should have been thought through and made, is not a satisfactory answer.

Though its force as a challenging issue is vitiated by Muskie's admission of error, his earlier position on Vietnam sets the tone for the irritated and suspicious view in which the politically aware hold him. It also provides a way to get at a characteristic which they find troubling but harder to define—the question of his commitment to the other great issues. It is not that he fails on issues per se. He is distinctly and beyond question a liberal. Year after year his voting record has fluctuated around 90 percent on the ratings scaled by Americans for Democratic Action. His quick remark that one hardly rises as he has in the last sixteen years without vigor and courage is valid. When you search his record you find it strong. The problem is that you do have to search, that he fails to project a clear and exciting image in relation to issues.

Again and again one hears people who care about these things complain that they don't know where Muskie stands. The reason they don't know automatically is that although he has been right on the issues over the years, he has not often been a leader in them. He has not expended himself and his political capital year in and year out at the front of the great fights. The reasons that he has not done so are found in his nature, his practice of politics, the quality of his growth, his relations with Maine and a host of other factors that sum up the man—but the end result has been to leave his overall leadership capacities in question.

There have, of course, been various exceptions to this rule, the chief of which was his fight against pollution of the environment. Muskie engaged that beast years before most of the politically aware knew of its existence. But even today—as we choke on our own effluvia—the pollution fight does not seem very exciting and is not well understood. Though it challenges the corporate giants of America and of the world and though it ultimately may change the most fundamental patterns of life, most people regard the pollution fight as easy, and the politically aware give Muskie little credit for the lonely battle. Instead they focus on the fights of the last decade which they saw as great at the time —civil rights, civil liberties, the reduction of defense spending, hunger, poverty, welfare, health, the easing of the cold war, the challenge to neo-imperialism. In the fight for the Civil Rights Act of 1964, for instance, which President Johnson powered from the White House, and Humphrey, then Majority Whip, drove through the Senate, Muskie made every vote—more than a hundred in total—and never failed to vote with the libertarian forces. He spoke on the subject near the end of the debate, as is his way, and brought to it a note of hard logic and decent good sense. But these are the areas in which the politically aware believe that a man who aspires to national leadership should be known, and by his actions should demonstrate a visceral commitment to humanity. The result of his relaxed posture has been the often expressed feeling of the politically aware that, yes, Muskie's instincts are all right, but they tend to be smothered in caution and a distaste for contention. This is the source of the common charge that he waits to see where the other liberals go and then follows at a leisurely pace. How, the politically aware ask, can such a man bring about the change that must be made?

Furthermore, Muskie's aura of a practical man from Maine who believes in getting things done has led to a tendency to view him as a technician of government instead of a leader. He is a pragmatist and a compromiser and believes that is how government goes forward, but in the liberal mind these qualities have taken on bad connotations. Pragmatism has come to suggest that the test of right is whatever works. Compromise has come to be seen as an excuse for giving away the public good. This is not very realistic, since making things work and compromising to accommodate the interests of others are fundamental aspects of people living together, in single households or in full societies, but it is also true that the political practice of compromise has given it such a bad name as to obscure this simple fact of life. Therefore, in ways that are hard for the politically aware to state clearly, their hunch feeling is that Muskie is too oriented to things as they are. In this context, even his insistent dedication to the American system becomes suspect. Most of the politically aware want to work within the system, but they want to make it function not as it often has but as it was intended to, and as it could function with new leadership. That happens to sum up Muskie's own feelings accurately, but his position on the 1968 ticket with its obligation to the Johnson administration, his reputation as a Senate regular with emphasis on pragmatism and compromise, and his lack of a fighting image on the great issues, all lead to a suspicion that in his heart Muskie holds to the old view that seems to confuse the interests of the system with the interests of those who happen to control the system.

Muskie's general style also is more attractive to the mass of people who support him than to the politically aware, whose suspicions it tends to exacerbate. Muskie is a quiet man by nature. He speaks in an easy, gentle voice. He is honest and candid to a fault. This might appear a virtue, but in practice it often leads to his unwillingness to strike some viscerally exciting blow in this cause or that. He dislikes the personal attack. He is willing to attack a man's policies but not to impugn his motives. In 1970 he went to California to campaign for John Tunney against the Senate incumbent, George Murphy, that old actor turned right-wing politician, and someone asked him if he was against Murphy. Muskie replied that he was for Tunney, and though the point seems very small his liberal critics managed to seize it as evidence of lack of leadership fire. But in Maine they don't do things that way, and Muskie is a Maine man. In elections at home, which Muskie contests vigorously and wins by handsome margins despite the state's strong Republican orientation, he rarely mentions his opponent's name, let alone attack him. He dwells instead on his own positive (and pragmatic) approach to problems and his idealistic view of how politics should be conducted. Throughout the campaign he waits hopefully for his opponent to strike, in desperation, some more or less low blow in response to which Muskie can become magnificently outraged. Then, voice trembling with indignation but still without mentioning his opponent's name, he chastises the opposition for stooping to such levels, and thus manages to introduce a little color into the campaign. Usually the opposition obliges him: "I can always count on the Republicans doing something stupid," he once said with satisfaction. In 1970 various people urged Muskie to campaign nationally to pick up political IOU's and cut down on his campaign for reelection to the Senate from Maine, since he was sure to win it anyway. His refusal to do this was taken as further evidence of his lack of a national feel. (In fact, for Muskie to have ignored people whom he is paid to represent in order to solicit national credit for himself probably would have been poor politics.)

The problem is that Muskie's style just turns off people who consider themselves hip. He is so dull, they say despairingly, so uninteresting, he really doesn't grab me at all. Writing in the *New York Times Magazine,* Susan Sheehan noted, "Muskie's niceness and the other old-fashioned virtues attributed to him, like moderation and thrift (*sic*), are not the qualities that attract his critics, who prefer the chic virtues that Muskie lacks: pizzazz, savvy and chutzpah. To them Muskie is a Horatio Alger hero and Horatio Alger heroes are from Dullsville." Obviously the savvy to which she refers is not in the halls of Congress, the value of which the politically aware discount in Muskie's case, but would appear to be rather a certain street chic associated with the gall which "chutzpah" implies and which is much more at home in Manhattan than in Maine. Mrs. Sheehan continues in the same vein to point out, however, that his critics "think of Maine as a hick state," not at all to be considered with New York or California as a homeplace for politicians.

As a result of these feelings that Muskie induces, much of what he has done since 1968 as he moved into a genuine leadership posture has gone unnoticed or at least unappreciated by the politically aware. He did take a party to Jackson State. He was the first senator to endorse Campaign GM, the liberal attempt to assert a role in the affairs of General Motors; the step was merely the latest in a succession he has been taking for years to try to open society's processes to common people. He wrote legislation to force auto companies to make the first clean automobile engine in history. He spoke at the anti-war rally Allard Lowenstein organized at Providence in April 1971. In 1970 he and Abe Ribicoff took Joe Duffey (then a Senate candidate) into two of Connecticut's toughest Polish districts and demanded and got applause. He has written a revenue-sharing bill that bases its allocations on need. He was responsible for the passage of the Model Cities bill and is clearly identified with the need to salvage the American city; still more important, he faces up to the great changes that will be required not only in systems but in values. He criticizes the FBI's overzealous surveillance and its director's intemperance and has proposed a declassification board to control the Pentagon's penchant for secrecy.

But these factors are lost in the rash of adverse feeling he inspires, which probably means that for all their interest in issues, the politically aware also make their political judgments perceptually—and simply find a different kind of political personality exciting. For, of course, these people also want leadership that seizes their hearts and forces their response. They want commitment to issues demonstrated with rhetorical impact and they want the villains damned in clear-cut language. They too fear what is out ahead and they want reassurance that the man they follow has the courage as well as the insight to deal with it.

It is the stylistic problem that most disturbs Muskie. He knows that the ambivalence of the politically aware is an important and potentially dangerous problem for him, but the stronger feeling probably is his personal sense that these people should be with him. He stands for what they stand for—and he does so in terms that do not alienate the larger mass of the people who in the end control the future and who find the rhetoric of violent change unsettling. Perhaps quality of rhetoric is at the heart of the equation. His national speech on Election Eve in 1970 called the President a liar in so many words, and that, as Muskie once said, "is hardly Pablum." Yet the thrust of the speech was healing and soothing, an appeal for an end to hatred and political division, and that is how it was taken. Muskie sees change not in radical but in incremental terms. He sees leadership as identifying problems, altering people, persuading them to a course of action and assembling the political muscle to put it through. He avoids the apocalyptic as frightening to most people and unproductive, because accomplishment comes with moving many people. In essence, however, he wants the same decent society his critics want and in actual practice his approach probably would not be sharply different from theirs. Why, then, the impasse?

When he dwells on it and becomes irritated—which follows almost immediately—Muskie turns back to the question of rhetoric. "It's because I won't get up there on the platform and give them what they want," he says. "They want demagoguery—they like to hear people called sons of bitches—and I won't give them that." The politically aware do have a certain susceptibility to liberal demagoguery, but since on balance they include the best-educated and the most intelligent people in the nation, to say that they have a taste for demagoguery alone is much too easy an answer.

The real answer lies buried deep in the complexity of Muskie's nature, his attitudes and his political practice, which are difficult to unravel and which make up the body of this book. The split view in which he is held resolves itself and becomes one in fully understanding him—which is much more important than understanding his record.

The importance of the dichotomy is that it provides a referential framework in which to clarify one's estimate of the president Muskie would make. The worried complaints focus not on the man but on the potential President; the troubling question for anyone who cares and who feels drawn is whether he should support Muskie and work for him, or resist him, or ignore him. Thus understanding the man answers a political question that is increasingly important as the time of decision approaches. In the end, however, whether understanding answers complaints depends on each complainer, for Muskie's course won't change much: "If I bend and twist to suit everyone, I'll be no more than a pretzel. I am what I am and that's how they'll have to take me."

2

The
Man from Maine

Edmund Muskie was born in Rumford, Maine, just before five o'clock on a Saturday morning, March 28, 1914, on the first floor of a three-story six-family building that still stands in a working-class district near the center of town. Rumford is an undistinguished town of seven thousand people on the banks of the Androscoggin River, which nature made one of the most beautiful and a whole series of pulp and paper mills have made one of the filthiest rivers in America. A pall of smoke and a sour odor seeping from the single mill that dominates Rumford hangs overhead like a rich uncle's foul breath which everyone resolutely ignores. Muskie's father, Stephen Muskie, a tailor, was born in 1883 in Poland and came alone to America in 1903. Muskie's mother was born in 1891 in a Polish enclave in Buffalo and she met her husband there. They were married in 1911 and moved immediately to Rumford, by the chance that a friend had gone there and liked it. Eventually Stephen Muskie opened his own tailor shop.

Edmund, their first son and second child, was a shy little

boy with a taste for books, who displayed a ferocious temper at home but was unusually accommodating with his friends. He is remembered fondly but not very well in Rumford today; he was a good student and was valedictorian of his high school class, but he showed little of the sense of power that he reflects now, and he rarely thrust himself into things. In the fall of 1932, amidst the excitement of Roosevelt's campaign, Muskie entered Bates College, a small liberal arts college with traditional ivy-covered buildings at Lewiston, forty-one miles from Rumford, which he could afford only with scholarship help. Roosevelt's campaign and his first hundred days made an indelible impression on Muskie; he discovered himself a Democrat natural-born in a state where Republicans reigned. He developed his talent for debate and graduated from Bates in 1936 as class president and a member of Phi Beta Kappa. He graduated cum laude in 1939 from Cornell Law School and the following year took over a law practice whose owner had died. The practice was at Waterville, a town of nineteen thousand in central Maine seventy-eight miles from Rumford. In 1942 he joined the Navy and served as a sea-going officer on small ships in both oceans, and in 1945 he returned to revive his practice.

It was a modest practice at best and he did little to expand it. When he closed it permanently in 1954 as governor-elect of Maine, it was of little more significance than when he had taken it. In this period he met, courted and in 1948 married a pretty Waterville girl named Jane Gray, who is thirteen years his junior and who still treats him—five children and a quarter-century later —with an engaging blend of deference to his age and stature and marvel that he should have been so fortunate as to have snared her.

Later in the book we will take a closer look at Muskie's actual political career. As we shall see, he ran for the Maine House of Representatives in 1946 and won by a narrow margin. In his second term his fellow Democrats elected him Minority Leader, an honor less surprising than it might seem, since Democrats were so poor in both numbers (they held a sixth of the seats) and quality that there was little competition for the post.

Maine was a Republican byword. It was one of the two states that Alf Landon carried in 1936 and there had been only two Democratic governors in Maine since the Republican Party was organized. In 1954 Muskie and a small group of young men picked up the party reins that aging leadership had dropped in exhaustion and began rebuilding the party. Muskie ran for governor less as a matter of desire than because no one else would, and he certainly did not expect to win. When he was elected, Democrats were as dumbfounded as Republicans. Although the Legislature was Republican by a ratio of about 4-to-1 at the time, Muskie proved himself a remarkably agile governor and pushed a majority of his program through. He did so by choosing his battles with great care and then taking them directly to the people.

In 1956 Muskie was reelected by a wider margin and in 1958 he easily unseated an incumbent Republican in the U.S. Senate. In Washington he clashed under odd circumstances, as we shall discuss, with the Majority Leader, Lyndon B. Johnson, who relegated him to the outer edges of the Senate. In the next decade he worked his way steadily into Senate power, and by 1968, though unknown to the general public, was on any knowledgeable list of the handful of most effective men in the Senate.

Throughout this time, Muskie stayed close to the interests of his people and to his assigned areas, and he conducted himself in ways consistent with the ways of Maine. He does so still, though his scope is broader today. The attitude one finds in Maine is unusually definable and related to place. Maine's isolation, its near-zero population growth and its lack of urbanization all have helped it escape the dilution of attitude—and the profits—that onrushing change and the migrations of a restless society have imposed on much of the rest of the country. Most people there are state-of-Mainers, born and reared. They are proud of their state and its rigors (they refer to natives who live elsewhere as Mainiacs) and they tend to carry on the old attitudes.

The state's extraordinary beauty draws visitors from all over the world and rather hides the fact that Maine really is a hard place. Its winters are cold and interminable; snow covers the ground from late October until early May. In its colder areas the snowfall ranges up to 110 inches a year and there may be fifty days when the temperature does not rise above zero. In Muskie's hometown of Waterville in the winter of 1970–71 there were fourteen consecutive days when the temperature remained below zero and evergreens thought to be impervious to cold were dead in the spring. Such weather makes outdoor work cruel and makes every facet of life—going to work or to shop or to school—difficult and monotonous and occasionally dangerous.

Maine is a poor state. It ranks in the lowest quarter nationally in per capita income, and its people's weekly wage rates compare with those in the poorer Southern states. Its isolation reduces its commerce and its young people leave to find jobs. Its farmland is beautiful, but much of it is stony and poor; barns invariably are attached to houses by a series of closed sheds in testimony to the effect of temperature and drifting snow. Fishermen take little boats onto the cold Atlantic and lobstermen's lines freeze as they haul their pots in the fog; they earn no more than a subsistence living. Farms and fishing are giving way to industry and many Maine towns are dominated by a single big plant, factories that produce shoes or clothing or wood or fish products, and mills that produce textiles or paper. That odorous mill in Rumford pays about half the town's taxes and a huge Great Northern plant pays some seventy percent of the taxes in Millinocket. If an official in the towns so dominated by a single industry wants to put up a new school, as Muskie once said, "he'd better go down to the mill and see how they feel about it." Textiles and shoes are pressed by foreign imports and most of the factories pay on a piecework basis. People stand in mindless concentration before machines that punch out piece after piece, each worth some fraction of a cent. Maine's industries generally are the sort that require relatively low skills and pay correspondingly low wages. Unions are weak and their officials often are employees of the plants with which they negotiate. But while wages are low, prices are high. Property taxes are surprisingly high. Food costs are measurably higher than in urban areas. Fuel and power costs are the highest in the nation—which deters industrial growth and adds to the burden of winter. Summer visitors are a valued crop but in another sense they inhibit a more sound economy and produce jobs that are both seasonal and low-paying.

Thus, remote and on the economic fringes, Maine did not cash in on the nation's postwar boom, and while this now can be seen as something of a blessing emerging shyly from disguise, that has not been the way its people saw it over the years. They were painfully aware that while it sometimes took hard times six months to penetrate their fastness, good times often never arrived at all. One can overdraw the picture, of course; while income averages are low, there appears to be relatively little real poverty, perhaps less on a percentage basis than in some richer states where income averages are higher but the income itself is less evenly spread, where the comfortable are more so and the poor are poorer. Overall, life in Maine appears pleasant. The natural beauty enthralls Maine people as well as visitors, and if beauty doesn't feed the stomach, still it feeds the spirit. Maine is a state of pleasant small towns and rural communities (the largest city, Portland, has about 70,000 population) and most people live in wooden houses that are neat and well kept, with generous barns and tall trees in the yards. The impression of a visitor is that Maine people are happy and content with their way of life and rather proud of its rigors, but that the terms of their lives are considerably more hard and direct than those of most Americans.

It is in reflection of this heritage that a visitor can generalize about common denominators that seem to reflect the Maine attitude. Judgment is valued in a country where the consequences of poor judgment can be serious. From their harsh and sometimes dangerous environment it follows that they prize endurance, caution, attention to detail, doing things as they should be done; it follows that reliability should be seen as a greater asset than sparkle and élan, that foolish and careless men should be held in unusual contempt. They have a strong sense of propriety—a man should follow a proper course and one who does not understand propriety is deemed unsound by definition. Their wisdom appears in country homilies that apply good sense to immediate things; their humor turns on good sense deflating urban puff. This humor suggests a caustic quality, but in encounters they emerge as calm, pleasant, courteous and slow to take offense. Independent, hard working, usually plain-spoken, they find virtue in making do and being glad with what there is. They care about balance and fair play and modesty and do not admire men who promote themselves unduly. Maine is practical, pragmatic, interested in what works. One afternoon in Biddeford, Maine, I came early to a political rally and at the end of the hall saw a formidable woman behind a table which held a coffee urn and a platter of doughnuts. It had been a long, difficult day and I asked her for a cup of coffee. She gave it to me graciously, but I noticed that no one else approached the table, and I asked her why. Because, she said, they knew she would not open the table—except for an obvious visitor—until after the speaking. "If they're eating and drinking, they won't be listening. And anyway, so long as you haven't served, they won't leave." I said I thought that sounded like a basic Maine attitude. " 'Tis," she answered.

Muskie takes great pleasure in these people. He trusts their instincts and when he is among them he watches their faces. They are not, he once said, "a demonstrative people. I think that what you sense is that they are at peace with themselves and their environment. They are not loquacious. They are conservative politically and in other ways, but it is more a matter of style than of ideology and philosophy. I think they judge people by the way they do things . . . they don't categorize me, you know, as liberal, conservative or anything else. They know me as a man who has dealt with them for some sixteen years and this is how they measure me. This is how they measure anybody. And they take plenty of time . . . they won't accept a stranger quickly. They want . . . to come to know what he represents, what he is, how he does things . . ."

Though Maine people voted for Landon in 1936, they rejected Goldwater in 1964 because they perceived him as a radical conservative and they do not care for radicals. They are upset by violence, extremes and loud voices. Temper is not admired, nor is the cut and thrust of partisan politics. A man should state his own case rather than belittle his opponent. In Maine, Muskie's refusal even to mention his opponent's name is taken as the height of propriety and dignity. When Muskie was traveling in 1969 the wire services tended to single out his criticisms of President Nixon as his most interesting comments and file them. The Maine papers carried the remarks and soon the people were irritated: after all, didn't the President ever do anything right? Politics is politics, Ed, but let's be fair. One afternoon in 1969 Muskie exploded on the Senate floor and gave J. William Fulbright a tongue-lashing. Muskie is effective at this when the mood takes him, and afterward Ernest Hollings of South Carolina caught him in the cloakroom and cried, "Ed, you were *mad* out there—I wish you'd get mad and stay mad right through 1972." Muskie liked that, of course, but his pleasure soon faded. "Evidently I was effective," he said sourly, "but what did the Maine papers say? 'Muskie blew his cool.' "

Every critical comment from Maine in those days stung Muskie. "That's what all those people down in Washington just don't understand—or if they do, they don't understand why," said George Mitchell, who now heads Muskie's political operation. Mitchell is deeply devoted to Muskie, and though twenty years his junior he is one of the few men with whom Muskie is fully comfortable and whose company he invariably enjoys. He is an intelligent, practical and politically skillful man who uses, in the Maine fashion, an unusually pleasant manner to cover a fierce and stubborn temper. "They're always telling him—these people who think they know how to make Presidents—that he should be doing this or that, and what they don't know is that he always takes into account what the people in Maine will think. Oh, sure, as his campaign takes more force, as he becomes more truly a national figure, the Maine calculation probably becomes less important, but it's always going to be there to some extent, and until you understand that you really don't understand the man."

In Maine one day, when his focus still was more clearly on home than on the whole nation, Muskie said, "People have an investment in you. Many of these people started their first interest in politics with our campaign in 1954, which was bright and exciting and youthful after years of colorless one-party rule. So they start with you and they follow your career. They make you part of their lives and they feel they have helped make you what you are, and that is true, too. And this is a danger—it becomes a burden that you always carry. If you fail them, they will turn on you with a particular sense of betrayal. That's why you don't rant and rave, no matter what advice you get in Washington. You don't throw these people away after all these years."

All his life Muskie has accepted these people's values as his own. He is a strong man of independent mind but he never was a rebel. He and his father often fought, but in the end the son was submissive. He played the same role in college, where an examination of his correspondence reflects an unquestioning acceptance of authority. This was partly related to the financial pressure under which he went to school, of course, but seems to have indicated attitude as well.

It does not follow, however, that submission came naturally to him. He is a man of deep emotion with a quick, hot temper and he radiates personal force. "I'm always boiling on the inside," he once told a startled reporter, "but it doesn't often show." His boiling qualities appear as wisps of steam penetrating his Maine cool from time to time. He is what he is—but sometimes the Maine attitude seems to have given him a sense of what he ought to be as well. And that, in turn, explains a great deal about Muskie.

Most of all, it explains the impact propriety has on him. Everyone has propriety, every place has standards, but Muskie seems to interpret his very strictly. It explains his natural aversion to many things which in other parts of the country are regarded as good hot-blooded politics. It explains his dislike for impugning men's motives, for extreme rhetoric, for overstating his own case, for personal attacks or even for indulging in (he would say "stooping to") personalities, and his quickness to perceive demagoguery in what others might see as simple rhetorical exaggeration. It explains why he needs a solid platform and why he finds it difficult to keep himself in the limelight between legitimate political occasions. Staying plausibly in the limelight when there is no natural reason to be there is one of the keys to taking national leadership. It is something that Edward M. Kennedy does very well and it is one of the reasons that he has remained a force in American politics. The Maine attitude helps explain why Muskie often is not the first to speak on vital issues and why his national campaigning has a soft note disturbing to people who yearn for exciting language. It explains the quality that keeps him from thrusting himself into various situations. It explains the note of balanced and reasonable (and therefore often lengthy) good sense in his answers to questions even when more simple (he would say oversimple) answers have a way of drawing headlines and attention. It explains why he often refuses the urgings of his staff to say and do things in order to seize attention. It is why in the period after 1968 he found it difficult to elevate himself to national leadership—a post for which in fact there are no invitations—when a man with more gall might have felt quite naturally that his leadership was just what people needed. Propriety, as practiced in Maine, says a great deal about Muskie.

Some of the painful growth that Muskie underwent in the period after 1968 involved struggling past the inhibitions of the Maine attitude. While what he was saying and doing nationally seemed not enough to many potential followers, it often seemed a bit too much to the people in Maine. This was further complicated by the early opening of the 1972 political season. The people in Maine, far from the center of things and relatively content, found it strange for their senator to perceive and discuss the nation's ills so actively. When he did things that moved toward national leadership, he was bombarded with irritated questions from home. "Why, Ed's just running, that's all," said one of his supporters in this period. "Turns out he's no different than the Kennedys. They've always been running." This is one reason that the 1970 campaign for reelection to the Senate from Maine was important to him. Not only was it proper for him to be there soliciting the votes of his people, it was necessary. They are independent and do not enjoy being taken for granted, and while it is hard to imagine his being defeated, he certainly could have been embarrassed. But more important still, it was his way of keeping faith with his people. When the election was over it was as if a load had been lifted, freeing him to go on the greater quest. Obviously, winning a new six-year term had a practical political effect in freeing him, but the emotional effect probably was more important.

Muskie's emphasis on thoroughness and hard work are clearly consonant with the Maine attitude. It is a trait he carried from boyhood, and much of his success, particularly in the Senate, rested on it. James R. Calloway, now staff director of the Public Works Committee, remembers: "The first time I ever dealt with Muskie he was a freshman and he was handling some very minor bill. He asked me such detailed questions that I wound up preparing a sixty-page memorandum for him. I gave it to him and the next morning he not only had read and digested it, he had prepared a memo of his own critique-ing my memo." When Muskie was elected governor, he engaged a quiet, pleasant man named Maurice F. Williams to help prepare his budget. Williams, who now is Maine's Commissioner of Finance and Administration, went on to become Muskie's administrative assistant in his gubernatorial period. He remembers how quickly Muskie grasped the complex of figures that ranged across the state's affairs. "And he really had them. Toward the end of the budget-preparation period, I remember he gave a long discussion citing them from memory and it was very impressive. But it was two years later, when we prepared the budget for the second term, that I found out how well he had learned them. He gave another discussion comparing the new figures with the old, and now he had both sets in mind with a sort of built-in comparative analysis." On the golf course one afternoon Muskie fired a shot that did all the wrong things but by a fluke landed near the flag. "I don't know whether I'd rather have a bad shot with good results or a good shot with bad results," Muskie mused. "I know which I'd take," his partner said. Half an hour later someone asked Muskie abruptly, "Which would you take?" His mind was in the same track. Without hesitation he said, "The good shot with the bad results."

This is the attitude that makes Muskie feel it is inherently unfair to criticize a man's policies without offering an alternative solution. (What would *you* do, Ed? the wise voice cries from the Maine audience, and he always takes care to have an answer.) It's just a cheap shot, he says—easy, fun, but cheap—to criticize the President without taking account of the realities which the President must face. That this made things difficult for Muskie and his staff when he began to move nationally did not have much to do with it; that was merely another in an endless series of problems, but what counted was that the propriety of the situation demanded certain standards. He was miserable when he felt that he had failed those self-set standards. Flying in one night from some desperate cross-country dash he said in angry frustration, "I like to be *thorough*—and it just seems impossible in this damned situation."

There has always been a practical tone to Muskie's approach to government. This is the Maine way, and it also is true that there are so many unmet economic problems there that they naturally draw a man's attention. But it also relates to the polite texture of Maine campaigning, which is different from the practice of politics elsewhere. Earl Long, it has been said, once undertook to bite off the ear of an opponent as they wrestled on the floor of the Louisiana Legislature; within quite recent memory, Ralph Yarborough of Texas and Strom Thurmond of South Carolina squared off in the halls of the Senate; but in Maine, that sort of thing is not done. It is not that Maine campaigns are easy or that the people don't care, but that the style is different. Furthermore, Muskie wins his campaigns by a near 2-to-1 margin in a state in which Republicans outnumber Democrats. He and other Democrats have succeeded not by inspiring those cool, conservative State-of-Mainers with the violence of their rhetoric but by offering better solutions to real problems. That approach made substantive as well as stylistic sense.

Muskie took these attitudes to the Senate. His tendency to come late into debates with a quiet, sensible statement seemed about right to the people at home. They would have been startled to have seen their senator leading first this fight and then the next. "Maine people," Muskie once observed, "don't expect to hear from their representatives with every breakfast. If they did, they would wonder if he had taken leave of his senses." This also is related to Muskie's willingness to stay indefinitely with poor Senate committees. He plunged into work which led to knowledge which focused his interest on the problems involved. Eventually seniority and his growing prestige opened the way to more volatile and nationally exciting committees, but by then he was deeply engaged on his own ground (his first move was in 1971 and had become essential, from Banking and Currency to Foreign Relations). In terms of effectiveness and contributions, his two areas of legislative strength are satisfying, but they do not burnish his leadership image as others might have.

When Muskie was asked in late 1968 to comment on Nixon's election to the Presidency, he observed that "in Maine we have a saying that there's no point in speaking unless you can improve on silence." As his own candidacy grew, he moved beyond parochial limitations that seemed artificial at the national level and began responding to the larger electorate. This growth, however, was more expansion than basic change.

The Maine attitude obviously adds to the stylistic disfavor in which the politically aware hold Muskie, but it probably has an opposite effect on the larger group who keep him high in the polls. These people might find the Maine attitude cooler than their own practice, but it would be consistent with their own sense of propriety and many would find it reassuring. The bulk of America, after all, is a good deal more like Maine than like Manhattan. Furthermore, there is a new appreciation for the way life appears to be lived in places like Maine, where people seem to have time for each other and to be in touch with the rhythms of life. It relates to the great land hunger that grips the country and it concerns the style of life, not of region. There is appeal in the hard weather of Maine, the importance of the seasons, the image of the farmer who plows when the ground thaws, the fisherman who deals with the sea. It is as if life is still real there and nerves are still sound and when a man goes to bed at night he feels he has done something worthwhile. Or so it appears, which from this view is as good as the fact.

Muskie is a plain, open, direct man; or rather, he appears to view this as proper and desirable and consistent with his nature and with his heritage, so he is open and direct even though his nature is a good deal more complicated than this suggests. Nevertheless, it is the way of the Down-east Yankee trader who prized straight talk and direct manners, and was amused by elegance and disgusted by arrogance.

When Muskie was preparing for his 1970 campaign in Maine, the initial radio advertising was prepared in a New York studio and included an announcer saying reverently, "Edmund Muskie is a great man." Muskie listened with predictable irritation and rejected it. "Why can't we just say, 'Ed Muskie is a good senator,' " he said. "That's the truth. I am a good senator. That's what we're trying to get over. And let's say Ed, not Edmund; Edmund is an odd name, it's hard to say. I like plain Ed."

Plain Ed. He is an unpretentious man who doesn't seem to find marks of status appealing. He does not flee to secret hideaways. He drives his own car, his friends have his unlisted numbers, he goes to regular restaurants and gets on and off planes with everyone else. He readily stops on the street to talk government with anyone who questions him and sees it as a duty to do so. He is not arrogant and dislikes the trait in others. Of a Democratic governor whose opinion of himself rose rapidly after his election, Muskie snapped, "My God, you'd think he was born to the office." He accepts and seems to enjoy jokes at his own expense.

Muskie had almost no national experience until he was forty-four. Though he has had a world-wide range of sophisticated experience since then and is no longer confused by multiple forks, his tastes are essentially modest, more rural than urban, more solid than chic. He has little taste for wines or fine foods, for the theater or great restaurants. His sense of art is active and true but unlettered. He has been observed eating with his knife. His clothes are good but utilitarian, with fashionable striped shirts and vivid ties, and many of his suits come off the rack. He likes bird hunting and is an avid though not very good golfer. He swims in the sea off the Maine coast, going far out despite the chill. His sense for figures makes him powerful with cards and he once was a cribbage champion. He reads eclectically, watches television occasionally, follows professional sports lazily. He and his wife go to resorts from time to time, but they are not given to frequenting the fashionable watering holes where photographers await the mighty. Women like Muskie, but his friends choke on the idea of his having a flirtation. "Huh," snorted one who sees himself as a real swinger, "not that straight son-of-a-bitch!"

In a Kansas City hotel room years ago someone asked Muskie if he needed anything for the night. A friend who was along has never forgotten his answer: "Well, I am all out of toothpaste." His host had a tube sent up. During the 1968 campaign Muskie found a quote from Thomas Jefferson that he liked and used widely until his staff pointed out that in the modern idiom it took on an obscene connotation. Muskie found the whole thing irritating. He enjoys a drink and at one point in his life fancied boilermakers, which did not appear to have great effect on him. Apparently he has not been intoxicated in years, though when he is tired his mood is sharply improved by an Old Fashioned. The Muskies go to parties which Muskie sometimes enjoys, though parties are part of Washington's political life and might better be seen as work.

These modest tastes are reinforced by the fact that Muskie always has been poor. He is one of those men who do not care enough about money to pursue it. He often is frustrated by the shortage of it, but the actual making of money bores him. The

Rumford Muskies lived in modest circumstances, and Muskie struggled to get through college. His law practice was never lucrative. He broke his back the year before he ran for governor and still owed five thousand dollars in medical bills when he was inaugurated. The governor's salary then was ten thousand dollars a year. Muskie's Washington house (which technically is just across the line in Bethesda, Md.) is worth about sixty-five thousand dollars and is half mortgaged; his Maine house is worth about half that and also is half mortgaged. When he made his assets public in 1968, Muskie listed the two houses, some fifteen thousand dollars in a mutual fund and a small checking account. An aide suggested that he had overlooked savings accounts. There was a painful pause during which the aide realized his faux pas: there were no savings accounts. Muskie's face got red and he began to discuss a point that strikes him now and then: I must be mad to have opted for public life and no money when this society is full of people making plenty and not facing half the pressure I face, but oh, no, not me . . ."

In 1966 he bought his second Maine house, a handsome yellow cottage at Kennebunk Beach, and sold the house at China Lake. The lake house did not sell immediately, however; Muskie pointed it out to a friend once and said casually, "I bought the other house and then sweated six months trying to sell this one." At that point he had been in the Senate eight years. Since 1968 his income has soared because of speaking engagements and book contracts, though he has put most of this back into politics. First, however, he had his houses repaired and repainted. An acquaintance, seeking to compliment Muskie on not having used his office to enrich himself, once commented on the modesty of his Washington home. Muskie stared at the man coldly; in fact, his home was a considerable achievement.

George Mitchell has a vivid recollection of a trip Muskie made in the early 1960s that further demonstrates the point. Travel is always hard, but the rich manage it in a flurry of attendants and special treatment, which contrasts with Muskie's style. "The senator used to make his annual summer trip to Maine by car," said Mitchell, who was on his staff at the time, "and I usually was delegated to drive the other car. The senator hated that drive; he always was in a foul humor. Well, one year Jane found a lot of bargains in children's clothes in Maine and she bought the whole winter wardrobe for all the kids. She packed them in boxes and of course, when they started back to Washington there wasn't room for them in the car. The senator had a Valiant station wagon with one of those racks on top, so he put all the boxes up there, threw a tarp over them and tied it down. When we got down in Connecticut, on the Merritt Parkway, I saw the tarp beginning to come off, so I drove alongside his car and tapped my horn and pointed up at the tarp. He stopped, madder than hell, saying, 'Damn it all, what's wrong with you?' I showed him the loose tarp and he tied it down quickly and drove off and I fell in behind. In a little while it was loose again and I drove up and he scowled and stopped and cussed and tied it down again. This happened another time or two, the senator getting madder and madder, and finally we were over on the Jersey Turnpike and the tarp came loose again. I drove up alongside and tapped the horn and pointed and he scowled and waved me off. So I fell in behind and pretty soon the tarp came clear off and those boxes rose up in the air like an airplane taking off and flew back and crashed against my windshield and clothes went flying everywhere. Well, it takes a half-mile to stop on the Jersey Turnpike. I blew my horn and flagged him over and he got out saying, 'Oh, I hate this damned trip.' Jane said, 'We've got to go back,' and he said, 'Like hell we'll go back, leave them there,' and Jane said, 'That's the whole winter wardrobe for all the kids, we *can't* leave them,' and so we set off down the Jersey Turnpike picking up clothes, the senator muttering and cursing."

Muskie is often irascible, but his easy moments usually are fun. At a Senate hearing which dealt, among other things, with the dangers of oil spills, someone made a flamboyant remark about the Boston Tea Party, to which Muskie instantly responded, "I wouldn't want to use oil as they used tea." These cracks come quickly and sometimes they are more heavy than funny. He is famous for the poor quality of his puns, which his friends suffer with restraint. Standing in a hotel in Portland that has glass corners and thus gives a startling view of the street below, you mutter, "God, that's eerie," and the quiet voice comes immediately from behind you, "No, it's Portland."

His formal humor soon reverts to Maine stories, which he probably uses to key himself quickly to the state and its cool virtues. Maine stories are monotonous, since they all seem to turn on the countryman confounding his victim, who may be merely a cityman but more likely is that genuine butt of the Maine view, the out-of-state tourist. A tourist comes to a fork in the road. Signs indicate that each fork leads ultimately to Portland. The tourist looks at the farmer who is poised expectantly on hand. Does it matter which way I go? Not to me it don't. Roars. Stories of this nature demolish Maine audiences. Still, they are generally inoffensive. A columnist once sniffed that during an unexceptional appearance Muskie told a story about horse manure. But it is not such a bad story. The cityman takes his horse to a farm and asks the charge for boarding the animal. Fifteen dollars, the farmer says, and I keep the manure. At the next farm, the price is ten dollars and the manure. At the next farm the price is five dollars. Curious, the cityman asks why no interest in the manure? Well, says the farmer, at five dollars you've got to understand there won't be any manure.

During the 1968 campaign Muskie went all over America telling about the Maine farmer who met the Texas rancher (one must be very naïve to doubt the outcome of that encounter). The Texan had shiny boots and a big hat and whipcord breeches. "How big is your place?" he asked the Maine man. "Oh," the farmer said, "couple hundred acres." "Well," said the Texan, "I'll tell you: when I get up in the morning I get in my car and I drive hard all day and maybe I'll get to the end of my place and maybe I won't." "Yes," the Maine man said, "I had a car like that once." The press people traveling with Muskie got so that they would breathe that punch line in unison, a massive whisper from the press table: "I had a car like that once." When he came home to Waterville on election night they had a little ceremony and gave him a silver plaque with a battered little car attached and under it the words, I HAD A CAR LIKE THAT ONCE.

It is not his usual way, but in certain warm moods Muskie demonstrates considerable charm, a quality that every politician must have to some degree. Once, campaigning through a grocery store, he noticed a handsome stack of watermelons. "Do you know," he said abruptly, "that the Russians raise watermelons with red seeds? Yes. Some Soviet Luther Burbank decided black seeds were unpolitic . . ." and he shot down another aisle to seize a shopper's hand. I remember the morning he hypnotized a lobster on the streets of the arch Republican town of Rockland. Lobsters are a Maine symbol which Muskie enjoys. When I said I not only had never seen one hypnotized but doubted it could be done, he was delighted. He seized a big one from an outdoor tank with his left hand just behind the menacing claws, which were still unpegged, and began stroking the tail, folding it down. Gradually the lobster quieted until Muskie could set it on the sidewalk, poised immobile on its head and its claws. When he picked it up the spell was released and the big claws snapped angrily. He dropped it into the tank and bounded smiling up the street, shaking hands and saying, "Excuse my clammy hand, I've just been hypnotizing a lobster."

Muskie is a candid man. Candor has become unusual because something interesting and sad is happening to many public figures in this image-conscious era. They are developing a sort of double-talk for press and public that is designed to put a noble coat on whatever they touch. They do not lie outright but nevertheless what they say and the interpretations they offer are further and further from reality and therefore increasingly unbelievable and useless. By contrast, Muskie talks to people and to the press in an open and often introspective and self-revealing way. He doesn't bother to hide irritability or problems because outsiders are present. If he hasn't thought something out he is willing to say so, even though he and his questioner know that he long since should have done so. His considerable problems with the press never go to candor. He is reserved and feels no obligation to tell all that he knows or thinks about everything, but the fact is that there is little difference between what he says in public and in private. The only subterfuge I have ever encountered in him is his willingness to stand on a platform and describe every man there as exemplary. Once he remarked to a group of reporters, "I wouldn't want to say, even about myself, that I believe everything I say. There is a political license as well as a poetic." Perhaps he was thinking of all those shambling men whom he had endorsed over the years.

On September 7, 1971, Muskie made a statement in Los Angeles that suddenly brought his candor to everyone's attention in a most controversial manner. He said he did not believe a ticket which included a black Vice Presidential candidate could be elected in today's climate. The results were interesting and are worth examining in some detail.

The statement was in answer to a question at a meeting with thirty-five black leaders in Watts, the deceptively pastoral black ghetto over which the freeways of Los Angeles fly. There was no transcript of the meeting, but soon afterward Muskie's answer emerged through Thomas Bradley, the black Los Angeles city councilman who nearly defeated Sam Yorty in the Los Angeles mayoralty race in 1969. There has been some confusion about what Muskie actually said. At a press conference the next day in front of the Century Plaza Hotel, this is how he described it: The purpose of the meeting, Muskie said, had been to discuss "how we could move effectively to deal with the problems that concern black people." So, he said, "I was asked in that context whether a black candidate for Vice President could be considered for the 1972 election if I were a candidate for the Presidency. I said that in my judgment such a ticket was not electable now. I said I regretted that—it shouldn't be so—[but that] my judgment [was that] such a ticket would be defeated, and that if it were it would be a setback . . . to equality for blacks in this country . . ." He also told the black leaders, as he described it later in a conversation, "I think more shocking than that is the fact that a black child has a forty percent greater chance of dying before its first birthday than a white child—I said *that's* the thing we ought to be correcting. Which is more important now, if you've got so much political good-will and muscle, where should you apply it first, to correcting that condition or to running a losing campaign for a ticket with a black on it? These are questions that everybody has to answer."

The black leaders with whom Muskie met did not appear offended. Bradley issued a statement saying he disagreed but that he appreciated Muskie's candor and added, "Such honesty is a fresh breath of air on the political scene and we need more of it." When the statement went on the news wires, however, there was strong reaction around the country. Many black leaders were affronted. President Nixon said it was "a libel on the American people" to suggest that they would vote against a man on the basis of his color—which seemed an unlikely statement from him. Various Democratic competitors said that it was not true, or that if it was, Muskie still shouldn't have said it. Nearly everyone said they believed that no one should be denied anything on the basis of race, but of course Muskie had said that too. More disappointingly, considering his own high reputation for candor, George McGovern was quoted by the Associated Press as saying, "I am confident the American people will not vote on the basis of such consideration." Charles Evers said he thought Muskie was right. Shirley Chisholm said that Muskie had made "a terrible political boo-boo."

Mrs. Chisholm's comment was most appropriate, for the question was purely political. We are so used to hearing conventions spoken in politics that the truth burns the mind. The fact is that while it should not be so, the statement *is* true and everyone in politics knows it. Saying otherwise is mouthing the conventions; believing otherwise is naïveté. It seems clear that we are a racist society, but even that is not the issue. The point is political; it is not whether everyone would reject such a ticket, or what would happen if that was the only issue or that a ticket including a black would lose no matter who it ran against.

American elections are decided by relatively narrow margins. President Nixon lost in 1960 by 112,803 votes and won in 1968 by 510,315 votes out of some 73 million cast (the deciding electoral vote margins were greater, of course, but the point remains valid). Landslides based on some situations so overriding as to make a black candidacy immaterial are rare. It's unlikely that President Nixon will win or lose by a landslide in 1972. A ticket including a black Vice Presidential candidate would lose in a situation of narrow margins because a relative handful of people could defeat it—and they would. It simply is nonsense to say otherwise. (A Republican official attempted to refute Muskie on the basis of a 1969 poll in which 67 percent said they would vote for a black President. In addition to the notorious unwillingness of people to admit prejudice to pollsters and the meaninglessness of a political question asked in general instead of in particular, the position was neatly blocked by Bernard Brodie of the University of California at Los Angeles in a letter to the *New York Times:* he noted that such a poll should be calculated against one which asked whether those polled would vote for a *white* man for President, and since he assumed a working answer of 100 percent yes, he felt the margin of difference was ample to make Muskie's case.)

The real question was not the truth of the statement but whether Muskie should have said it. When he heard it, Berl Bernhard, staff director of Muskie's campaign, sighed and said, "Well, that's what happens when you've got an honest candidate." Aside from whether it hurt him politically, the important question is whether what he said, true or not, "has placed a ceiling on the aspirations of millions of his fellow countrymen," as Hobart Taylor, Jr., put it in a bitter article in the Washington *Afro-American.* Taylor, a leading black Democrat who was a White House aide in the Johnson administration, said Muskie's statement "dims the future of black Americans," and that "this kind of prediction may express public opinion but it also can form it." Much of the discussion the remark provoked strayed from the remark itself; thus Taylor said in something of a *non sequitur* that since black votes tend to go to one party, ". . . we expect those who receive the benefit to be prepared to bear some of the risk and burden of sustaining the legitimate aspirations of this segment of their support . . ."

The charge of insensitivity which results in negative leadership shifts the issue from truth and has no answer. Muskie's judgment that people want to hear the truth and are willing to accept it, and that dealing with problems openly is the best way to start solving them is one side of the argument, and Taylor's is the other. It was not something, however, into which Muskie slipped insensitively and without thought. He was meeting widely with black leaders who are increasingly focusing on political action, and the question was obvious. He had considered it and his answer. "I could have slipped it," he said. "I've been in politics long enough to know how not to answer questions." The black response he must live with, but some of the pious needling from the politically aware irritated him. "I didn't say it in Alabama or someplace, to an audience that wanted to hear it. I said it in Watts to an audience of blacks. Sad as it is, it's just the truth." Muskie's response to the question was practical and direct, quite within the framework of his heritage. It is too early to judge its ultimate political effect, but no matter the outcome, it will stand as one of the gauges of what Muskie is.

Men who travel with Muskie—and travel has become the *sine qua non* of national politics—develop a lasting image of a tall figure slumped in a seat, long legs folded uncomfortably, knees shot out at odd angles, chin cupped in hand as he gazes silently out the window. In this busy age, travel is one of the few things that immobilize a man and yet free him from routine. Other men talk or sleep or snap open their ever-present briefcases, but Muskie gazes out the window and it doesn't matter if he is in the front seat of a friend's car watching the Maine countryside or in a jetliner six miles over land that is hidden in sun haze. He looks without seeing in silence that lasts for hours, and the assumption is that he is revolving in his mind the things that other men discuss and analyze and ponder aloud as a matter of course.

Muskie is an intensely private man. One of his central characteristics is a lonely internality. The apparent contradiction is not real: the plain and open ways of Maine are standards of propriety; the lonely, silent quality is part of his nature. His candor and willingness to talk freely lead people to imagine quickly that they know him. Actually, one of the basic steps in getting to know Muskie is to come to understand that you don't know him. It is a point that not many people reach and very few pass. That is why journalists have trouble understanding him even though he talks freely, why he is so stubbornly unwilling to do things that people expect him to do, why he counsels best of all with himself and seems most at home in his own mind. Often the men around him don't know what he is thinking and await with interest the offhand remark that will key them to his ideas. Because he is a natural speaker, these ideas that he turns in silence and touches in occasional oblique remarks sometimes emerge full-blown in extemporaneous speech, forced into whole cloth as other men produce ideas under the pressure of conversation.

He can be implacably stubborn when he thinks talk is being forced on him. Loye Miller, Jr., of the Knight Newspapers once mistook an invitation to ride on Muskie's campaign plane in Maine as an opportunity to interview him. When they were airborne, Miller, a very pleasant man, said, "Senator, could we discuss the ingredients that will go into your decision as to whether you will run for President?" Muskie looked at him. "Oh, it'll depend on how I feel the morning I decide," he said. Miller paused and then with an obligatory smile said, "Well, could we discuss the factors involved in how you'll feel that morning?" "Sure," said Muskie, "It'll depend on what I had for breakfast." There was not another word spoken on the flight.

Unless Muskie decides formally to take questions, he dislikes interviews with their interrogatory format. Of a *New York Times* reporter he likes, Muskie said, "At least he doesn't approach me like a damned district attorney." The best conversations with Muskie are those that become discussions of ideas and conceptual politics; these pique his interest and set his mind flowing and sometimes last for hours. He does not enjoy reminiscing, which is basic entertainment for most politicians. Things of the past that are related to facts instead of ideas bore him. When he returned to Waterville after the war he rarely talked about his experiences, and his friends found he'd been nicknamed Moose at sea only when congratulatory telegrams so addressed arrived when he was elected governor.

He is a prickly and often defensive man and one never knows how he will receive a comment. A friend who was thinking of the dangers inherent in unstable crowd situations, asked him if he had considered the risks involved in giving young Rick Brody his platform that day in 1968. Muskie, who is one of the ranking debaters in the Senate, which in turn is the central forum of the nation, threw back his head with an irritated look and said, "Well, I didn't imagine that he would demolish me in debate. Instances of one debater destroying another are very rare, you know. I thought I could hold my own."

He often seems uncomfortable in social situations that are not also political and usually refuses small talk that is not in a political context. He has a wide spectrum of friends who do not seem to mean much to him, and the number of people with whom he is genuinely easy is small. This is the real importance of his relationship with George Mitchell. Muskie once was close to a Waterville contemporary named Dick Dubord, a man of wit and charm, quite the opposite of Muskie's silent intensity. Dubord traveled on *The Downeast Yankee* in 1968 as a kind of friend-in-residence, but he died soon after and no one has been able to fill the vacancy he left.

Even Muskie's relations with members of his staff have jagged edges and he is distant with all but a few of them. For years his Senate affairs funneled through a single man who had access to him, and though this made trouble he did not change it until the pressures of his Presidential campaign literally forced him to open the system. That he did so was one of the signs of growth involved in lifting himself from Maine man to a national man.

Another small but clear sign of growth was that he began to thank people gracefully, though that is less a personal than a political fact, since Presidential efforts depend ultimately on volunteers and while volunteers demand very little they do demand thanks. All his life Muskie has found it difficult—as did his father—to thank people or to apologize. His oblique approach when forced to take one of these steps was clear the evening in the 1968 campaign when he gave George Mitchell an unwarranted tongue lashing in public. Mitchell, who had taken leave from his Portland law firm to help run Muskie's campaign, sat in silence trying to control his own sharp temper, and finally Muskie said in a quite different voice, "George, how does it feel to give up your law practice and work without pay and spend months away from your family so you can get this kind of crap?"

One of the roots of his lonely internality—one of the sources of Muskie's complexity—is shyness. Though he usually is seen in lively political situations and though his personal force often overrides the quality, he nevertheless is shy and has been all his life. He has learned to deal with it, of course, though not without cost; mulling it over one day, he said, "I don't think my family ever understood the agony I went through in overcoming shyness."

Muskie's mother and his four sisters still live in and around Rumford; his younger brother, Eugene, is a steelworker living in California. The elder Mrs. Muskie is an interesting woman who blends something of the sparrow's charm and the hawk's strength. She passed eighty in good health and does largely as she pleases and says exactly what she likes in a high, clear, faintly accented voice. She laughs often and is cheerful with visitors, as if she is determined to be happy whether she is or not. In 1968 she attained modest fame when a reporter asked her somewhat patronizingly if she intended to vote for her son. "Unless someone better comes along," she snapped, and became a national story.

Her recollection of Stephen Muskie's courtship says a good deal about her. She was nineteen, a pretty girl with dark hair and a willowy figure. A cousin brought the young immigrant to her house to meet her. "A few days later," she said, "I got a letter from him. He said he was thinking about me and wanted to know if he could come to call. I said yes—I thought, if I don't like him, I'll just throw him out."

She lives alone today in a boxy mustard-yellow clapboard house her husband bought more than forty years ago. It is in a hilly section of Rumford known as Virginia, not for the state or the queen or even the holy mother but for one Mr. Virgin, an early settler whose name still provokes bursts of innocent merriment when it is mentioned. She sits in her neat kitchen and gives you coffee and talks merrily in a sort of combative defensiveness, and it comes finally as a surprise to realize that no matter what she thought about her prospective husband in 1911 she too is a shy woman. Her husband was much more gregarious and outgoing than she—in fact, her unwillingness to have any social life was a source of quarrels. She still dislikes being away from her home—which is more than a mere characteristic of age. Once when she was visiting Muskie in Washington she suddenly announced that she had to go home, for there were things to be done there. What things? Well, the porch needed sweeping. But what could it possibly matter, since she lived alone and wasn't there? Well, it was getting dirty, the leaves were flying, one must care for these things and so she must go. Muskie sighed and took her home. Among his sisters' strongest memories is their mother's refusal to go to the door. If she was alone with the children and heard a peddler's knock she would hiss them into silence and they would all crouch motionless, the children fighting off giggles, until the man outside tired and they heard him walk away.

Ed was the shyest of her children. His mother shakes her head at the thought of her oldest son. "He was an odd one," she says. When he was a little boy he followed her from room to room and when she settled, usually in the kitchen, he would climb into a window and sit there for hours, gazing out in silence. She would ask what he was watching, what he was seeing, and he would smile at her and shake his head; he could not say. He baffled her and he still does. When he was three his father took the family to Buffalo for a visit. "It was a long train ride," his father told a Boston *Post* reporter in 1954, just after Muskie was elected governor, "one that would make most children cranky and restless. Not Ed. He'd put up his hands for me to lift him so he could look out the window. My arms [got] so tired they'd pain for hours. But Ed was happy, just watching the scenery as the train moved." The image, so like his silent rides at thirty thousand feet today, appears again in a high school friend's recollection of Muskie gazing serenely out a bus window while the rest of the basketball team roughhoused in the aisle.

Muskie himself told the same Boston *Post* reporter of a birthday party given him when he was five. "I became awed by the sight of so many kids. In fact, I became frightened. I took my ice cream and cake and went into my own room and ate it." His older sister, Irene Chaisson, took him to school on his first day; he buried his face in her skirt at the horror of it. Later the teachers thought he might be ill, he was so silent, and in some alarm Mrs. Muskie took him to a doctor who established his health. Friends from the first grade recall the child sitting alone on the school steps at recess, staring into the distance.

His natural shyness was somewhat exacerbated by the prejudice he encountered in his first school. It was 1920, and as he once said, "there was this antiforeigner feeling, against the Germans and the Poles and the rest of us from Eastern Europe." The Ku Klux Klan was active in Maine and he remembers crosses burned on the hillside. He was called "a dumb Polack" a few times. But after the second or third grade the Muskies moved to the house in the Virginia section and he remembers no more prejudice. He had already made a good record at the school he was leaving. The teachers there told his father they were sorry to see the boy go, which surprised Stephen Muskie because, as he said later, "I knew they had had trouble trying to get him to play with other children."

Apparently by instinct, Muskie did not reveal himself to his friends. Their memories today are almost always of what he was like, not of things that he did. He was with them, around, on the edges, the shy boy who is liked well enough but remains peripheral. Muskie remembers his boyhood as happy. "I had lots of friends," he said once, a little defensively. "I had to overcome shyness, especially with girls, but hells bells, we played baseball, football, skiied in the pasture on barrel staves, went fishing, roamed over those hills in back of the house, played cowboys and Indians. We skated on the river in the winter and built bonfires on the shore. How can you grow up in a town like Rumford and not have fun? You step out your back door and go tree-climbing, building tree houses, picking strawberries in the summertime, oh, so many things we did—we were busy all the time."

Just the same, he was never gregarious. "He was a loner," his sister, Irene, said. "He just liked to be alone." He discovered reading early, as do many shy and intelligent children. The librarian told Mrs. Muskie that she thought Ed read every book in the library, an indicative exaggeration. He learned to croon in the style of Rudy Vallee and even went to dances, but he was very uneasy with girls. He developed crushes so violent that at times he sat beside a girl he liked and quivered but could barely speak, and it turned out that Rumford girls did not find this very appealing.

Muskie remembers high school as a time of adventurous awakening. Teachers liked him and sometimes in their absences he took over their classes. A young teacher, Mrs. Lucille Abbott, who taught a surprisingly unstructured class that ostensibly covered history and government but more accurately dealt with the changing institutions of the United States and may have been one of the true starting places in Muskie's life, remembered four decades later his "logical, orderly way of thinking," and said with unusual penetration, "He was just an average boy who was much more than average." He also was developing the competitive spirit that is vital to politics, though he usually concealed it. He was president of his class, president of the student council, valedictorian—and when it appeared briefly, through some administrative slip, that the latter honor would go to another, Muskie literally was sick with disappointment, crushed, pale. When word came of the error, he erupted with joy.

He was mildly popular in high school and coached the other students without making them feel inferior, though they always saw him apart. Once the basketball team won a game in Lewiston. "That night we were all running in the halls of the hotel, raising hell and celebrating, and I remember looking in Ed's room," a teammate said. "He was sitting on the bed studying. But you couldn't hate the guy."

He was cautious, even then. "He would never go with us to steal apples and things like that," a friend said. "He was afraid of getting into trouble." Frank Anastasio, now a barber in Rumford, said reflectively, "You know, it was as if there were two sides of me in those days, one with Ed and one with the others. We'd get together on Sundays and shoot craps and play cards, and that was very bad. But Ed didn't do that and we didn't invite him, we didn't suggest it. He was different." After Muskie was inaugurated as governor of Maine there was a reception and a receiving line. Frank Anastasio went through it and when he reached Muskie and shook hands they chatted a moment. Nervously, Anastasio's wife plucked at his sleeve to hurry him along. Muskie still had Anastasio's hand and he said, very softly, "Take it easy, Frank; let 'em wait."

He was a tall boy, very thin, awkward, who had to work hard at athletics, a striver and an achiever who may have been cautious most of all because he was vulnerable. "Poor Ed," his sister, Lucy Paradis, next younger than he, once said, "That was his nature. He was just as God made him, shy and withdrawn—and now he's grown up and he's smarter than all of us."

In high school, and even more important in college, Muskie went out for debate, which was one of the great turning points in his life. At Bates College he fell under the tutelage of the late Professor Brooks Quimby who made Bates a power in the debating world at that time and who was by all accounts an extraordinary teacher. He was a vigorous, opinionated, articulate, fiery sort of man and his attitudes were precisely tailored for the field of debate. On the one hand he delighted in a good fight about any subject whatsover; and on the other, he had a punctilious sense of form, propriety, the standards of a gentleman. He was intelligent and very quick and he gutted a shallow argument. A more combative boy might have been put off by his demands, but Muskie, who was receptive and unassuming, was enthralled. He never lost his feeling for the old teacher. Quimby was dying of cancer during Muskie's 1968 campaign. When Muskie heard he broke out of his schedule and called. "Brooks," he said, "I've been wanting to go over some points in the campaign with you." They talked for an hour without mention of Quimby's illness and then Muskie went back to the race.

The footing that Quimby gave Muskie in debate is fundamental to his career. It had many effects on him, but one of the clearest was that it gave him a structured form in which to escape shyness. It gave him a reason to stand up and talk and a forum for doing so. The rules of debate forced him into channels with the rest of the contestants, and once he was moving, his quick mind and his developing ability to cut to the heart of an argument were free to rove across the problem and bring up his capacities.

Unlike many shy men, Muskie has a powerful ego and his self-confidence appears always intact. Debate did not give him something new—it just released him. It also led him naturally into politics. Although he did not consider politics as a profession until he was forty years old, a review of his life shows that its skills were the only thing which he always was good at and which he always liked.

"I guess I need politics," Muskie once said, "or something like it, because without it I wouldn't really feel alive." It is a raison d'être; it is coloration, it is another vent that frees him. If debate is a structure in which to focus argument and channel speech, politics is a structure in which to deal with people, and it seems to make Muskie an extrovert. He arrives in political situations smiling and happy, full of banter and often clever small talk and camaraderie. He shakes hands, massages shoulders, hugs women and is the pleased center of attention. On the rostrum he can wax sentimental over shared recollections or sail into sweeping speeches or break up over his own quips. At a fund-raising dinner in Minneapolis one night in 1971 he was so taken with a series of jokes he was making at Hubert Humphrey's expense that he choked to a momentary halt, clinging to the rostrum and grinning helplessly at a thousand people. Away from politics he is an introvert. The change between the two is startling and often abrupt. He rides to the political event in lonely silence, staring from the car window. He goes in the hall and erupts. He comes out, exuberance already fading, tiredness setting in and sinks into silence, watching the road slip by.

Shyness holds a man tight as a vise and is just as uncomfortable. The rest of Muskie's family seem to have escaped its effects. As often as his mother has said she really didn't understand Muskie, she has said that it was his younger brother, Eugene, whom she enjoyed. It was not a matter of relative affection; Eugene was lively, laughing, full of fun, and Ed was shy, introverted, his mind in the distance. The others in the family have loud, hearty voices and they laugh readily. Eugene's friends in Rumford remember his resistance to his father's urgings that he should emulate his older brother. "Be like Ed! Be like Ed!" they remember him snapping long ago. "I don't want to be like Ed; I want to drink beer."

Muskie is a man of strong and effective personality despite his native shyness. This is not always immediately visible because he often allows his personal force to lie quiescent until something triggers it. Personal force is an ambiguous quality compounded of emotion, force of intellect, the capacity for anger, the ability to dominate men and situations, and it is much easier to recognize than to describe. Perhaps its central ingredient is the least definite of all—native toughness, both intellectual and personal.

The equation begins with and could hardly exist without a solid personality. Despite his shyness, Muskie never seems to have doubted his own value or to have seen himself in small terms. He has been in authority a long time and he is used to being the center of attention, to giving orders rather than taking them. Muskie is competitive but he takes failure easily. During Arthur Goldberg's gubernatorial campaign, Muskie spoke to some fifteen hundred leading Democrats at the Americana Hotel in New York City. A few months earlier he had spoken poorly in New York, and this time he wanted to recoup, to shine before what is probably the toughest audience in politics. But that morning he had been campaigning in the potato fields of Aroostook County, Maine, hard against the Canadian border where winter's chill comes early, and by the time he reached New York he had a cold and was tired and edgy and his speech failed. It was flat and badly written, and after a while he put it aside and spoke extemporaneously and that didn't work either. It was an opportunity to star—other than an obligatory speech by Goldberg, he was the only speaker—and he failed it. In doing so, he lost another chance to swing a segment of the politically aware in his direction. Returning to Maine on a small plane that night, Muskie gave no hint of recrimination, toward himself or anyone else. He talked briefly with his aides and then sank into his usual silent abstraction, gazing out into the night as the plane took him home. When things are done they're done—as in the furor that followed his discussion of a black running mate—and he shrugs and goes on. This quality of confidence and some clearly (though internally) defined standard give Muskie a consistency which is important to his broad support. People see the same man each time and thus confirm and solidify their feelings.

Muskie brings a powerful intellect to the equation of personal force. His mind is considered one of the best in the Senate, which, despite occasional obvious lapses, is an arena of powerful minds. The range of his thought when he is engaged makes his conversation very pleasant. He has a subtle, flexible way of shifting perspective in midstroke, so that the question shakes into a juxtaposition that you had not considered. New ideas pop out carelessly, often in the form of reflections that draw distant and abstract things into tight relationship. Overall, however, the clear impression that one draws is not of brilliance but of strength, sharpness, quickness and the capacity to drive to the heart of a problem. It may have been unusual in terms of international politics that Premier Kosygin of the Soviet Union spent nearly four hours talking to Muskie in the Kremlin in early 1971, but the fact that he found Muskie's mind worth engaging for that time is not surprising. They are both practical men of state.

Muskie is not an intellectual and does not pretend to be. His education was good, but he gives the clear impression today that it was a beginning base from which he moved rather than a central part of his life. Literary allusions are very rare in his conversation and his occasional historical references usually deal with American history. He does not seek out the company of intellectuals or seem interested in their concerns or their theories, except for the ones which might offer solutions to public problems. Once he was given a luncheon at the Harvard Club in Boston with a dozen guests, about half of whom were among the ranking intellectuals in America. The guests told Muskie generally of their concern for the country, and he responded with what amounted to a short, intelligent speech, though it was given in conversational voice. It was during the 1970 campaign, and as I listened, I realized that he was saying essentially what he had been saying on the stump all over the country, even using some of the same phrases and illustrations. Later several of the men said they were favorably impressed, which may mean that in the end we all seek the same comforts from politics. Muskie's schedule forced him to leave the luncheon before any genuine give-and-take could develop—which did not disturb him at all. His interest in intellectuals runs along practical lines—positions papers, backgrounds on things like foreign policy and the economy, speech drafts, novel solutions to problems—and when he talks about intellectuals it is likely to be in terms of building a system for seeking their help, monitoring and using what they offer and seeing that they are thanked.

The force of Muskie's mind is most clear when it is applied to problems. His reputation as governor and as senator grew on his hard focus on problems, and as one of his associates once said, "If you accept the idea that the brain is a muscle which develops with exercise, you see he's been growing ever since through cerebration." He brings a hard skepticism to his treatment of problems. He is known in committee for the searching examination he gives ideas, turning, probing, analyzing and, if he finds one weakly buttressed, often shredding it definitively with a casual, almost absent air. He dislikes the fuzzy and the incomplete, and his mind tends to skip ahead, absorbing and moving through the next three and four stages of the argument or the consequences that acting on the argument can be foreseen to produce, and focusing on some ramification well down the road. What then? he suddenly demands of the idea's proponent, who quite possibly has not yet traveled that far and thus finds the question disconcerting. He has a way of shaking out the argument —"Just sharpening the issues," he says with a faint frosty smile— and recasting it with a whole new set of conclusions which are seen to flow naturally from his opponent's position, but which at the same time serve quite effectively to undermine it.

John McEvoy, Muskie's administrative assistant, once summed up Muskie's thought processes this way: "I think he's at his best in terms of problems. He devours alternatives. He rejects an a priori argument, rejects things that are not factually based, not founded on data, that one can't explain and defend. Many public men prefer not to have alternatives, you know. They prefer to have a staff they trust develop a course of action which they then approve or disapprove, and in the latter case the staff then rethinks the problems. Muskie is always interested in alternatives, and usually has some of his own. I noticed immediately an ability to break a conclusion into its parts and examine each part. He is very fast and seems to do this in a reactive way. He deals with mirror images of ideas; that is, he sees the backside, the opposite side, which means he sees the whole idea and thus the fragments into which it can fall and the effects it can have. Often enough he asks questions as if they appear as part of the problem when in fact he has gone through to the conclusion and broken it into fragments and now his questions are tracking back from the fragments. So you see, he takes an idea and splits it, as if he perceives immediately that it is not just one but perhaps five ideas, which is another way of saying that he sees the complexities that are hidden from many people who see only the vague outlines of the idea."

Muskie's ability to handle people, which is part of his success over the years, also relates to force of intellect. In the Senate, fellow members quickly recognized his political sense and found they could trust him to make judgments and take positions that were consistent with the political realities. What gives him a sure-footed way through the shoals of problems is his ability to recognize quickly where the real interests of the various sides lie and to maneuver with these interests and their implications fully in mind. He is able to supply some guidance long before the other fellow sees where the situation ultimately leads.

"You know," McEvoy added, "he has a very canny ability to say just the right thing to bring the other guy along. He sort of leads him up to the precipice and then induces him to jump. It takes great patience. He's willing to listen to the other fellow a long time before he starts talking, but then what he says brings the man along, usually unaware, until the guy finds himself doing what Muskie wants him to do. It doesn't always work, of course, if the other guy sees where he's being taken, or if it's someplace he really doesn't want to go, but lots of times it's just that he hasn't thought it through and Muskie has, so Muskie can shape it as he goes along and see that it all falls out where he wants it to."

Another factor of intellect in Muskie is the capacity to sense common denominators of human experience and feelings, and then cast the issues that trouble people in those terms. In such a framework issues become understandable and real, something which people can deal with. Some of Muskie's appeal to a broad range of the American people seems to be his capacity to get to the root of their feelings and fears and thus offer directions. While such a quality clearly is intellectual, it also depends upon intuition and emotion.

One of the more misleading facts of Muskie's nature, considering his cool, Maine-bound attitudes, is that he is a deeply emotional man. Emotion pours from his extemporaneous speeches, sometimes in disturbing amounts, as if released by the format of speaking. It is all a little startling, since it seems contradictory. But it is there, held in tight control that cannot really keep it down, and it probably explains why Muskie is widely perceived as a warm man despite his coolness. People admire cool restraint, particularly in a hot and ugly time, but they are not drawn to a man who is truly cold.

Muskie's father could and often did cry real tears over his memories of Poland and the family he had left behind. In 1959, three years after his father's death, Muskie visited the village to which his father had never returned. It was an emotional experience for him, and when he returned he wrote his constituents about it. It is a curious document, warm and yet couched in such formal restraint that he could describe his approach to the village and remark quite naturally, "I became profoundly moved as I considered that in a matter of minutes my eyes would see fields, streams and trees, and possibly even faces, that my father's eyes had seen last more than half a century before." Muskie once discussed his father at length in a filmed interview, and as he recalled his father's view of life his voice softened until it was almost tremulous. The camera's long lens was in tight and Muskie's face filled the frame. In the finished film the moisture is plain in his eyes and there is intense emotional thrust in the passage.

The contrast between the cool and the warm in Muskie is plain in his relations with his mother and sisters. There is an element of estrangement between them. They see little of Muskie, and even when he is with them there is little communication; his world is sharply different and sometimes they feel that the only common ground left is memories. They learn more of what he thinks by watching him on television than by what he tells them.

And yet, he makes it plain that he wants and needs his family around him. When there are political events in Maine—particularly dinners or ceremonies—tickets and transportation arrangements for the Muskie family always appear. Once there, they find him surrounded by politicians and pressure and he has but a moment for them, a handshake, a hug, an awkward instant, and then he is swept away.

On the night in 1968 on which he lost the Vice Presidential election, his sister, Lucy Paradis, and her husband, Henry, took Mrs. Muskie to the Waterville motel where his party gathered to watch the returns. Through that long night he sat in silence watching his defeat. At about four in the morning, though there was a room for her in the motel, Mrs. Muskie insisted on being taken home. She could not sleep in a strange bed, she said. Lucy finally yielded. First, however, she looked around for her brother. The gaiety was over, the loss certain, and someone said he was napping. Reluctantly she and her husband drove Mrs. Muskie the seventy-eight miles back to Rumford. The next morning Muskie called his sister and said, "Well, you skipped out on me." There was pain in his voice, a vulnerable sound, and Lucy has never forgotten that, nor the pain it caused her. "I guess he does need us somehow," she said. "Maybe we are where it all began."

Muskie is devoted to his wife and to his children, though he often handles them in cool ways. Jane Muskie travels constantly with him, and while she is herself a considerable political asset with a charm and vivacity that Muskie lacks, the main reason he insists on her going is that he likes to have her near. They seem very comfortable together, often quiet and relaxed, occasionally sharing a faintly bawdy joke. He does not invite her to all his conferences, but it is apparent he tells her the results because she always knows what's going on. Though he wants her along, he feels no constraint to talk to her, and when they travel he is often silent and distant. Sometimes, raising her eyebrows, she turns and talks brightly to whoever else is along, obviously leaving the bear to himself.

He was thirty-four and she twenty-one when they married

and the difference in age has given her both an advantage and a disadvantage. She handles him with an odd mixture of devotion and insouciance and manages never to lose her temper with him in public. This is a bit more than he can manage—when he is irritable he snarls at her readily. She is the only person with whom he can really afford to lose his temper, she once said delicately, "and, well, he does. And then I lose mine. And we say a lot of cruel things to each other and sometimes we hurt each other a lot. And then we make up."

It is one of Jane Muskie's important qualities, her brother, Howard Gray, once said, that she can handle Muskie's emotional force and not be absorbed or diminished by it. When Muskie talks about her the extent to which he needs her and relies on her is clear. She has borne him five children, not to mention three miscarriages, and she has always been part of his career. He made her the youngest first lady of a state in America, he has taken her all over the world, and now she is running too on the longest, hardest campaign of all. When Muskie talks about her, he makes it plain that he appreciates her.

Muskie is an emotionally volatile man, as is reflected in his sharp and sometimes explosive temper. As his move toward national leadership became increasingly serious, his reputed temper surfaced as a political issue. When he offered no demonstrations, talk about it gradually died down, but a single public explosion could revive it as a serious and possibly critical political issue. There is no doubt that he has a strong temper and that he exercises it from time to time. When he does so, it has a startling and to some people frightening effect. To those who know him, his temper is almost a cliché, but nevertheless it raises an entirely valid question which must be answered. The real terms of the question, however, are not whether he has a temper (a man without temper would hardly be worth describing) but whether it goes out of control, for only then does it imply weakness and becomes dangerous.

Muskie's reputation for temper may be increased by the fact that he often is ill-tempered, which is quite different from losing one's temper. He is irritable, complains, snaps, feels sorry for himself, turns waspish. He fizzes, as if venting pressure with a whole string of complaints. He is not pleasant company in these moods, and the people around him operate in strained silence. They tend to ignore the complaints he makes in this vein and sometimes, so common is his habit of growling, they tease him about it.

Even as a boy his temper was fierce and real, though he usually displayed it only at home. His sisters remember his eruptions over this transgression or that, and he often clashed with his father. As a man Muskie learned to focus the verbal capacities that made him strong in debate, and he could be rough in anger. His temper was slow to fire, but when it did, people remembered it and those who had suffered it did not invite it again. "He could peel a man when he really cut loose," an associate remembered, "and it wasn't very nice."

Muskie also is physically imposing, which adds magnitude to the force and a certain seriousness to the anger. He is six feet, four inches and weighs more than two hundred pounds. He has big bones, and though he is deceptively slender he is a strong man with good stamina. A story told by a hunting companion of a day in the Maine woods nicely catches Muskie's physical capacity. "We were out for woodcock, me, Muskie and another fellow," Bob Wood of Waterville said, "and we came to a log stretched over a pretty busy stream. It was a cold day and there was ice at the edge of the creek. I walked across the log and the other man sat down and bumped across. Ed started over standing up and in a minute I heard a big splash. There was Ed in water to his waist. He came wading out and the other man looked at me and I saw he figured we were done hunting for the day. But Ed sat down and pulled off his pants and his socks and wrung them out and put them back on freezing cold and said, 'Let's go.' "

Talk of temper irritates Muskie now that it has grown into a political issue and he sniffs at the idea that he might explode. Over the years, however, he has had sharp encounters. There is a somewhat choleric quality in the Senate anyway, since strong men frequently clash over issues each considers vital. Muskie's reputation there is more for moderation and quiet than for temper, but he has had fights and made enemies and it is not difficult to find people who have felt his bite. In Maine his political opponents have been trying for years to lure him into a public explosion. Once he scheduled a television debate, for which he prepared carefully. Later he found his opponent had prepared by huddling in a hotel room with a group of friends trying to think of things he could say "to get Ed mad, you know, get him to blow up on TV and look bad." Muskie's supporters in Maine who have known him better over the years than they know the man he has become still get apprehensive when they hear his voice go up and see that glitter in his eyes. One day a thick-necked man accosted Muskie at a beery Democratic picnic and attacked one of his votes. When Muskie started to explain his position, the man cried, "Oh, Ed they're leading you around by the nose." Muskie stiffened. He got a bad look on his face. "You shut up," he said, "and listen to me." He set out his position in a tight voice that started to rise. Jane tugged at his arm. He ignored her. "You get this straight," he said, glaring at the man, "no one, no one leads Ed Muskie by the nose. Not you, not anyone, and don't you forget that and don't you ever say that again." The man looked dismayed; he had been drinking and suddenly he was in deep water. "I didn't say that," he said. "You did," Muskie said. The man shook his head, and Muskie's hand came up and with a faint smile in which there was no humor he shook his finger slowly in the man's face, half remonstrating, half warning, and walked away.

The first time people see Muskie's temper they are usually startled by the changes that come over him and some are frightened. He gets bigger, he seems literally to swell up, his face reddens, a sense of pressure comes in the room. Almost invariably a tense silence falls. Then, in a controlled way that suggests he is restraining himself with difficulty, Muskie opens fire. It *is* startling: suddenly this remote, quiet man is raw and vibrant, his eyes are bright, the very features of his face seem intensified and force pours out of him. Yet he holds to his point and it is obvious that he is focusing what he is saying for effect.

Of a vivid eruption that took place one night in a Tel Aviv hotel room, Jules Witcover of the Los Angeles *Times,* who absorbed much of the brunt of it said later, "No, he wasn't out of control. He held to the subject; he was pertinent. And he had a right to be angry. We had challenged him on some procedural thing that was really none of our business. He was tired and irritable and so he let us have it, but we parted friends. In fact, when we went back to our rooms the hotel had put baskets of fruit there and we had one sent to him, kind of a joke, you know, but also a gesture . . . I found the whole thing rather invigorating."

The raw change that overcomes Muskie, the sudden outpouring of personal force, is what has given him his reputation for temper. Some people find this force very startling, even intimidating. This quality is an ingredient of any situation in which Muskie finds himself, though he often allows it to lie quiescent, just below the surface. It is why some of his own staff members are afraid of him. He does nothing to frighten them; it is just that his presence contains a quality that some people find intimidating.

A man who has watched his staff for years with a clinical curiosity said, "It's just there. They can't help it, but it takes the edge off their judgment and it affects everything they do." Muskie does nothing to exacerbate this fear, but neither does he do anything to allay it, and it is difficult to say if he enjoys it.

The answer to the question of Muskie's temper, then, is that it does not go out of control and therefore it probably is not dangerous in any total sense. It is strong and he seems to let it run more often than he needs to, and its expression is unusually vivid. It has become an old saw in Washington: "I asked Muskie about his temper—and he lost his temper." In this respect, he has brought the criticism down upon himself, though as he has grown in national leadership, his temper flashes have been increasingly modulated. Were he to become President, his voice magnified by the power of that office, expressions as vivid as some he has made in the past could be terrible in effect. Of course, to assume that he would let the fire that is in him flare as strongly in the White House as it has before is to return to the crucial question and suggest that his temper runs out of control. I think it does not. I have seen him in many outbursts but I have never seen him near losing control. I know many people who have suffered the brunt of his temper and not found it pleasant, but I have yet to meet one who describes him as having been out of control. Therefore, should Muskie become President, his temper would not rule him. On the evidence of what he has been, he would not act and react in anger and he would not terrify the world with intemperance.

Muskie's idealism is one of his most clear-cut traits. He believes in the American dream. He believes in the efficacy of the free individual. These beliefs spring from his nature and his experience, but their clearest derivation is the same as the framework in which he most often articulates them—his memories of his father and his father's faith. In a way, almost all of us believe in the American dream and in another way hardly any of us still do—and Muskie is not a damned fool about it, either, and neither was his father. When Muskie became governor of Maine, his father told a friend, "I just hope he can stay honest." Cynical? No, Muskie once said, his father just understood the pressures.

Idealism is difficult to discuss in this slick era without sounding naïve or hackneyed. But this is just another failure to reconcile what we are and what we say we are, for idealism is a strain that still runs deep in the American personality. Believably articulated, it still draws an honest response. Muskie makes idealism credible because he himself so obviously believes in what he says and because he makes himself personally believable. His demeanor and his conduct force people to take him seriously. Though he is a realist who trades regularly on the Senate floor, one rarely hears about Muskie the whispers of self-serving deals common to many politicians. The only serious questioning of his integrity I've ever heard was the assumption made by some people that he spoke for the Administration plank on Vietnam in 1968 as the price of his place on the ticket. There's never been a shred of evidence or a hint of a specific quid pro quo. Perhaps if he hadn't spoken he wouldn't have been chosen and there's no doubt the choosing made possible what he is today. He says he spoke for the plank because it seemed the best thing to do at the time, and to conclude that he did so against his conscience is inconsistent with the rest of his career.

It is clear that the most formative influence in Muskie's life was his father, the immigrant Pole who never lost his wonder at the gift of a new life in a new country nor lost sight of what it meant. Stephen Muskie *believed*—and he appears again and again in his son's speeches and private conversations. Muskie often casts his own vision of America in terms of his father's experience. By every account, Stephen Muskie was an extraordinary man, and his son was deeply devoted to him.

When Muskie represented Waterville in the Maine House of Representatives, he sometimes went to Rumford for the weekend and returned to the capital with Lucia Cormier, who then represented Rumford. Miss Cormier remembers stopping her car one cold morning where Muskie and his father were waiting on the sidewalk. When he saw her, Muskie turned to his father, said goodbye, kissed him and got in her car. She has never forgotten that kiss and how easy and natural it was. "There was great warmth there, between father and son," she said.

Stephen Muskie was a slender, gentle, emotional, pleasant man with a low voice and a modest manner, but he was also strong and firm. "He could control his children with a cut of his eyes," a boyhood friend of Muskie's said. When Edmund Muskie was born his parents were undecided on a middle name for him. Stephen Muskie opened the Book of Saints and paused at the name Sixtus.

"I don't like that name very much," Mrs. Muskie said.

"Sixtus was a pope, a good man," her husband said. "We will name him that."

Like his son, he got what he wanted, usually without raising his voice. He was intelligent, sensitive to what went on around him, interested in the affairs of the world, and he is remembered in Rumford today, fifteen years after his death, for his pleasant manner and for the quality of his talk. "He always had the nicest smile—somehow he put a light in your eyes," Miss Cormier said. After he died, a woman they hardly knew told his daughters, "I certainly miss your father. He always tipped his hat when he passed me in the morning and somehow, it made me feel good all day."

He made suits in his tailor shop, though more often he measured men for suits that were made in a Baltimore factory and on which he did the final fitting. His shop was an agreeable place, a narrow, deep, rather dim room, warm and a little steamy from the pressing machine. The times were unhurried and the town small, and people often came in—as in a barbershop—as much for company as for the mending that was the other part of his business. A young politician, Rupert Aldrich, who was running for his first office when Muskie was in high school, fell into the habit of visiting the shop. "It was very pleasant," he said. "All kinds of people stopped in. I was soliciting votes and I met a lot of people there. Steve Muskie was a generous, honest, likable man. He read and he always knew what was going on. He'd have something to tell you when you came in, this or that had happened, and what he thought about it. He really was a lot like Ed."

"My father thought he was as good as anyone," Muskie's sister, Lucy Paradis, once said, meaning that he relished the egalitarian stance, and he enjoyed talking to everyone who came into the shop. Most of all, however, he appears to have enjoyed talking to his oldest son. "Ed was the only one in the family who really listened to him, I suppose," Mrs. Muskie said one day, and then, a nettled expression crossing her face, added, "They always *whispered* to each other."

Stephen Muskie, then Stephen Marciszewski, was born in 1883 in the tiny village of Jasionowka, some twenty miles north of Bialystok, near the Russian border in what the deputy foreign minister of Poland would describe to Muskie seventy-five years later as "the saddest part of Poland." The family lived on a noble-man's estate, of which Stephen Muskie's father was manager or overseer. Stephen Muskie often told his own children of his boy-hood, of accompanying his father to the fields where the people cut and stacked the hay, of the apple orchards heavy with the sweet ripening fruit, of learning to fish with his father, of the big duck pond, of being given cookies in the kitchen of the great house, which he always called the *palaz*.

When Muskie visited Jasionowka in October 1959, the first thing he saw as he approached the village was that building, "large, white, somewhat shabby but clinging to the shreds of an ancient dignity." It had been converted to a state farm. Old buildings, some in ruins, surrounded it. The duck pond was intact; the son saw it as small. In the village Muskie located an aunt, widow of his father's brother. The villagers gathered in the street outside the old woman's house and welcomed him. A two-man police surveillance team had followed him in and now stood watching at the edge of the crowd. Muskie invited them to pose with him for pictures which he said he would show the deputy foreign minister later that day and the villagers were amused when the policemen "rather shamefacedly refused." In his letter later, Muskie went on to describe the people and "the barenness of their lives," and added, "But for my father's dream of freedom and opportunity, this would be my life—the life of my children."

Russia occupied that part of Poland when Stephen Muskie was a boy and regularly pressed its young men into her army. The boy's father decided early to send his son away, and in the situation, of course, it had to be forever. Stephen was apprenticed to a tailor in the village where he learned his life's trade, and just before his seventeenth birthday he walked away. He left at night and for the rest of his life he carried an indelible memory of that empty path; he turned and waved to those he left behind and then walked on alone.

After three years in England he came to America in 1903 and worked at tailor shops in Massachusetts, Pennsylvania and finally in Buffalo, New York. He was cheerful, but it wasn't easy.

Years later he told an interviewer, "I was so lonesome, so home-sick, that I would sit on the curbstone and I couldn't walk . . ."

In Buffalo he married Josephine Czarnecka and for a honey-moon took her to Rumford, Maine, simply because a friend de-scribed it warmly. He had planned all along to stay in Rumford, Mrs. Muskie now says rather sharply, though *she* thought they were going only for a visit. It was five years before she saw Buffalo again. The cousin who had introduced them had assured her that she would not like Rumford, and he was right. "It was awful," she said. "The streets weren't paved—oh, I cried every night. I wanted to go back where I belonged."

Instead her husband found work in a Rumford tailor shop. Soon she was pregnant and he bought her a sewing machine, the Singer she still uses today, and taught her to sew. His name was hard for Americans to pronounce and he decided to change it. His choice of a new name says a good deal about him. "Muskie!" he said not long before he died. "I guess there isn't another name like it in the whole world because I made it up myself." Eventually he opened his own shop and his reputation spread, for he was an excellent tailor, combining a liking for the work with conscien-tious attention to detail. In the early 1920s he bought and re-modeled the house in the Virginia section of Rumford and later bought the house next door. This modest burst of prosperity was ended permanently, however, when the depression struck Maine.

Ultimately there were six children, and though Ed was shy, they seem to have been a lively, loud, happy family. Stephen Muskie played with his children, read the newspapers, joined the Elks, took the family fishing and berrying in the summer, played cards and games, enjoyed an occasional drink, made kraut in the cellar and a good-quality home brew and seemed to find life sweet if not easy. Once when Ed came home from college wearing new maturity like an ill-fitting suit, his father offered him a drink of home brew and the boy cried, "Oh, no, Father. I learned to drink in college. Get out the whiskey."

Late one night in the study of his Washington home when he had come in exhausted from the incessant campaign in which he lives, Muskie fell into a nostalgic reverie about Christmas. "Oh, sure, the presents were modest," he said, brightening, throwing off some tiredness at the memory. "My father didn't believe in spoiling kids, but we always had books for Christmas, the girls had dolls or my mother would make a whole new wardrobe of clothes for last year's dolls. Well, we are too damned lavish with our kids for Christmas these days and there was nothing like that in my father's house, but on the other hand, we always had plenty of games, and the dinner table at Christmas just groaned. My mother was a marvelous cook and there would be a big turkey and—oh, puddings and pies and cakes and all those vegetables, fabulous meals. And my father would go into the woods and pick the Christmas tree and bring it home. We didn't have electric lights on the tree, but we had candles. How they ever managed it I don't know—I remember a hundred and fifty candles on the Christmas tree and every night they would light it. Imagine that— it must have been beautiful; I remember it as beautiful. I mean, they just went all out to make Christmas in their warmth and love."

Prayer was a basic part of the family's life. Stephen Muskie was always up first in the morning's darkness. He would light the furnace, kneel by the dining-room table to pray and then rush outside to exercise. Muskie's sisters still whisper prayers in Polish and a college roommate remembers Muskie kneeling automatically beside his bed each morning. Muskie still does not miss Sunday mass, at home or on the road. When he travels over the weekend his staff locates the nearest church and he slips in the back as the mass begins, offers the response in a soft, clear voice, drops a little money in the plate and slips out again, threading through the crowd and away. Without quite saying so, though occasionally he takes a friend along, he keeps mass a private affair. Oh, yes, he said once when asked, "I think a man needs— especially at this time—some way to seek that kind of inner guidance and solace and comfort and strength; I get a great deal out of going to church." He leans on it heavily, he said, particularly in times of tension and strife. Catholicism no longer is much of a political issue and Muskie probably makes it less so because his attitudes in these areas are fixed more by ethics than by religion. He long has been in favor of government support of birth control, for instance, but still is disturbed by the idea of indiscriminate abortion, and it appears obvious that both reactions grow from internal reasoning rather than religious teaching. It is plain that the whole Muskie family was and still is devout, but in a relaxed way, with very little sense of the peril of hellfire.

That old doom-sense view of religion would never have been Stephen Muskie's way. He was a moderate man, relaxed and judicious with a pleased view of life. He spoke in the low voice that his son inherited and always deliberated thoughtfully and at length when the children wanted to do something. Then he set out clear rules for them to follow and they had the comfortable knowledge that so long as they did they were safe, for their father would not change the rules. He was close with money but he could be generous. "He bought us things we would enjoy," Muskie said, "ice cream, hot dogs, things like that. He didn't stint us on what he thought we needed, and his test of what we needed was generous considering how he had to struggle . . ." He took pleasure in his work and he did not charge much for it. "He told me," his oldest daughter, Irene Chaisson, once said, "when I went out to work, to do my best, exactly as I would want someone else to do it for me." He irritated his family in hard times because he spent hours on meticulous reweaving to repair holes in garments but rarely charged more than a dollar. "It's such a little thing to charge for," he said, "and yet they need it." He disliked hearing ill spoken casually of another. "If you said something bad about someone," Irene said, "he would right away bring out something good about the person."

His oldest son's stubborn temper developed early and father and son often clashed. The boy's weapon was silence, which infuriated his father; nothing, including real whippings, could induce him to answer. Irene hated those bouts. There was something raw in their faces that cut her and she would run upstairs to her room when they began. Once Stephen Muskie bought the boy a yellow slicker raincoat and rain hat, and the boy decided he looked foolish in the rain hat and refused to wear it. His father said that he would, the boy said that he would not, and a confrontation began. It is a legend in the family today; they all remember the rage, the noise, the implacability. But oddly, no one remembers how it came out. It is as if in foreshadowing the future, Muskie and perhaps his father as well were demonstrating a certain political ability: perhaps they delayed the battle until it stopped raining and then never allowed the subject to arise again. When Stephen Muskie lost his temper a terrible look would come across his face and he would strip off his belt. Once in his anger he caught it by the wrong end and gave Ed a crack with the buckle. Perhaps sensing his tactical advantage, the boy, who was about twelve, "screamed and cried," Mrs. Muskie remembered. "Oh, it must have hurt him awfully. My husband turned white. He didn't say anything. He went in the living room and sat down." That was the last beating Stephen Muskie ever gave his children, all of whom felt that Ed had suffered in good cause.

Perhaps they fought hardest because they were closest; they had a special relationship, one that neither the other children nor the mother shared. "I can see so much of my father in Ed today," his sister, Lucy Paradis, said, "the same way of thinking, the same expressions, the same serious attitudes." Mrs. Muskie, who is quick, abrupt, not given to elaborate reflections or recollections, remembers their talks well. "Somehow he could talk more with Ed," she said, "it was as if they thought alike, even though they often differed, often quarreled." Muskie's father liked to talk. He would sit in an overstuffed chair in the living room with his paper and sooner or later the boy could come and their low, slow voices would begin.

In high school Muskie was friends with a boy named Charles Taylor, who often came to the Muskie house and was fascinated by Muskie's father, whom he remembers as "one of the most perceptive men I ever met." He was "tremendously grateful," Taylor thought, "for what the United States had done for him." The old man was unusual in that after years in this country he had not lost his acute consciousness of his new equality. He liked to talk about it and to spell out to the listening boys how important it was to him as a human being. He never let them forget how different his childhood had been. He was proud also of Poland and his heritage, and he talked, as good teachers do, in stories, fables and parables. He talked to the girls about the world's dangers, by which, Irene said, "he meant men," and he talked to the boys about life. Many of Ed's friends regarded his father with awe and dreaded his talks, from which, as Frank Anastasio put it, "we were too polite to leave, we had to stay and take it." But Charles Taylor, who saw more of Stephen Muskie than any of Ed's other friends, remembers him "oh, very vividly, after all these years, and that's why I'm so sure he had such a powerful influence on Ed." Taylor remembers too that "Mr. Muskie didn't command the audience, either. We just gravitated toward him. I'd often be there in the evenings and we'd sit down with him for a while. I was editor of the high school paper and Ed was a writer for it and we often went to meetings at night. But before we left we would talk a while and I think Mr. Muskie enjoyed that. They weren't really conversations—he did most of the talking. His voice was low, his English broken, and one had to listen carefully to hear him. Looking back, I can see his depth more clearly now than I could then. One absorbs most lessons in retrospect, you know, but the strength of the memory assures me that the effect was real. What did he talk about? Well, of course, it wasn't so much what he said as the impressions he conveyed, the attitudes, his sense of the proprieties, of man's place in the world, of politics and man's responsibility to his fellows, of values and what was important and what was ephemeral and how a man should live his life. That's really what he talked about."

Once Muskie and Robert Maynard of the Washington *Post* were talking about their immigrant fathers, and Muskie observed, "As I look back, my father was a very strong man—in a well-defined sense of personal values and standards and objectives . . . he always had a clear message that you've got it in you. He was full of stories, but they all came around, all the things he used to say and stand for, came around the strong character. Nothing in my life is going to give me as good a test of what's in me as he had. He met it, surmounted it. Of course he was strong."

In that filmed interview in which Muskie betrayed such emotion at the recollection of his father's effect on him, this is what he was saying as the long lens drew close:

"Well, I suppose the effect was more unconscious than conscious—I'm sure it was. Because thinking back, here's a man who came to a strange country as the result of a deliberate plan which his father had put together for him. The objective must have been clear from the beginning: that there was no future in his home, no future in his own country, not in the eyes of his father, at least. And he was to be sent to a new country to find a future and to build one. And I'm sure without knowing really what passed between his father and himself that he understood that in order to build such a future its quality and its characteristics would depend upon the kind of man that he was, the kind of man that he became, the values that controlled his life. And it seems to me as I think back upon that part of his life that I knew, that these things were always uppermost in his mind, that he thought consciously of such things as integrity, being true to himself, self-discipline, obedience, truth. And I can't recall his ever departing from what can only be described as a very rigid standard."

And to an audience of white ethnic Americans he further explained:

"Everybody in this room is either an immigrant or descended rather recently from immigrants . . . somebody had to struggle to make it possible for us to be here tonight. Someone had to believe in something, believe in it deeply enough to sacrifice a great deal, to assume heavy burdens, to risk disappointment, for us to be here. My father used to talk to me about it. And running through his stories was the lesson he was trying to teach us of the importance of the individual, of his rights, of his opportunities to be free and to work. He was teaching us about the values of such things as self-reliance, self-restraint, self-discipline and self-respect . . . [instead of] selfishness. He understood, coming from a part of the world where the individual was nothing, how important it was for the individual to be free to grow, to become something bigger and better, stronger, wiser, more enlightened."

When Muskie entered politics in Waterville he did so as a Democrat. He supposes his father was a registered Republican because at the time a man had to vote in Republican primary elections to have any voice in local affairs, but he also is sure his father voted regularly for Democratic Presidential nominees.

But it is an oddity characteristic of their relationship that it did not occur to him to ask his father how he voted. Of course he would not have done that, he said once, rather primly; a man's vote is his own and one does not inquire. And for all of the father's sentimentality about his Polish boyhood, he was not a particularly demonstrative man. He found it difficult to say thank you, Muskie has said, and he simply did not, apparently ever, compliment or congratulate the boy on his academic and elective achievements in both high school and college. Muskie very much wanted his father's approval, and though he sensed he had it, he hungered for overt tokens. Once, "when we were having a little spat," Muskie challenged his father on this and the older man snapped that he expected his children to do well and saw no reason to compliment them when they met his expectations. "Well," Muskie said much later, "he didn't believe in showing affection very much except in the things he did for us . . . He didn't believe in praise, and I thought I did very well in high school and I rather resented—oh hell, I really knew, I just was being petulant . . . feeling sorry for myself."

When Muskie was elected governor, his father's pride was obvious if still unspoken. That he could leave the old country in the dark of the night, come to America and live to see his son elected governor of his state must have been proof of all he had believed. He had a serious heart condition by this time and had sold his shop with an arrangement to continue working there on a limited basis. His son was gone, grown, caught in the press of events, and their long talks were finished. On the night of the election, which almost no one expected Muskie to win (Muskie himself was torn between hope and pessimism), the old man told his wife, "Tomorrow you will be surprised when you wake up and find our son is elected. But to me it will be no surprise because I am sure now that he will be elected." Mr. Muskie had been ordered to give up cigarettes, and though the family knew that he still had one occasionally, they were startled to see him pacing the house restlessly that night smoking constantly as the returns poured from the radio. He stayed up most of the night listening, though his wife tossed her head, said she could wait until the next day for the news and went to bed.

Stephen Muskie enjoyed the governor's mansion. He and Mrs. Muskie went to the Legislature for their son's inauguration; they were announced when they entered the crowded chamber and there was a round of applause. At the mansion he took off his shoes and napped on a couch, an egalitarian touch that appears to have pleased him. And once he did voice his approval: remembering the beatings he had given the boy, he said to Irene, "See how smart Ed is? I should have licked the rest of you more."

He died on January 25, 1956, when he was seventy-two, a bit more than a year after the inauguration. His health had been failing and he was working less and less. He was a devotee of the ancient art of predicting the future through the fall of the cards. Every night, his daughter Lucy said, "he would lay out the cards. I think he knew when he was going to go." For some time he had wanted to clarify his wife's social security status, since she was to be sixty-five the following March. It had meant sending to Buffalo for a copy of her birth certificate and she had been reluctant, not wanting to be bothered. He persisted, however, and the paper eventually came. He and Lucy took it to the social security office and set in motion the necessary formalities and one day a letter arrived which confirmed her eligibility. After lunch he sat in the living room and studied the letter with obvious satisfaction.

That day now has a crystalline quality in Mrs. Muskie's memory. "After he read the letter he called me in and sat me on his lap and held me. He didn't often do that. He explained the letter and what it meant, and then he kissed me hard and he said, 'Well, I guess I go now.' " He went to the Elks Club and spent a long, pleasant afternoon playing cards. He came home on a bus that left him a block from his house. There was a driving north wind and he walked against it and in that block he had a final heart attack. He reached his own front yard and lay down in the cold and died curled on the ground with his steel-rimmed glasses neatly folded in his hand. His family found him there. Mrs. Muskie has never stopped thinking of that day. Her wash was freezing on the line and if she had gone out for it she would have found him; if she had sat in the window watching for him, as she often did, she would have seen him fall; but she did not.

He had spoken in the past of a modest funeral, but Muskie was adamant. His sisters remember Muskie, face drawn, saying, "He didn't get much out of my success, but he'll have that, at least." Muskie had given his father a watch; he saw that it was buried with the old man. It was an elaborate funeral, at which Stephen Muskie's son arrived in the gubernatorial limousine, Maine One. But the actual service was small and private. It ended at a cemetery that lies high on an open plateau from which you can see for miles, where the Rumford hills are dark and distant all around and the sky seems bright as morning. When press photographers appeared, Muskie drove them away.

3

Metamorphosis of the Down-east Yankee

In every situation in which Muskie has found himself since he was forty years old, his potential has reached far beyond the expectations that anyone held for him. It is an odd point to make of a man who went in sixteen years from small-town lawyer, and none too successful a one at that, to Presidential candidate, but it also explains a lot about Muskie. It explains why his record seems curiously remote and even unimpressive, considering his position and it contributes to a general confusion about what the man is. It is as if he is always running ahead of himself, as if his past never quite explains him.

The patterns in which a man grows delineate what he is more than do his actual capabilities. There was never any question of Muskie's intelligence, competence, diligence, grasp. Growth is the widening of horizons, the enlargement of self, the expansion of consciousness that allows a man to apply his abilities at a higher, wider level. In Muskie's growth, there is none of the usual sense of a successful man developing like a tree adding rings year by year until it is the largest in the forest. Nor is his growth that of the usual ambitious man, fires within burning hot and visible so that everyone sees that he's a comer. No one ever thought Muskie was a comer. He simply rose as the situation opened, moving at the speed necessary, sometimes in a few weeks, sometimes over a period of years. For the first forty years of his life, he hardly moved; there was a curiously unfulfilled quality about him that he did nothing to change until suddenly the way opened before him. He decided to run for governor. Then in less than a month his performance was that of a different man and a few months later he amazed the state of Maine and made headlines from coast to coast.

It is odd—but Muskie seems to rise from one plateau to the next simply because the opportunity appears. Until it does, he stands by, not fully content but doing nothing very active to force it. And in these waiting times he seems to have had no particular expectation that the next step would come nor even to have thought much about it. It is as if he had no idea how far he might go—or even whether he would go at all—if the situation had not opened up to him. Once it did, he moved into it with authority and rose steadily until he had reached its upper limits—and there, once more, he hovered, bumping slightly against the upper edge but doing nothing apparent to break through.

It would libel Muskie to imply that rising from small-town lawyer to Presidential candidate was all sort of an accident, that he floated up like a balloon cut free of its string. He rose, when the way was open, on sound abilities that were the more surprising because they had not been very apparent. His growth was not accidental but its triggering mechanism was unusual. This is important in understanding Muskie as a person and considering him as a Presidential candidate. To be seen fully, Muskie must be seen in process: he defines himself best in the act of becoming.

This makes for confusion: look at what he has been and you see little of what he is becoming. See him as an unhappy lawyer and you cannot imagine the gubernatorial candidate he became. See him elected governor by what appeared to be a fluke and you cannot anticipate the success he achieved. See the newcomer banished to the Senate's outer edges who worked his way to the center of its power, the unknown nominated for the Vice Presidency who became a sterling candidate, the modest man from a minor state who became his party's leading Presidential candidate. Take any of these in place and you've no reason to suspect the next will follow—but each did.

The quality adds to the conflicting view of Muskie. People who perceive politicians see movement, not record. Their reaction is sensory, not specific. The same things may draw the politically aware, but when they turn to examine, they examine not what he is becoming but what he has been. Naturally, in Muskie's case, the process is irritating, since he seems to promise more than his record justifies; actually he simply is moving beyond his record and defining himself more in his movement than in his past.

This also is one of the causes of his failure to take national leadership much earlier in his career, a central shortcoming in his Presidential candidacy. The other side of rising only to challenge is that one doesn't bother to rise unless one is challenged. There is a suggestion in this quality of someone easily satisfied who does not generate his own excitement and involvement. At a time when ambition and a sense for great issues were propelling Hubert H. Humphrey, for instance, into the center of national affairs, Muskie seemed to feel no such thrust. He was moving along his own path, doing what came naturally, rising in the arena that clearly was open to him, which then was the Senate and not the national stage. This is not a fatal flaw—the White House, after all, provides its own thrust—but neither is it an advertisement for leadership.

There is a destructive side of ambition that Muskie seems also to have missed. He is not hungry for power; he apparently likes it, but he seems to have no more drive to acquire it for its own sake than he does to acquire money. That is one reason he never bothered to rule the Democratic Party in Maine, though it is almost his own creation. He and a handful of others took the reins when they were dropped by an old guard that literally had exhausted itself in internecine fighting and futile challenges to the Republican majority. Muskie was elected governor that year, the only winner on the slate, and by his conduct of the office he made the party viable; though still in the minority, it has been able to win elections. It has depended on him ever since. He even supports it financially; in 1970 he gave the state committee some twenty thousand dollars from his own fund-raising to keep it solvent.

But Muskie exercises no authority over the party. This was never more evident than when Bill Hathaway, a Maine congressman, turned on Muskie at the Democratic State Convention in 1968. The issue was a move to unite the Maine delegation to the national convention behind Muskie as a favorite son. In Maine, at least, his chances for the Vice Presidential nomination were discussed widely and it was clear that a united delegation would support Humphrey. Hathaway, who supported Robert Kennedy, attacked the favorite-son plan in a bitter speech. Muskie, listening in silence, took it as a personal blow. After Hathaway's motion was defeated, Muskie made an angry speech in which he pointed out emotionally that he had not sought this honor, nor had he sought *any* personal advantage from the party. Hathaway was momentarily abashed, but the point is that in the disciplinarian school of politics he would have been punished. Instead, though Muskie is usually prickly and quick to suspect unfriendliness, he did not let this incident rattle the party or change his public attitude toward Hathaway, with whom he still plays golf. Maine's young governor, Kenneth Curtis, likes and admires Muskie, but he makes it clear that he is of a subsequent generation of Democrats and has his own power base which operates independently of Muskie. That is true, but only because Muskie allowed it to develop so; a different man would have held the power to himself.

The nature of Muskie's growth accounts for his quiet beginning as a Vice Presidential candidate. At a press conference in San Francisco early in the campaign a reporter began by noting that Nixon had just said that he would continue to eat California grapes and drink California grape juice. Was that Muskie's feeling too? The reference, of course, was to the strike and boycott which César Chavez was leading on behalf of Chicano grape pickers against the big growers of the San Joaquin Valley. This was a cause with which Robert Kennedy had identified himself and Chavez had staged a widely discussed fast earlier that year. The boycott against California table grapes had reached Europe; there had been picket lines in New York City protesting their sale. But Muskie responded, "I don't know. I like California grapes. I have eaten them. Why, did he have some special reason for saying that?" Someone explained the situation briefly, and Muskie, face darkening, realizing that he had slipped into trouble, said shortly, "I have no position on it as yet. I haven't had a chance to study it, which (*sic*) has developed as a California issue."

The oddity of that answer so late in the day suggests that Muskie had not started the campaign as a man who long had thirsted for a national voice. He was widening his scope daily, moving from the base of what he had been, a respected Senate regular, which is a position far below the requirements for national leadership. His speeches and press conferences at the beginning of that campaign strongly suggest the newcomer from Maine feeling his way over strange ground.

Yet the other side of his unusual pattern of growth—the speed with which he can move when the way opens and the situation demands it—is equally evident in his quick success in that campaign. It was not just a matter of inviting students to his platform or of giving refreshingly candid answers to questions. What made him exciting was his political expertise, his grasp of the sense of widely differing crowds and the striking of a genuine theme. He went all over America finding ways to talk sense and decency to people, ways that they found believable. He went into Polish and other ethnic centers, particularly in the industrial states, and threw their taste for George Wallace into their faces. The likes of George Wallace was not why *his* father had come to America, he cried, nor was it why their fathers had come. He forced men who believed they were voting their interests to see that they were repudiating their heritage—and he carried it off smoothly and warmly. By the end of that campaign, Muskie was a handsome national candidate, a man whose dimensions had expanded far beyond what there had been reason to expect. He was not yet a Presidential candidate, which is still another level and one that he did not really reach for another fifteen months, but he was a vitally changed man.

Years ago, when Muskie was practicing law in Waterville, he was offered a lucrative law partnership in Rumford. He turned it down after much thought, he once said, because he couldn't imagine living the rest of his life in the stink that seeps from the great pulp mill there and pervades the town. That may not be a remark to be taken at face value (though when you have been to Rumford you can believe it), but the interesting point is that had he taken the offer and were he today a comfortable attorney unknown beyond the borders of his town, there is hardly a soul who would have thought that Ed Muskie had failed to develop his potential; he still would have been one of the success stories of the Class of '32, Stephens High.

When Muskie returned to Waterville after World War II he was thirty-one, a naval officer and lawyer, and was soon elected to the state legislature. And yet, clinging to him like an overtone of Rumford, as the smell of the mill clings long to your clothes, was an unformed quality more likely in a man years his junior. It was not a matter of competence. He was diligent, hard-working, attentive to detail. He hurried around Waterville, a tall, gaunt figure in bow ties that clipped to his collar and suits that hung loosely on his big frame, and he busied himself in the town's civic clubs. The unformed quality was an intangible impression that nevertheless is widely recognized by people who knew him then, as if he did not quite know what he wanted or why, as if he had not yet crystallized his sense of purpose. Nor did it seem to be the familiar decompression that so many returning veterans were feeling then; it was more as if he had missed compression altogether.

Perhaps it grew in part from the fact that he never found himself in the law. As we have seen, his practice obviously never satisfied him; even the way he came to it was haphazard. He finished Cornell Law in 1939 and taught school briefly in Rumford. Rupert Aldrich, the young politician who enjoyed Mr. Muskie's tailor shop and probably was instrumental in leading Muskie into the law, heard of the Waterville practice for sale, drove Muskie to Waterville and they examined it together. There is no indication that Muskie gave any thought to whether it was the right kind of practice for him or whether he would enjoy it. It was established, with books, files, records and most important, customers. Since the depression was still on in Maine in the early 1940s, the customers were the attraction, but they also turned out to be the problem. Most of the practice's clients used it for bill collecting, which is harrowing work, dealing in hectoring letters sent debtors and backed by the threat of lawsuits. "I hate collection work," Aldrich said, "and Ed did too. You have to be a mean stinker to be good at collecting." Mulling it all over, Aldrich said, "Ed was really deeper in the law than that. He was well educated and he liked complicated legal problems; he was interested in constitutional matters."

Probably as a result of the original nature of his practice, Muskie never got a foothold in law, though he soon began to shift the practice and eventually he dropped collecting. But the rich and the exciting side of law eluded him. Some lawyers work their way into the business world until they are part of it, some break new legal ground, some find cases that expand human rights and dignity and thus expand civilization itself—but Muskie did not find these cases. "I never did really get involved in the law," he once said. "I never found the satisfaction there that I did in politics. I'm not good at chasing dollars, I guess that's my trouble." It is obvious that this is how the law appeared to him. "I didn't like the fact that I couldn't pick my cases on the basis of interest but had to pick them on the basis of money, those that would pay a fee. It's a matter of people's troubles translated into dollar signs, and that's kind of distasteful."

Soon after Muskie returned to Waterville he began to court Jane Gray, who then was eighteen, a plump and pretty girl who worked in a small dress shop that had a state-wide clientele and was surprisingly exclusive. There is a photograph taken of Jane when she was seven, which seems an innocuous picture of a little girl bearing some resemblance to Shirley Temple until you notice the mouth: it is the mouth of the woman today, firm, set, determined. She was the last of five children, the baby and the star of a family that had little room for stardom. Her father, a millhand who had emigrated from England through Nova Scotia and into Maine, was ill most of her life and died in 1937 when she was ten. The family lived in poverty, the older children working and Jane's mother holding it all together by cooking and serving three meals daily in her home to some sixty young men from Colby College in Waterville. Jane was close to her mother, who, despite the hardship, was a very cheerful woman who managed always to find the bright side in whatever happened, a quality which Jane inherited and is reflected in her ability to maintain the grinding political rounds she now faces. Growing up as the pet of sixty young gallants who swarmed in her house, she could hardly have helped gaining confidence, but there also is a sense of strength and well-defined values obvious in her. Mrs. Alvina Lewia, one of the owners of the shop in which she worked, once said, "She had quality. After Stephen, her first child, was born she came in the shop one day with a package that had just arrived from Ed's mother. She opened it and it was a baptismal gown that Mrs. Muskie had made." Standing in the smart shop, surrounded by lace and silk and hats that sold for fifty dollars, the women looked at the little gown. Mrs. Lewia's voice dropped at the memory. "It was nice, but it was—well—rude. It was made of unbleached cotton, I think, and the embroidery was elaborate but quite rough. And Jane said, 'Wasn't it nice of Ed's mother to do that?' One of the girls in the shop who was quite young said, 'You're not going to put that on your baby, are you?' and Jane said, 'Well, of course—he isn't going to know the difference.' All five of her children were baptized in that gown. Jane always knew what mattered."

The shop was a real source of pleasure to Jane and it is endlessly grand in her memory. "It was one of those scary shops," she once said, "where you know everything is going to be so expensive that you don't even dare go in and ask, where there's just one thing in the window and maybe a jewel and a bottle of perfume or something and—well, I wouldn't have dreamed of going in . . ." She was working at Montgomery Ward when the impossible happened: the formidable Mrs. Lewia appeared before her desk and offered her a job; it was too much to believe. She was clerk, model, salesgirl and, dressed in its finest, a walking advertisement for the shop. The ladies taught her early the virtues of good clothes, lessons which, considering the state of Muskie's purse over the years, have brought him no great pleasure. They also took a maternal interest in her future and that of Florette, the second girl in the shop. In their eyes, the future tended to converge on that eligible bachelor, Muskie, who handled the shop's legal affairs.

It is Jane's recollection that she was entirely neutral in the matter and had no particular interest in meeting Muskie, though she also added a few minutes later that she had begged her brother Howard to introduce her to Muskie and he had refused, warning her sternly that Muskie was much too old for her. One night Muskie called a meeting of the AmVets, of which he was president, to discuss the formation of an auxiliary, and Florette persuaded Jane to attend. Afterward Muskie offered rides home to those without cars, which included Jane and Florette. "Well, he took me home last of all, which I thought was nice," Jane said, her expression still reflecting the pleasure she felt at this turn of events.

The next day he asked her for a date—to a political meeting with a cup of coffee afterward—and from then on he saw her every day. Jane was very happy, though things were tense at the shop for a while. Her mother was startled and her brothers were suspicious. In retrospect, however, it appears they were under-estimating Jane; in fact, because she was sweet, somewhat self-effacing and invariably younger than Muskie's crowd, for years there was a tendency for her husband's associates to overlook her strength, intelligence and growing political acumen.

The courtship lasted for more than two years, until Jane was twenty-one. Muskie was sharply aware of the difference in their ages. "He was hypersensitive to the charge of cradle-robbing," Jane said, "and I think that's why we carried out our courtship in the open." He came daily to the shop and took her to lunch, to the same restaurant and usually to the same table. At night they went to political and civic meetings, at which she was expected to be quiet and ornamental. They bowled and went to the movies and talked. Did they laugh, dance, play? "No, not really. He was always enjoyable to be with," Jane said, "but he was quiet. He wasn't what you'd call a live wire."

What was he like, then, from her special vantage point? "Well, he was stubborn. He had all the bachelor's faults. He was much more stubborn than he is now—why, now he hardly has any faults left." She paused and her eyebrows went up in a quizzi-cal expression. "But then he was like any bachelor, selfish, in-considerate, demanding. I thought then, well, I'll change that, but one doesn't. Still, he's much more outgoing now. He was very introverted then, very quiet. He was always well liked in Water-ville, but you had to get to know him before he opened up. He liked people though—he always liked people."

For all her sunny good nature, Jane is as volatile as her husband. "Summers were the worst time because we fought so much," she once said. "Oh, we had lots of fights." Many of them turned on an isolated lake cottage which Muskie owned. Jane was not allowed to go there unchaperoned and she accepted this as natural and proper. Perhaps because he was older and more realistic, Muskie was irritated, and it probably was her bland acceptance of the rule that turned his irritation to rage. She was a saucy young lady entirely confident of her own charms, but she also was young enough to see Muskie as an older man and consequently dangerous, and she was cautious. She moved slowly, even reluctantly, into the association which at the same time she quite ardently wanted. "I've always had a lot of respect for my husband," she said. "I admired him—had I been a man, I would have liked to be like him. But he *was* a lot older than I and I was leery of him too. I didn't want to get in over my head and get hurt—I held back and I suppose I was protecting myself.

"He would say he was going to the cottage, and if I didn't want to go that was fine—and I'd tell him to go right ahead, but not to be sure I'd be waiting when he got back. I had been interested in a very nice young medical student before Ed came into the picture, and one day Ed and I had a big blow-up and Ed said he was taking off a couple of weeks and demanded that I come along, and I kept saying, 'But I can't. There's no one down there. Girls just don't do that,' and so he stormed off. Just by chance the medical student came home that same day and I was so mad at Ed that I walked—oh, I shouldn't have done that—I walked the length of Main Street hand in hand with this boy for everyone to see, and Ed saw. He came by in his car, I forget which it was now, he always named them and I think this one was Silver Lightning—it was a Studebaker—and he passed us like a bullet. Oh, he was angry. About fifteen minutes later he turned up at my door and he was *roaring* he was so angry. He was shouting at the front door." She was smiling, looking pleased at the memory. And what happened? "Oh," she said, her eyebrows rising, "we made up."

At this point Muskie was thirty-two years old. They were married on May 29, 1948. She converted, Baptist to Catholic, Republican to Democrat. Stephen was born on March 18, 1949, and Ellen on Sept. 22, 1950. (Ultimately, they had five children. Melinda was born December 27, 1956; Martha, December 17, 1958, and Edmund, Jr., known as Ned, July 4, 1961.)

Even in the midst of love, marriage, children, there remained an unfulfilled quality, something aimless and frustrated, about Muskie's life in Waterville. He seemed to be seeking something without quite knowing what. He did not allow many people to know him well, but one who did, a man who now holds a high position in the Republican Party in Maine, described it this way: "Well, in retrospect, I didn't think it was a good time for him. He sure as hell wasn't the most-likely-to-succeed sort of fellow. He had his own ideas and he was likely to insist on them. He blew up in a hurry and he was very impatient with anyone who disagreed with him, even his best friends. There was a raw quality, a kind of irritation and impatience. He was a good cardplayer, that sense of figures he has makes him a wizard sometimes, but God, how he hated to lose. He was a good drinker in those days, too. I never saw him drunk by any means, but he could get pretty boisterous. I remember a night he met some of my wife's family for the first time and pretty soon he was telling one of them off. We got to playing poker and he was losing and he got mad. About two in the morning he lost a big pot and there was this big dramatic scene. 'Get the grocery money, Jane,' he says, glaring around the table." The man paused, remembering, smiling and yet somehow irritated at the recollection. "Oh, God, it was too much. You know, if Muskie had stayed here in practice, I think he would have been an unhappy fellow. He seemed so frustrated. But he wasn't a climber, you see; he was balked and he could have stayed that way because he wasn't really doing anything to change it."

Probably the point should not be overdrawn. The personal force later so evident slipped out from time to time. Mrs. Lewia, remembering when he was her attorney and prepared her tax returns, said, "Well, you know, he was strong. You weren't afraid of him, exactly, but he had authority."

Muskie and Jane bought a four-room clapboard Cape Cod house that had an unfinished loft with dormers, and after two children were born, he added bedrooms upstairs. He did the work himself, and when he was finished he stepped back in pleasure to survey it, sat on a railing he forgot was temporary and fell backward to the floor below. His back was broken and for weeks he lay on the edge of death in a Waterville hospital. For months it was not clear whether he would have the use of his body again;

through the summer of 1953 he crawled grimly from his lake cottage to the water, lowered himself in and swam, forcing his muscles to work again. It was in the hospital that Jane's new faith came to focus: nuns lined up outside his door praying and she was there fifteen hours every day, the chapel and prayer the only relief from the sickroom. "He could have died in my arms," she said, "and I found prayer very helpful."

Though his fellow attorneys kept his practice open, it deteriorated further during his months away from it. Then, just as he returned to work, the hospital that had saved his life ran out of money and prepared to close. The nuns needed $100,000 to remain open, and Muskie decided to raise the money. While his practice limped along he staged an impassioned campaign; from September 1953 to February 1954 he raised $120,000 and the hospital still operates in Waterville today.

In the midst of this campaign, in January 1954, Muskie received that offer of a partnership in a prestigious Rumford law firm. It was a firm with the sort of clients and income that Muskie had not achieved in fourteen years of practice in Waterville. He would be forty in two months, he had two little children and anticipated more, and he was deeply in debt from medical expenses. He agonized for weeks over the offer, tempted on the one hand and yet plainly not really wanting it, and finally, with a palpable sense of relief, he refused it.

This was a critical shift in Muskie's life, perhaps the most critical of all, for thereafter his real career began and the searching tone that had marked him so long came to an end. In effect, the avenue for growth suddenly opened before him, though neither he nor anyone else recognized it as such. In April of that year, 1954, Muskie decided to run for governor. It struck him much more as a duty than as an opportunity because there was no chance for a Democrat to win. The last Democratic governor had been elected in 1936 and for years Democrats had been losing by a consistent two to one, an impossible margin. There was an element of duty to it because when the new group of young men took over the party, there seemed a possibility that eventually they could make it visible. Muskie was national committee-man at the time, but he was no one's choice to run for governor. The slot was offered formally to at least three different men, all of whom declined, before it fell to Muskie. "He was calling people up all over the state and asking them to run," said his friend, Dick McMahon, now director of federal housing in Maine, who managed his campaign that year, "and they all turned him down because no one wanted to be the sacrificial goat, and they kept telling him, 'Listen, if you're so goddam hot for someone to run, why don't you run yourself,' and when that got hard to take, he did."

Then, to everyone's surprise, Muskie won the race and was elected governor of Maine. The details of how he did it are important in understanding Muskie, but they are more fairly seen in another context. The point here is that the insignificant at-torney had grown suddenly into a powerful candidate. As he would again in 1968, he caught his stride quickly, struck a theme and soon was outrunning everyone's expectations. Reviewing the campaign, one is struck with the smooth solidity of the man. McMahon, who traveled constantly with him and may have known him best of all at the time, believes that "the basic man was set by then. He knew who he was and what he was about and it was impossible to throw him off pitch. The rest of us were often impatient, but he rarely was. He never got excited and he never slung mud; he never hurt anybody and he never wanted to. And his timing was beautiful." At the end, it wasn't even close: Muskie won with 54.5 percent of the vote, and national reporters drove all night from Boston to interview the Democrat who had top-pled a Republican in Maine.

As in 1968, it was not that Muskie had been without experi-ence or background until then but that there had been nothing (by the peculiar terms of his nature) to cause him to grow. He actually had considerable political experience, and as if fore-shadowing the direction he ultimately would take, he demon-strated a natural flair for it. He practiced politics with a confident efficiency and pleasure that quite belied the frustrated Waterville lawyer.

From his earliest public office, when Muskie was elected to the Maine Legislature in 1946 he immediately found that he liked government. He enjoyed the process by which legislation converts ideas into laws and policies and he studied it diligently. With his capacity for hard work when his interest was aroused, he soon knew a lot about it. He liked the parliamentary form with its relationship to debate and was capable of fierce combat on the floor. Of the 151 members in the House, only 24 were Democrats that year. Muskie soon proved himself particularly adept at marshaling this tiny minority in order to assemble the combinations with various Republican factions which was the only real weight it could have. As we have seen, in his second term he was elected minority leader, and while there was no chance for Democrats to put their own ideas into effect, he kept them sufficiently organized to have some voice in the ideas of the opposition. This beginning in politics appears to have had a powerful effect on Muskie's political style and on his attitudes.

He also impressed the Republicans, who eventually sent a reporter, Peter Damborg, as their emissary to make a serious offer. Muskie smiled and said, "Listen, you fellows just don't understand—I'm a Democrat because I believe in the Democratic Party. I just don't like the way the Republicans run this state." When he left the House the majority made a series of speeches of genuine warmth and gave him a standing ovation, an honor rarely accorded Democrats.

In 1947 Muskie lost a race for mayor of Waterville to a strong Republican, partly because the Democratic Party (which has its greatest strength in a few towns, including Waterville) was in its usual disarray. McMahon remembers that Muskie was friends at the time with an old Frenchman whom McMahon characterized as "an old bum, a man whom the French wards despised," for reasons that now retreat into the past. Muskie refused to repudiate the man—"Goddammit," he told McMahon, "I'll pick my own friends!"—and the French wards went against him. Afterward, one of the ward leaders went to Muskie's office and berated him. "You see," he told Muskie, "you'd have won if you hadn't had such a friend." Muskie sat in silence at his desk, but the leader complained later to McMahon, "And you know, Muskie never offered me a drink. He had a bottle, too, I saw it right on the filing cabinet, and he never offered me a drink. Can you imagine that?"

Muskie was named state director of the Office of Price Stabilization in early 1951. The job sent him all over the state and let him build a priceless network of acquaintances, but the nature of the job was probably even more important. It was a post of limited authority in which persuasion was much more important than enforcement. It was a matter of investigating people's problems, finding the roots of their interests, making adjustments that accommodated at least part of those interests and then persuading everyone to an understanding of his view. It was a challenge that fitted Muskie's style and which he enjoyed; at the same time, of course, it further conditioned the political attitudes that he was developing.

These were the same qualities he used later as governor, and again to everyone's surprise, he was highly successful—in another surge of growth almost as soon as he took that office. As we will see, no one had supposed he would be the candidate he became, and no one expected him to be a strong governor. Republicans said his election was merely an unfortunate fluke which they would correct two years hence and then issued disciplinary statements cautioning him. The people of the state themselves seemed a bit startled at what they had done and they may have been waiting to see if they had made a mistake. Newspapers warned sternly that the coming legislative session, which began on the day the governor was inaugurated, would have to be, as one put it, "a hold-the-line session unless—and heaven forbid—we are to have new or heavier taxation."

And in fact, the Democrats did begin with very little program. They had concentrated on the campaign, not on a govern-

·ment that might follow. The only explanation that Muskie has ever offered for his sudden bursts of growth came in connection with his moving into the governorship: "I have a rather large capacity to ponder to myself the question, What if?" he said. "What if this or that happens, what will I do, how will I make it work? And driving around Maine in the campaign I had spent a good deal of time thinking about what might happen and what I would do if I was elected."

What he did in fact do was plunge immediately into his governorship and begin building on the relationship with the people that he had developed in the campaign. At the same time, he proved himself extraordinarily dexterous in driving his program through a legislature that the Republicans controlled by about four to one. By the end of the six-month session, the reversal in political position was stunning. Republicans were openly predicting that Muskie was unbeatable in the next election—which, one newspaper countered, would be "no great tragedy." In 1956, when Muskie won reelection by 59.17 percent of the vote, the Republicans were demoralized, and one newspaper, reprimanding them editorially for the violence of their rhetoric, suggested that "the only explanation for these tactics, so alien to Maine custom, is that the Republican Party apparatus is badly frightened." Muskie's second term continued the pattern of success and in 1958 he easily unseated a Republican incumbent to win election to the Senate by more than 60 percent of the vote.

And yet, though Muskie had certainly grown handsomely to meet the gubernatorial challenge, it is even more interesting that he did not appear to have grown much beyond the confines of an office that while grand to a Waterville lawyer, was still small on the national scale. There is a revealing naïveté implicit in an incident that took place that same fall when Muskie appeared in the campaign of Governor Averell Harriman of New York, who was trying unsuccessfully to beat off Nelson A. Rockefeller's challenge. They were in Harriman's limousine in a cavalcade roaring along a freeway when a motorcycle policeman stopped them and gave Harriman the speech for his next stop. Harriman opened the envelope, oblivious to Muskie, and began to read. Muskie was intrigued. "What is it?" he whispered to a friend. "It's his speech," the man said, puzzled. Muskie, who ran the government of Maine with two aides and several secretaries, said, "You mean he has a speech writer?" "He has two," the man replied, and Muskie's eyes widened.

The same quality appeared again when Muskie arrived in Washington in January 1959 and crashed head-on into the powerful Majority Leader, Lyndon B. Johnson. It was a contest he could not win, and the fact that he would let it arise suggests that he really had not grown far beyond Maine. He may have arrived with an exaggerated view of himself, since he had been in considerable national demand. The Maine election at that time came in September instead of November (in 1960 it was changed to November). That made his victory in 1954 the first major Democratic success since the Eisenhower sweep of 1952; this, coupled with the oddity of Maine going Democratic, made banner headlines in New York, Los Angeles, Seattle, Milwaukee and many other places. *Time, Life* and *Newsweek* carried stories on Muskie. He campaigned in seventeen states that fall for various Democrats as a harbinger of what did in fact turn into the Democratic recapture of Congress. In 1956 and in 1958 he was again in demand. His early election to the Senate made him the first of a surge that year that solidified the control of Congress that the Democrats have held ever since.

A certain friction with Johnson may have been inevitable, for both he and Muskie are men of great personal force. The quality emerges differently because Johnson uses his powers openly and with gusto and Muskie is more likely to hold his quiescent until something triggers their sudden release. Johnson by then was famous for his pleasure in the exercise of power; even today discussions of the various approaches to Senate power are likely to include "the Johnson blackmail method." Since Muskie's attitude to power is radically different, as his handling of the Maine party indicates, he is cool to the Johnson method. Furthermore, a man in whom personal force is a striking characteristic is quick to sense and resist pressure. Muskie was a successful and stubborn man with a demonstrated willingness to fight and it would be surprising if he did not approach this meeting with some determination not to be awed, some anticipation of metal clashing on metal.

The crucial issue as the 1959 session opened was a proposed change in Rule 22, which determines the vote necessary to break a filibuster. The Senate traditionally has been reluctant to override a determined minority. At that time it required a two-thirds majority vote to impose cloture and stop debate. Through the 1950s the strong and well-organized Southern bloc had used the filibuster to stop civil rights legislation, and as a result angry liberals in the Senate had developed real momentum toward a simple majority cutoff of debate which would have eliminated the filibuster as a parliamentary maneuver. (Today, of course, the changed situation implies some virtue in holding fast: now the old Southern bloc has collapsed, the civil rights fight has moved out of the Congress and liberals are using the filibuster to their own ends, as in the fight led by William Proxmire of Wisconsin against the supersonic transport.) Johnson, always the operator, had developed a compromise plan on Rule 22 to head off a bruising battle. Debate would be cut off not by two-thirds but by two-thirds of those present and voting. The compromise was more apparent than real since on critical issues senators leave hospital beds and come onto the floor in wheelchairs to whisper their crucial votes, as did Clair Engle of California, shortly before he died.

Muskie knew that Johnson would bring up Rule 22 at their meeting. Furthermore, he knew that Johnson controlled the committee assignments he would get and that committee assignments determined—at least at the beginning—what kind of a career he would have in the Senate. Johnson's successor, Mike Mansfield of Montana, is much more likely to let things work themselves out in the open, but Johnson's style always was to button them up in advance. The liberals felt that his compromise was a small concession, but it was nevertheless a concession and Johnson stood on it. A veteran of those days remembers, "Jesus, it was rough. Lyndon was going around with two lists in his inside coat pocket. One was for committee assignments and anything else you wanted and the other was for Rule 22. He didn't talk about the first until you'd cleared on the second and that's all there was to it."

"I was interested in meeting Johnson," Muskie said. "From what I'd heard of him I thought he did things in ways that I could appreciate. He was a practical fellow who understood you had to give and take in politics to get things done, and that's the way I had learned to work in Maine." Muskie arranged for the meeting and at the appointed time went to the Majority Leader's office, a beautiful room of carved wood, marble, wide mantels and crystal chandeliers that lies just off the Senate floor. They talked about forty-five minutes in an easy, pleasant way and Johnson gave Muskie some good if rather avuncular advice. He talked about the problem of adjusting to the role of senator from that of governor. He talked about the proliferation of issues and how hard it is to keep up and thus always vote with confidence. "There'll be times, Ed," Johnson said, leaning back with a smile, "when you won't know how you're going to vote until they start calling the M's."

Then Johnson explained his compromise plan and when Muskie did not respond, Johnson finally said, "Well, Ed, you haven't much to say on Rule 22." Muskie, of course, was not ready to commit himself. He actually favored still another compromise, a three-fifths-majority cutoff, which he thought had a better chance of succeeding than the simple majority the liberals favored. On the other hand, he felt strongly about civil rights, and at showdown he would vote with the liberals and lose, as he eventually did, and Johnson certainly knew that. It is reasonable to suspect, therefore, that Johnson's irritation went more to the style than to the substance of Muskie's answer.

Muskie has a penchant for the one-liner that makes everything clear in the laconic style of the Maine farmer, the tart remark that devastates the butt of the joke. Now, asked about Rule 22, the Maine farmer took the straw out of his mouth, hooked a thumb in his overalls and said, "Well, Lyndon, we haven't gotten to the M's yet." Zing! I had a car like that once.

Muskie has a way of grinning when he fires one of these cracks and suddenly that personal force surges out, raw, vivid, almost triumphant—and one can imagine his sudden change of manner in the Leader's ornate office adding to the effect. Muskie has always insisted that, as he once put it, "I thought it was a pleasant way to let him know that I hadn't made up my mind yet." But this happens to be a style of wit not at all appreciated in Texas, where manners are less acerbic. Johnson was angered.

It was mildly funny and not very important except for what it says about Muskie. He himself seems rather bemused by it all today. His supporters make a case for his courage, of which he has plenty, and his dedication to the liberal cause no matter the penalty. But this was, after all, his first meeting with the leader, a man well known for prickly pride. Muskie was a small-state fresh-man, while Johnson had been ten years in the Senate, six of them as leader, and with Sam Rayburn in the House was the effective alternative voice to President Eisenhower. Furthermore, his ques-tion was reasonable and couched in an affable manner; whatever its content, Muskie's answer could have been in kind. On balance, Muskie's part in the affair appears somewhat gauche.

The story is told on the hill that soon thereafter Johnson overheard Muskie repeating his retort with gusto at a cocktail party. That may be apocryphal, but the retort got around and it certainly worked its way back to Johnson. Bobby Baker, the majority secretary who then was close to Johnson, publicly dis-missed Muskie as "chickenshit," a favorite Johnsonian term for people and things that displeased him.

And so, as if his swift rise as governor had never happened, Muskie began his Senate career on the bottom, for Johnson gave him what appeared to be disastrous committee assignments and did not even deign to speak to him for months. Muskie was frozen out of the process, and the fact that he drove his way back in is a demonstration of his capacity for growth. Most senators, particularly those from obscure states, remain on the fringes. The betting then—had anyone been interested enough to bet—would have been that Muskie too would have stayed on the edges, for he had neither position inside nor extra constituency outside nor natural flamboyance to thrust him forward. Instead, with nothing going for him but his own capacities, he grew steadily. This time, however, instead of quick response to an immediate situation, his growth was steady, smooth, logical, quiet, almost imperceptible. Slowly the Senate experience toughened him and made him wiser and more skillful.

His Senate career can fairly be seen as ranging from 1959 to 1968, for though he remained a member and put through some of his most important legislation after 1968, he obviously was much more than a senator by then. Searching that period, one finds little real excitement. There were no great moral crises, no plunges into fire from which a man emerges fully tempered. He did not involve himself deeply in the great issues of the times. He did not become an originator of great ideas or a champion of causes, except for the control of pollution which then was hardly seen as a cause. Instead there is a technical, managerial quality in Muskie's Senate career which seems related only obversely to the leadership he now seeks and which doesn't do much for his leadership image.

His first years in the Senate were quiet, lonely, not very happy. He spent his time with the minutiae of legislative detail, and as late as 1963, Donald R. Larrabee, a Washington reporter who services a series of New England papers, said in the Bangor *News* of Muskie's first term that he had "virtually buried his nose in a book." Muskie, he reported, was "satisfied that his plodding pace was the right course—for himself and for Maine." Later Muskie told Larrabee that he liked the story except for the headline some anonymous deskman had appended: "First Term for Building, Effectiveness Comes Later."

New senators customarily ask for the committee assignments they want and then wait to see what happens. Muskie asked for Foreign Relations, Commerce and Judiciary. The first is a prestige committee rarely open to freshmen, but Commerce was basic to his Maine interests and a reasonable request. The Steering Committee, chaired by Johnson, gave him Public Works, Banking and Currency (which had been his distant fourth choice) and Government Operations. Public Works is important since it deals in so-called pork barrel grants for federal construction projects, but at the time it was the place where the leadership sent young malcontents so that Robert Kerr of Oklahoma could ride herd on them. Dennis Chavez of New Mexico was the nominal chairman, but he was already ill and he usually deferred to Kerr, the rancher-oilman-legislator who was very close to Johnson and was generally considered the second most powerful figure in the Senate. Kerr ran the committee and he did not encourage initiative from newcomers.

Banking and Currency was a quiet committee. Many of its areas had crystallized into independent agencies such as the Federal Reserve. The Joint Economic Committee had further usurped the attention it once drew. Finally, its chairman, A. Willis Robertson of Virginia, was opposed to most of the legislation that came before it and therefore did as little as possible.

Government Operations was classified as a minor committee (senators then could serve on only two major committees) and though its importance has increased, it was not very active then except for its investigating subcommittee, dominated by the chairman, John L. McClellan of Arkansas, with whom Muskie never became close.

Sympathetic leadership or even sympathetic committee chairmen might have swept Muskie into the new experience of the Senate. Instead he was at sea, getting his bearings on his own and suffering the dejection which Johnson had predicted and which most governors encounter upon reaching the Senate. The move usually is seen as promotion, but the difference was that in Maine Muskie was the center of things and in Washington— "Well," he said one night, "you come down here after having run your state and find you don't amount to a damn. It is a very depressing experience for the first few years." Another time he described it as "like playing crack-the-whip on ice skates. When you're a senator, you're just the tail of the whip." His aide, Don Nicoll, said, "The governor can control things, you know. The Senate is very different and things are usually out of control and the best one can do is to pick up the pieces as things keep getting broken."

The Senate is a place of great confusion and of arcane ritual that swirls around a man at first as he struggles to find a place in it. But Muskie had another problem which was particularly serious for him: he did not have a clearly defined place—a proper platform from which to operate. Ron Linton, then staff director of Public Works and now a consultant in Washington, who took a quick, firm liking to Muskie, said, "Muskie has to be working. His worst times come where there is not a legitimate place for him to work. He gets upset about wasting time, he wants to know his role—and at that point, in effect, he was serving on committees without any real role." Another Senate staffer said, "He had been put out to pasture and he sure as hell didn't like it. He wanted to do things, but he didn't know what." There is a report that Muskie once asked Mansfield, with whom he immediately felt comfortable, how long one was expected to stand on the edges; Mansfield dismisses the story today as apocryphal, but it does stand aptly for Muskie's actual situation. He was thoroughly frustrated in this period—a condition into which he falls readily anyway.

When he had been in the Senate a few months he had his first debate, with the formidable Wayne Morse of Oregon who was a difficult opponent for anybody. Muskie had been named a subcommittee of one to deal with a bill introduced by Paul Douglas of Illinois to dispose of some fifteen hundred acres of federal land near Des Plaines, Ill., and he had worked out what he defended on the floor as "a good Yankee compromise, a good trade for the taxpayers of the U.S. and a good trade for the citizens of Illinois." Morse, however, had developed a formula which he wanted the government to follow when disposing of land, and Muskie's compromise did not meet the formula's criteria.

John Donovan, who then was Muskie's administrative assistant, has always believed that Mansfield called the bill suddenly because he decided it was time to blood Muskie on the floor. Mansfield was Majority Whip, and contrary to Johnson's reaction, he liked Muskie immediately. Muskie and Mansfield are in some ways similar in nature. Both are modest, spare, quiet men from rural states of small population whose interest in power takes a more polite form than in men like Johnson and Kerr. In any event, the bill came up without warning and Mansfield called Muskie and said, "You'd better get over here and handle this, Ed." Muskie came onto the floor and Morse immediately opened fire. Donovan remembers that Muskie's hands were trembling (as they do today before he begins to speak) but he quickly caught the momentum of the situation and, knowing his subject perfectly, launched into a spirited defense. At one point it appears that both men lost their tempers, for they dropped the niceties that usually accompany Senate debate and spoke directly. Morse was an acerb and powerful debater with one of the quickest minds in the Senate, and it was an auspicious beginning for Muskie that the Senate voted a few minutes later to sustain his Yankee compromise. "I would not have recommended to myself," Muskie said after the vote, "that I indulge in debate with the Senator from Oregon in my first experience . . ."

As a member of Government Operations he saw his first important bill through the Senate, which with a similar bill introduced by L. H. Fountain of North Carolina in the House created the Advisory Commission on Intergovernmental Relations. The bill passed with an authorization to fund the commission, but it could not really be formed until the Appropriations Committee actually allotted to it a specific sum of money. At the end of the session Carl Hayden of Arizona, president pro tempore of the Senate and chairman of Appropriations, began to consider the supplemental budget which was the last hope of funding for all those varied bills which individual members cherished. This was the commission's opportunity— but Muskie then was a man of little influence.

Milton T. Semer, who then was on the staff of Banking and Currency and now practices law in Washington, described it this way: "Old Senator Hayden held a regular court and everyone was running around trying to get things through. Muskie had spent the whole year listening to that dreary, dreary testimony on intergovernmental relations and he hadn't had a single success. Boy, that had been a long, lonely year for him. I was on the floor one night when one of Johnson's emissaries came up and asked me, 'You think Muskie would go for fifty thousand dollars initial funding to get that advisory commission of his going?' I said, 'Christ, yes; anything so he doesn't draw a blank for the year.' 'Okay,' the man said, 'fifty thousand; the leader worked it out.' So Muskie got the commission funded. He was appointed a member at the start of the next session and he's a member today."

The importance of Muskie's teapot tempest with Johnson should not be overestimated. It resulted in poor committee assignments, but it did not mark him permanently. Though frustrated, he followed his nature and dug into whatever work he could find, and since hard work is appreciated in the Senate, this provided a ladder for him to climb. The Senate is an odd place, composed of a hundred members who operate with no responsibility to one another in an intricate tension of constantly changing balances and alliances. No ties, least of all those of party, are binding. Often enough, the two senators from a single state represent opposite parties and they certainly represent separate constituencies. Even the leadership has authority only to the extent that it can frustrate the desires of a Senate member if he does not obey, for there is no hierarchy of command. Furthermore, the interests of various senators are very diffuse, combining the constituencies they represent, the committees on which they serve and their own ideologies, antipathies and ambitions.

There are two basic approaches to power in this arena, other than election to the leadership itself which is specialized and carries such liabilities as to make it a dubious power base. One approach, followed by men like John Kennedy and Robert Kennedy, by Eugene McCarthy at the end of his Senate career and to

some extent by William Fulbright, is to use the Senate as a platform from which to address a broad national constituency. The
power these men had and have on the floor reflects national rather
than internal position. The internal course is through the mechanisms of the Senate itself, through seniority, though that rule can
be changed, through an understanding of the machinery, through
solid knowledge acquired by hard work and most of all through
the achieved trust of one's fellows. These are the ways—the last
the most difficult of all—to the inner "club" or establishment of
the Senate. The terms may be a little passé today, particularly
since Mansfield runs the Senate much more openly, but there
remains an inner circle.

Muskie worked his way into that circle by hard work and
force of intelligence. Members are very pleased when they learn
they can rely consistently on the knowledge and judgment of one
of their fellows because it lifts a little of the pressure under which
they operate. Every senator is asked to vote on every proposition
that comes before the Senate. Each man has his own position on
the great issues of the year, the ones involving huge sums or
major philosophic thrusts, but he can hardly keep up with everything. Primarily he relies on committees, which are expected to
and generally do produce sound bills. Committees achieve considerable expertise and are composed of a wide enough political
range to insure reasonably intelligent bills with the extreme edges
rounded off before they reach the floor. In addition, however,
when a man whom members trust assures them that a bill does
this, that and no more, they feel free to vote accordingly and
return to their own work. When a senator is willing to make a
real study of such grinding subjects as intergovernmental relations, his fellows are the more appreciative.

A reading of the *Congressional Record* in the early years
of his career suggests that he was watching, listening and learning.
He did not engage in much floor debate and when he did speak
he took pains to do so from carefully prepared positions. As he
became more familiar with the issues and with the subtle workings of the Senate, he fell into the habit of listening as the debate

developed and then, near the end offering a balanced summation statement that tried to cut through emotionalism and doctrinaire positions and make sense of the situation. There often was a cool lucidity to these statements; gradually they began to prove useful to other members who had not yet thought the issues through; in time they became helpful guides for which men who respected Muskie waited, often delaying their decisions (on bills that did not reflect their own vital interests) until he had spoken.

This same tendency toward studied, thoughtful positions appeared in his committee work. Muskie often waited quietly as fights developed and then late in the debate struck hard with a well-engineered substitute proposal which amounted to a compromise but still held to the bill's basic purpose. Because these compromises answered most of the needs of most of the views represented on the committee, and because they were well armored in good sense and therefore not vulnerable to immediate adverse reaction, often enough to be impressive they became the final bills. His fellow committee members not only found his judgment sound but, equally important, saw that he had a good political feel for emerging situations. Since the crux of government is the blending of constantly changing reality, administrative machinery and politics, this is a crucial asset. Gradually the Senate learned that when Muskie spoke he had something to say. He was sure of his facts because, in the phrase used endlessly around the Senate, "he did his homework." Indeed, his capacity to absorb and retain abstruse details was one of the talents which moved him toward power because it gave him knowledge that many colleagues were not willing to acquire and thus a command of certain situations that others found difficult to match. Furthermore, he was independent, not easily led, dangerous in debate, rough when angered. When he made up his mind he acted upon it and he was hard to shake. "Muskie can take care of himself," Mansfield said, "and he always did. He was independent. He was nobody's man. He really was a very good senator."

Muskie's position improved when President Kennedy took

office in 1961. He was not a Kennedy intimate, but they were friends and Muskie was one of the first in the Senate to endorse him. He helped swing the Maine delegation behind Kennedy, which was less important in actual numbers than to Kennedy's strategy of going to the 1960 convention with a solid New England base. Johnson became Vice President and Mansfield was Majority Leader. Mansfield named Muskie to the Legislative Review Committee, commonly called the Calendar Committee. Muskie is its chairman today. The committee was not very important, but Mansfield invited its four members to sit on the Democratic Policy Committee and allowed them to vote. In effect, therefore, they became members of the Policy Committee, which meets weekly and determines how the majority is to function and hence how the Senate itself is to function. Other committees control legislation; this committee controls the machinery. The Majority Leader is its chairman. Under Johnson it voted by voice, which made it difficult to oppose the leader. Mansfield introduced the secret ballot in 1965, thus purposely reducing his own power and further opening the process. Muskie's position on the Policy Committee was important because it gave him an inside view of the structure and operation of the Senate. He was an apt pupil and the experience added to his increasing skill.

By 1962 he seemed more comfortable in the Senate. His confidence was restored, he understood the machinery and he was beginning to sort out his roles. Late that year the situation changed radically on Public Works. Chavez, the Committee chairman, and Kerr, the Committee power, died in rapid succession. Pat McNamara of Michigan, with whom Muskie was close, became chairman. Muskie needed a wider legislative area and he told McNamara so. Meanwhile, Ron Linton, staff director of Public Works, had been looking into the increasing pollution problem. He suggested a new subcommittee and McNamara immediately agreed and appointed Muskie its chairman. In time, pollution became Muskie's primary field, as we will see in detail later, but the extent to which he then regarded himself as a national figure is clear in his reaction to his appointment: "I'm from Maine," he told Linton. "What the hell do I care about air pollution?"

But as it turned out he came to care a great deal. The pollution question, air and water, now provided a base for steady, exhaustive, enjoyable work, and Muskie became an expert. After completing his first bill, on water pollution, he turned to air pollution and in expertise soon surpassed Linton, who had been studying it for months. By the middle of the first big air pollution hearing, Linton remembers, Muskie was in control of the subject.

In the meantime, however, the bill that is generally conceded to have established his Senate reputation was on another subject and out of another committee. The Model Cities bill, introduced in 1966, was an exciting, imaginative plan for focusing the efforts of government on the collapsing inner city. It grew from the fact that cities were running out of money for services and federal programs that might help often were uncoordinated and haphazard. The idea was to coordinate the potential of all three levels of government and then pump enough money into a specific area to make it work and demonstrate what could be done for the cities throughout the country. The plan might have succeeded, though no one ever really found out because after it passed it became another casualty of the Vietnam war. It was never adequately funded, and when the Nixon administration came in, all enthusiasm for it evaporated.

Explaining the bill one day recently, Joe Califano, who then headed the President's domestic programs, said, "The whole concept was to say to a city, Okay, you pick a hard-core ghetto area of a size to deal with as a whole, a Hough in Cleveland or a Harlem, and you put together in a coordinated package all the city, state and federal programs, job training, urban renewal, sewers, even fire and police, health services, everything, and do it all systematically. It was complicated as hell, but if you tore down a block, for instance, you had some place for the people to go, you had job training for the kids on that block, and not just any training but training for existing jobs, and when they came back from that, in theory you had the block rebuilt for them. You made it all work together and this program was supposed to give you enough dough to do it."

As Muskie put it during the debate, when asked how the program differed from urban renewal, "the emphasis in this legislation is to supplement . . . the physical reconstruction of cities by programs designed to reconstruct the lives of people who live in those cities . . ."

From its inception, however, the bill was in serious political trouble. By 1966 the extraordinary Eighty-ninth Congress that Lyndon B. Johnson's 1964 landslide swept in was worrying about reelection. A rush of legislation in the President's Great Society program—more, in fact, than the administration yet had been able to administer—had already passed Congress. Model Cities was produced by a Presidential task force which endowed the bill with highly militant language which irritated the more staid members of Congress. Since inner cities now are populated largely by blacks, it could be seen as a bill for blacks and this aroused Southern and other racially conscious legislators. The bill proposed to pour $2.3 billion into what at one point was as few as twenty cities in order to concentrate its effect. This was better sociology than politics because it meant that most legislators would be voting on heavy expenditures that would have no direct effect on their own constituents. If you agree that in an urban nation the health of cities affects everyone's health, the proposal was entirely valid, but that is a proposition that America has yet to accept.

The administration maneuvered a version of the bill through a House committee, but there it stopped. In the Senate it went to the housing subcommittee of Banking and Currency and ran into a wall because the subcommitee chairman, John J. Sparkman of Alabama, would not touch it. Paul Douglas was willing but was considered likely to lose rather than gain votes. People began to think of Muskie, also a housing subcommittee member, who had given crucial help to Douglas the year before in the passage of the administration's controversial rent supplements program for low-income families. Milt Semer, who was then at the White House as counsel to the President, remembers a midnight supper with Johnson and several of his aides. Johnson was angry with the progress of Model Cities, which he considered one of the two most important bills of the year. "What the hell are we going to do with it?" he snapped, and Semer suggested that they persuade Muskie to help. Johnson immediately nodded his approval. By this time the old antipathy between Johnson and Muskie was long buried if not forgotten; indeed, Muskie had been among the dozens of people whom Johnson had allowed to wonder if they might be selected for the Vice Presidential nomination in 1964.

Muskie, however, was not enthusiastic. Califano persuaded him to study the bill, and while Muskie liked its ideas, he thought its form weak. He was irritated by the unnecessarily militant language and the mechanism for transferring federal funds (an area in which his intergovernmental-relations work had made him expert) was unnecessarily complicated. It also was obvious to him that the bill could not pass unless it was expanded to include a wider range of cities even if such a change diluted its effect. It was summer and Muskie was going to Maine. On the way to the airport he stopped at the White House for a steak luncheon in Califano's office to talk about the bill. When it was over he said he would sleep on it and decide the next day. By this time Johnson and Califano had agreed, as Semer put it, "to let Ed figure out what he can put through and we'll go with that."

The next day Don Nicoll, now Muskie's administrative assistant, called Califano and said Muskie would take the bill through the Senate if he could make certain changes. Johnson ordered Califano and Larry O'Brien, then Postmaster General and his chief liaison with Congress, to fly to Maine to work out the changes. Jane Muskie cooked a big lobster stew and served it and they talked for about five hours and came to agreement.

The bill, of course, was the administration's, not Muskie's. His only responsibility was to see it through the Senate. It also was true, however, that unless it went through the Senate it would not go anywhere. Before Muskie would let them leave that afternoon he insisted that O'Brien join him in a visit to the village post office in Kennebunk Beach. Senatorial visits to that post office were common, but at the sight of the Postmaster General walking in the postmaster lost control of the canceling machine and letters shot all over the room.

Muskie's contributions to the bill were political and parliamentary. He reshaped it substantially, reduced its militant rhetoric, improved its mechanisms and widened its impact, thus retaining its aims but making it more politically palatable. Then he saw it through committee and managed its passage in the Senate. The first crisis came in the housing subcommittee, which approved the bill's substance but balked over the $2.3 billion in spending which the bill authorized over the following five years. As usual, Muskie had prepared an alternative fall-back position in the form of an amendment reducing the spending to $900 million over the following two years. Since that was what the original bill had proposed for the first two years, it did not change the substance but it certainly changed the politics. Muskie checked by telephone with the White House, which quickly agreed, knowing, as Califano put it much later, "that there would be no trouble getting it funded later—a constituency always develops for these federal programs." The swing man who could tip the balance on the subcommittee was Thomas J. McIntyre, a conservative Democrat from New Hampshire who was up for reelection that year. If he could take credit for reducing the bill's authorization, he might view it as a useful political counter. Quietly Muskie offered him the amendment. McIntyre studied the paper a moment, and then, as Robert B. Semple, Jr., of the *New York Times* reported, said loudly, "Mr. Chairman, I have here an amendment I'd like to offer." The amendment was accepted, the bill passed the subcommittee and the committee and went to the Senate floor.

There the counterattack came in the form of an amendment by John Tower, conservative Republican of Texas, which would have converted the bill to another study of the problem and thus have gutted its force. The bill was two days in passage, and Muskie's performance is widely regarded on the hill as a tour de force of the parliamentary art. Those years of hard work were paying off: he had the knowledge, the expertise, the intuitive grasp of the interrelations of government to answer the objections, and counter the arguments brought against the bill, and he did so in a stream of dexterous debate. He opened with a graceful plea for the needs of the cities and then moved into a complicated discussion of the bill's actions. As the vote neared on the amendment that would have destroyed the bill, Muskie gave a short extemporaneous speech that by all accounts was emotional and powerful. In it he pointed out that he was from a small state not yet stricken with the disease of the cities and so not likely to benefit from the bill (which led Jacob Javits of New York to reflect his approval a few minutes later with an appellation that stuck: "It is wonderful to me that a barefoot boy from Maine could say it as eloquently as he has"). Unfortunately the force of that speech is lost; what appears in the *Record* is but a shadow of the original, pieced together afterward; the Senate's usually excellent system of recording broke down that day. The Tower amendment was defeated and Model Cities passed the Senate by a vote of about two to one, a startling change from the debacle that had threatened at the beginning.

"Ah, Model Cities," Mansfield said years later, "that's when Muskie made himself in the Senate." And he added, "It's the only instance I know of in which I could say that votes were changed on the floor by the way the bill was managed and presented."

In seven years Muskie had moved from the ignored edges of the Senate to its center. He had a comfortable little hideaway office deep in the basement of the Senate itself, a convenience limited to only a few. His counsel was sought, his support solicited. He would have made anyone's list of the most effective and respected senators; in 1971 Lee Metcalf of Montana told *Time* that Muskie "is the best of us all. If I rated all senators on a scale of 100, Muskie would be the first." A certain wary relationship sprang up even between Muskie and Johnson. The President always had an eye for a pretty woman, and he often told Muskie, "What you and I did, Ed, we both married above ourselves."

Since he offered this oblique compliment to many people it meant no more than a certain easy familiarity, but there were other signs. Johnson often invited a few couples in for a film in the evening and sometimes when Muskie and Jane were there he would ask them to stay after the others left. Then all four, the Johnsons and the Muskies, would gather in one of the little White House sitting rooms and talk politics, a subject they all enjoyed.

Once, in an odd and inconclusive conversation in the White House, Johnson offered Muskie what amounted to an unofficial role in his Administration; nothing came of it because neither man pursued it, but it does show how far Muskie had come and how much he had grown since that day when he began his Senate career with a Maine farmer's witticism. Ever since, in a process of slow, steady movement, following the way that was open, he had grown into a formidable figure who, though still within the boundaries of the situation, was resting against its top.

He did nothing, however, to go over its top. Months before the 1968 convention he knew his chances for the Vice Presidential nomination were strong. Humphrey told him openly that Muskie was his choice if he won the nomination and if he did not have to bargain the second position to hold the first. In the end it was a choice between Senator Fred Harris of Oklahoma and Muskie, and Muskie won. One cannot campaign directly for the Vice Presidential nomination, though many do so indirectly, but it is nevertheless interesting that Muskie seemed to have changed very little until the nomination actually came. Then he soared to meet its demands. But afterward, with the election lost and the way beginning to open toward the Presidential nomination, Muskie again grew steadily, responding as the new situation required. His ideas and attitudes and his concept of himself appeared to expand, the evangelical note that has always underlaid his pragmatism began increasingly to flower; gradually the tempo of this change hastened and since late 1970 it has been more and more perceptible from month to month.

Soon after the 1970 elections he came to a specific crisis that had been brewing for a long time, and because his handling of it is another measure of his growth, it is worth examining in detail. At first it seems minor, a matter that would be readily settled in normal affairs, but politics is never "normal affairs." The problem was the restructuring of his staff to fit that of a Presidential candidate. Had he failed to do this he probably would have had no real chance at the nomination or the Presidency; still, it was very hard to accomplish because of the ways of politics and because of his own nature and that of the man who blocked the way.

Don Nicoll was Muskie's administrative assistant for years. He is a quiet, intelligent, decent man who has a natural talent for the affairs of government and was widely considered one of the half dozen best AA's on the hill; Muskie relied on him totally. Since Nicoll is quite small and Muskie quite tall they often made a striking pair in the Senate halls. Nicoll had invaluable qualities: his judgment was sound, he remained calm when all threatened to collapse, an endemic condition in the Senate, and he was loyal. Professional politicians would put the last quality first of all.

In one way or another, Nicoll had been with Muskie since the beginning. The new group that took the Maine party's reins in 1954 was led by Muskie and Frank Coffin, now on the U.S. Court of Appeals. Coffin, as chairman, hired Nicoll, then twenty-seven and news director of a radio station, as executive secretary. As governor, Muskie had so little staff help that much of the legislation he proposed was actually written by Nicoll in the party office. In 1956 Coffin went to Congress and took Nicoll along. Nicoll joined Muskie's staff after Coffin lost a 1960 campaign for governor in an anti-Catholic tide brought out in Maine by John F. Kennedy ("Well, Frank," Kennedy said later, "we sure brought out the vote, didn't we?"). In 1962 Nicoll replaced John Donovan as Muskie's AA.

The Senate is surprisingly unstructured, considering its addiction to ritual, and senators use their staffs as they choose. Muskie soon found that he could trust Nicoll's judgment. Nicoll worked as hard as Muskie, knew Maine and understood government and the legislative process, and gradually Muskie gave him more authority. Nicoll became one of the few AA's who could speak for his principal without checking. He was one of those men with the capacity and the courage to make decisions—both rare qualities—and Muskie was willing to let him do so. Just how useful Nicoll became was demonstrated at that critical juncture in the Model Cities bill when Muskie offered McIntyre the compromise amendment. The document had been prepared in advance. According to Semple's account in the *Times*, it was Nicoll who whispered to Muskie, "Do you suppose McIntyre would like to offer this amendment?" In a moment McIntyre made the move and the crisis was over. "I worked on three major bills with Muskie," Califano said much later, "and I found Nicoll to be among the best on the hill."

It is an odd facet of Muskie's nature that he does not like to deal with his staff. This may be partly due to his shyness and his dislike for casual talk, but it also comes from the fact that he is bored and hence irritated by office detail. Among other things, it takes away time from the concentration on the substantive detail of legislation and policy that has been his focus in his Senate years. Today, spread thin from coast to coast, making the speeches, appearances and meetings that no one else can make for him, he has still less time or inclination to involve himself in staff affairs.

When Muskie is presented with something he does not want to deal with or thinks is not worth the bother, he often ignores it, gazing blandly at the questioner and saying nothing. This disconcerts his aides; its effect on a strong man is to force him to make decisions, but it tends to paralyze a weak man. Muskie believes that many problems are not really problems at all and are best ignored. It is a matter of deciding whether one is going to deal with minutiae or with broad themes, and Muskie chooses the latter even though it sometimes makes trouble. Under such a leader, Nicoll assumed more and more control of the staff. In time he became the single conduit to Muskie for the staff and for most people outside the office. By the mid-1960s he was doing the hiring and to most of the staff he was more directly the boss than was Muskie. Men who were not willing to accept such a relation-ship—usually the strong and capable—did not stay long. By the same token, Nicoll was not inclined to hire men who might challenge him. The unperceptive thought of Nicoll as a martinet hungry for power. In fact, however, the system operated as Muskie wanted it to operate. Nor was Nicoll's service as a conduit to Muskie a one-way matter; Muskie often was angry and Nicoll bore its weight. Muskie sometimes provokes savage arguments with his close aides in order to test his ideas, thrusting the aide into the position he is himself considering taking and then attacking relentless in order to expose the position's flaws. Once Maurice Williams asked in anguish why Muskie used him so cruelly, and Muskie was dumbfounded; that, he explained gently, if none too sensitively, was how he tested ideas. It is not always pleasant to be a conduit.

And in fact, Muskie and Nicoll were not close. They did not see each other socially and did not even seem very comfortable together. They may not even have liked each other much. Muskie's relations with George Mitchell, of whom he is fond, are sharply different from those with Nicoll. Nicoll in turn often appears edgy around Muskie. Milt Semer, who has watched them both for years, believes that "over the years, with all that pressure, they just wore each other out."

After the 1968 campaign, when Muskie became a national figure, the system he and Nicoll had built began to break down. The demands that fell on the staff were brutal. An office that once had been busy with the affairs of Maine now faced floods of letters, calls, offers to help and invitations to speak from the whole country, all of which had to be answered. Muskie spoke widely, and in theory, at least, each speech had to be arranged, scheduled and advanced, a man going in beforehand to be sure that the most advantage was extracted from the situation, the widest range of people and media covered, with extra visits to colleges and to local political leaders. People who helped had to be thanked and records of all who might help had to be kept as the nucleus of a political organization.

The substantive demands also exploded. They went far beyond the additional speeches that had to be researched and written. The ever-thorough Muskie considered substance most important of all and he may have been right, for at the beginning he had still to convince the American people that he had something to say. Furthermore, as a national candidate he was expected to have a sound position on every sort of subject, which demanded both research and the time to apply a broad range of critical judgment. These demands angered Muskie, but he also knew that the wrong answer, hasty, poorly thought out or foolish, could follow him forever. His old dislike of criticizing without offering counter-solutions of his own drove him toward developing positions that could be hardened into legislation and introduced. At the same time, he wanted to excel in his own legislative areas and use his new national weight to push tough air and water pollution bills through the Senate. In the midst of all this, the staff also was supposed to be assembling those black books of political intelligence, looseleaf folders, one for each state—without which no serious national campaign can function. When well done and kept current, they give a constant profile, brief but thorough, of each state and its economy, needs, problems, fears and disturbances; the educational, age and income levels of its people; its voting patterns, its convention delegates and how they are chosen; its politics and politicians and their fights and how to avoid them; and a hundred other details that scribe a place's life. Properly armed with his black book, a skillful candidate can fly into a state and with only a little dexterity seem a student of its affairs. On the other hand, the psychic strain as well as the potential for failure is enormous for a candidate who drops into state after state and without such information tries to feel his way.

The problem in Muskie's office was that too little of this mass of detail was being done. As Muskie had to grow, so did the staff—but the staff was Nicoll and he now began to appear constrictive, not expansive. It was becoming clear that Nicoll's strength was not in administration or national politics. He did not have strong people, would not hire them and would not delegate authority and thus responsibility. He was still the conduit and he kept his finger on every pulse. Though he assumed incredible loads and worked himself to exhaustion, things continued to pile up, plugged at the mouth of the conduit. The issue really was decisions, which Nicoll reserved for himself. It appeared, furthermore, that this was still what Muskie wanted, which is to say that the real growth issue lay with Muskie, not Nicoll.

At one point Muskie announced that everyone would make decisions and act on them, but as one young staff member said ruefully, "The first one he didn't like, that was the end of that." Nicoll was good at decisions, but eventually there were too many for one man to make. Decisions unmade are made by default; those that don't grow actively from policy tend to create policy instead. The candidate provides the genius and the scope of a campaign, if such it has, but the staff must handle the details, which means making endless decisions and hoping that a reasonable percentage of them will be correct. It is a truism that while a good staff cannot save a bad candidate, a bad staff can destroy a good candidate. When the staff fails, things are left undone, opportunities pass, people are turned away until an inept air of inaction comes to pervade the campaign. At the same time, obvious and embarrassing blunders become increasingly apparent. All of this quickly becomes public and the campaign is taken less and less seriously.

Letters to Muskie went unanswered. Calls—even important political calls—often were not returned. Speech texts rarely were ready in advance and so could not be released and publicized. When they were ready they often were poor, and Muskie frequently threw them away and went on the wing. He is a good extemporaneous speaker and can thrill an audience when the mood is on him, but speeches that inspire instead of offering substantive proposals make little news beyond the hall in which they are given. His scheduling was haphazard, rarely taking full advantage of any appearance. The lists of contacts lagged. Months went by without a visit to such a politically important state as, for example, Wisconsin. Fund-raising was not coordinated. There was hardly a beginning on local organization, even in the most critical primary states. He had assembled a group of experts to advise him, men of stature in foreign affairs, economic matters and national policy. But at least some of them found that their carefully drafted memos did not go directly to Muskie. They lay on Nicoll's desk until he found time to read them and attach a critique which often enough attacked their ideas but which they neither saw nor could answer. A chance to neutralize an old Kennedy operative in an attempt to keep him out of the McGovern camp was allowed to slip. When Muskie desperately needed a good speech writer a strong one became available, offered himself and was turned down. Muskie's 1970 campaign in Maine was a study in internal combat and by this time his Senate office and his downtown office were bickering. Through 1970 Muskie was often frustrated and angry, feeling that he was hurtling exhausted about the country, always behind, things usually out of control. But he wasn't doing anything about it.

The situation is summed up in the fight with Richard Goodwin that arose over Muskie's dramatic national telecast on Election Eve, 1970. It was amusing and though not very important of itself, it was a clear indicator of trouble. The chance to make the speech arose suddenly, on the Saturday before the Monday on which it would be delivered. It was a great opportunity and Muskie asked the staff to assemble a speech draft. Then he called Goodwin, who lives in a ramshackle farmhouse nearly two centuries old on top of a mountain in Maine. Goodwin is a brilliant writer and fine social and political thinker whose ego matches his other capacities. He served John Kennedy, Lyndon Johnson, Eugene McCarthy and Robert Kennedy—leading the *New York Times* to refer to him unkindly as a "typewriter-for-hire"—and he did a handsome job for each. His talents make him a marvelous asset for any political camp; his liabilities of arrogance and the desire to run things make him equally expensive. But any camp to which Goodwin is willing to extend ideas, advice and speech drafts is ahead, and that is the relationship that he and Muskie, maneuvering around each other warily for months, had slowly been evolving.

Now Muskie explained the situation. They talked for about twenty minutes, Muskie huddled in a restaurant phone booth while he sketched out what he wanted to say and the texture he thought such a speech should have. He asked Goodwin to prepare a draft and Goodwin agreed. Goodwin wrote all night and at dawn got into his jeep and drove to the Fenway Motor Inn in Waterville where Muskie was staying and knocked on his door at 7 A.M. Over breakfast he handed Muskie a magnificent draft. By every criterion it was excellent—rich, graphic and, most of all, alive. Such writing is rare any place, the more so in political speeches. With cutting and a few changes, it was the speech that Muskie gave the following day.

It is important here to be clear about the process. The speech was Muskie's. It reflected his ideas, his attitudes, what he wanted to say and how he wanted to say it. It was not Goodwin speaking to America that night; it was Muskie. Obviously it also represented Goodwin's thinking or he wouldn't have written it. Nevertheless, part of his special ability lay in how thoroughly he could capture Muskie's cadences and his philosophy. The original draft contained two things Muskie cut out because he disagreed with them and some phrasing he thought extreme which he softened. On the other hand, it was Goodwin's words that made Muskie so eloquent that night; with another speech he might have been less eloquent. Had Muskie been able to stop and write his own speech, it might have been as strong as Goodwin's. It might have been stronger. But Muskie also was finishing his own campaign for reelection to the Senate, and while winning was not a problem the margin by which he won was critical to his Presidential interests, as was pulling Governor Curtis back in for a second term. Muskie had to continue campaigning. On that Sunday night, while Goodwin and the staff (whose draft Muskie had rejected) fought over phrases in a long and agonizing "editing" session, Muskie went to Lewiston and gave a passionate, extemporaneous speech that in many ways was superior to the more formal televised speech. But no one can count on doing that for exactly fourteen minutes, thirty seconds, start when you see the red light, please.

In addition to writing the speech, Goodwin knew that it should be publicized heavily in advance. He felt that Muskie's staff was doing the job inadequately, so he made some calls of his own. The staff, already angry, believed that in these calls Goodwin left the impression that the whole affair was his. Equally angry, Goodwin developed evidence to dispute this. On election night, as is his custom and as he did in 1968, Muskie returned to Waterville and gathered staff, supporters, friends and press at the Fenway motel to hear the returns. Naturally he included Goodwin, who drove over from his farm. In his own ineffable way, Goodwin greeted at least three people there with the remark, "Well, I made another President last night!" The staff was seething, and Nicoll, who considered Goodwin an arrogant interloper and a prima donna as well, was particularly outraged. There was a hasty staff meeting in Room 341 in which everyone agreed on "the story," which turned out to be that Goodwin's was one of several drafts submitted, and that Muskie had assembled the final draft himself with no more reliance on Goodwin's than on others. The view was compounded of fury directed at Goodwin and protectiveness for Muskie, since the staff believed that credit for Goodwin would detract from Muskie's achievement. Muskie, who had already thanked Goodwin warmly, came into the meeting at one point and upon hearing their outrage said, "Well, that's the truth—it was basically his draft and we all know it." It was an excellent example of Muskie's unwillingness to interest himself in staff minutiae. Had he done so, he could have brought sense to the situation then. Instead he walked out and the staff continued to develop its united front for the press. The press did not believe the staff, but neither did it entirely believe Goodwin, who was well known, as one reporter said that night, "for putting himself in the center of everything and taking all possible credit."

Nor did that finish it. When the staff returned to Washington the story quickly leaked to the columnists Rowland Evans and

Robert Novak who wrote a waspish attack on Goodwin. One cannot measure the effect of squabbling that becomes public but it certainly doesn't help and it may have tarnished somewhat the effect of his speech. Someone read the column by telephone to Goodwin on his mountaintop, and he rushed to his typewriter and composed a very funny counterattack in which he shredded Muskie's staff in general and Nicoll in particular. Being rather isolated, Goodwin enjoys his telephone, and he called people all over the country and read them his riposte. He said he intended to offer it for syndication. The matter did not end—another tea-pot tempest blown into a mini-hurricane—until Muskie finally called Goodwin himself and asked him to let it drop.

Spelled out this bluntly, the answer seems simple: reorganize around Nicoll, fire him if necessary, but open things up. In fact, however, it was not at all simple. There is hardly a more difficult and painful thing in politics than shaking up a staff. In 1968 David Broder wrote a column in the Washington *Post* charging Humphrey with a fatal lack of self-discipline. First, Broder said, Humphrey would not force himself to stop talking, and second, he would not bring order to his chaotic staff, which in effect had two lines of command so that things were forever falling between the two and disappearing. It is not easy, nor was it easy for Muskie.

There was that loyalty factor, the loyalty that he gives people and demands of them. Loyalty is an ultimate virtue in politics. In the censure of Thomas J. Dodd of Connecticut, beginning as it did with members of his staff turning on him, it was not any mis-steps of Dodd's that shook the hill but the fatal word "disloyalty." Loyalty is the sticking plaster of politics, the tape that binds it all together, because there really isn't anything else. By the very nature of politics, a man puts himself constantly in the hands of others whose interests are bound to his own only through loyalty. He cannot rely on the party, which is equally the instrument of his competitors. He has none of the mutual interests that bind businessmen, the tenure of academics or even the simple day's wage for a day's work that holds most of us together. A politician is always vulnerable, always threatened. There is the entire army of the opposition working for his defeat and his own party is full of skilled, ambitious men who want his job and hopefully await his stumble. There is hardly another profession in which a man is so constantly in combat. That is why so many old politicians show tinges of paranoia—they have suspected too long and found trust too difficult.

Muskie remembers the thin years when the little band, which included Nicoll, set out to challenge the giant. He is where he is today—if you choose to see it that way—because so many little people in Maine have stood with him through the years. You see them when he campaigns in Maine, standing in knots on the curbs in little towns, awaiting the handshake and the word. Every successful politician has these people and the good ones don't forget it. Maurice Williams said, "I never worked for a man who was more loyal to me. You can be wrong but he'll see you as just fine. It's the way he's made—and you don't let a man like that down, you return his loyalty." And as Leon Billings, of Muskie's subcommittee on air and water pollution, says, "The highest recommendation in Washington is loyalty—the second is competence."

Nicoll returned that loyalty. He has buried himself and his own ambitions in Muskie's ambitions. The effect of being the man behind the public man is to subordinate one's own ego; one acts always for one's man, never for oneself. Many strong men cannot bear the role. Yet any man good enough to excel on the hill can have his pick of careers. Nicoll has sacrificed his own political hopes. He holds a master's degree and would enjoy academic life. Once when he had decided to leave Muskie for an attractive professorship, Muskie responded indirectly, but in such a manner as to keep Nicoll with him. Loyalty does work both ways.

People in Maine have complained about Nicoll for years and Muskie knows why. Nicoll was the man who said no. He was the lightning rod that drew the heat from Muskie. It is an ancient story: ask the leader and he says he'd love to help, he's not sure of his own plans, see his assistant and work it out; his assistant says no. It takes some naïveté not to understand the source of that no, but if the petitioner cherishes his sense of closeness with the great man, he persuades himself that the man would have done it but that goddamned assistant blocked me. Nicoll has taken this heat for years, and while his own curt manner may have added to it, Muskie cannot possibly have been unaware that Nicoll carried the psychic pain of being the man at whom many are angry so that Muskie could be spared.

Furthermore, he knew how hard Nicoll had worked over the years and since the flowering of Muskie's Presidential ambitions. Effective or not, there was the period when Nicoll was doing it all. And it was all very well to say that the staff was weak, but in fact Muskie *was* ahead. There is an old saying in politics that the good staff or candidate is the one that wins, the bad the one that loses. Nicoll had carried the weight for years, he was still carrying it and Muskie was moving ahead in the polls. It is entirely possible that Muskie, with his tendency to divorce himself from staff affairs, may not have had a clear idea of what was happening. Once when staff squabbling became especially bitter, he asked George Mitchell curiously what he thought was wrong.

And anyway, politicians hate to fire people; this reluctance is a congenital condition. Their nature is to try to soothe the public beast, and since their constituency is made up of naturally diverse elements, they seek to antagonize as little as possible. Often enough they are forced to a stand (which never pleases everyone) by principle or the situation, and so they see no need to take actions that would add gratuitously to the store of anger always building against them. When you fire a man, you make an enemy, you expose your flank, and before you know it he's working for the opposition and slandering you all over the state. Muskie is less vulnerable to this hazard than most politicians, but he shares their instincts.

And to be practical, if you lose a good man, who takes his place? Who does the things he has learned to do as you want them done? Muskie spent years learning he could trust Nicoll's judgment; if Nicoll was not to be head of his operations, someone had to take his place. The old saying that the man who represents himself in court has a fool for a client may have come from the lawyers' guild, but it certainly applies to a candidate who tries to manage his own campaign. He cannot do it: he will kill himself politically and may do so physically. So he will choose someone and what if that doesn't work? There is no going back on these decisions.

What's more, the situation had been long established by Muskie's acquiescence. He could have changed it but he hadn't, and now it was a point of pride with Nicoll, for they were moving on to the great adventure that over the years of slogging work no one could have anticipated. Nicoll had control and he would not surrender it voluntarily. Yet to lose Nicoll altogether would be a serious loss to Muskie; he needed Nicoll's expertise, knowledge, capacity for work and judgment. It is no wonder that through 1969 and 1970 Muskie turned so savagely on the many people who in one way or another urged him to fire Nicoll. One man, a close friend for a quarter-century, was so shaken and angered by the outburst he provoked that he swore, "I'll never give Ed Muskie another damned word of political advice." The incident is indicative of the bitterness that came to surround Nicoll.

The 1970 Election Eve telecast sharply changed Muskie's position and forced his staff problems to a final crisis. The fact that he spoke for the party in a face-off with the President—a contest he clearly won—served to focus what was already in people's minds: it ratified him as the front runner. He drew the opportunity, however, not because he was ahead but because he had the stature and the presence to answer a President and Vice President who were waging a cruelly divisive national campaign. The move to set up a speech countering the President's began with Geoffrey Cowan, a young Washington lawyer strong in the politics of the New Left who had been with McCarthy in 1968. He called Joe Califano and Larry O'Brien of the National Committee, both of whom agreed in principle. Sam Brown, youth coordinator for McCarthy and coordinator of the Vietnam Moratorium Committee, joined Cowan. A committee was formed, chaired by Averell Harriman and including a number of others, among them John D. Rockefeller IV, the rising Democrat of West Virginia. It committed itself to guarantee the television time, fifteen minutes on all three networks which would cost about $150,000 in total.

Since the out party in American politics has neither leader nor unified voice except during actual Presidential elections, who would answer the President? Lest it give undue advantage to an individual, the party itself would have been obliged to offer a formless committee of Democrats or the already stridently partisan voice of O'Brien as spokesman. But an independent group could do as it chose, and it chose Muskie. Cowan was quoted later as saying that Muskie was "the only guy with enough stature to oppose the President."

Cowan started on Friday and by Saturday it was together. They reached Muskie early that afternoon in Lewiston, where he was having a late lunch with Governor Curtis. Bob Squier, Muskie's television and media consultant, flew up from Washington and designed the speech format. On Monday morning Muskie taped the speech at a home on the Maine coast, with a second camera outside playing on the sea crashing clean and white against the rugged rocks of Maine for effective if somewhat blatant symbolism. The President chose a speech he had delivered several days earlier to a roaring crowd in Phoenix. It said what he wanted to say and it pleased him as it had pleased the crowd, but on television it had a raucous tone of intemperance that was exacerbated by the poor quality of the television tape which the White House delivered to the networks. The effect was to enhance Muskie's quiet eloquence and his plea for an end to raw division in politics.

Overnight Muskie was converted from being one of the candidates to being the leader. This had a galvanic effect on his campaign and in turn brought his staff problem to crisis. The new attention doubled and redoubled the pressure. Invitations to speak are a convenient index: they jumped from ten or fifteen a day to seventy and then to more than a hundred a day. Letters, calls, requests and offers to help all increased proportionately, and answers lagged ever further behind. The pressure on the political side was greater still. It was time to begin collecting endorsements from political figures all over the country, to concentrate on delegates, to focus on states with primary elections, to set up local committees, to rally special groups, to maintain a flow of accurate, current political intelligence, to balance Muskie's schedule between maximum exposure and time in which to rest and think, and—perhaps most important of all—to raise money to keep it all going. And since very little of this was being done and men who were powerful in the politics of their states couldn't even get their phone calls returned, it began to be obvious that the Muskie staff, oriented so long to substance, had no real political arm.

Opportunities of all sorts were lost. Asked about Muskie, John DeLury, the pugnacious chief of the powerful sanitationmen's union in New York City, was quoted as saying, "I wouldn't cross the street to see him; I wrote him asking him to visit and he didn't even answer." A routine request for Muskie to cosponsor the second McGovern-Hatfield resolution to end the war was ignored by the staff and it was weeks before Muskie quietly added his name to the bill. Ever since, people have seen this as a sign that Muskie waits "to see where the other liberals go," as one commentator put it. But both the staff and the commentator were foolish, for Muskie's position already was clear: he had endorsed McGovern-Hatfield the first time and had introduced a similar resolution of his own. Financial backing from Democratic contributors that the staff had counted on so confidently did not arrive and financial troubles piled up.

There was a disastrous trip to California in which nearly everything went wrong, the most public of which was the ludicrous spectacle of Muskie repudiating the language of a speech he was to give after the staff had released the text. All of this was obvious to the press, which wrote sharply about it, observing, as did his constant critics Evans and Novak, "irrational scheduling, uncoordinated speechwriting and tardy organization ordinarily add up to defeat." And finally, the ultimate indignity for Muskie the professional: professional politicians told him to his face that he was functioning as an amateur.

The crisis was real. Nicoll himself now saw this clearly and he proposed a solution. Muskie's reaction is the key to the story, for what Nicoll had proposed was the easy way out. By this time, of course, the staff had expanded and there were some strong people operating laterally to Nicoll with direct access to Muskie, though Nicoll kept overall control of directions. Bob Squier, a brilliant political television designer who ran Humphrey's media campaign in 1968 and has a long list of credits, was spending half his time running Muskie's media operation. A tough, intelligent young lawyer named John McEvoy, with experience that ranged from the Pentagon to the Hill, had taken over Muskie's Senate office with the guarantee of full authority; now he was awaiting the outcome of the staff crisis with a critical eye, sure that if Muskie could not solve it he could not be President. Berl I. Bernhard an attorney in Washington, who had been staff director of the U.S. Commission on Civil Rights under President Kennedy, a man whose easy manner accompanies a penetrating mind, was consulting on legal matters and politics while maintaining a full law practice. Robert L. Nelson, once Bernhard's deputy on the Civil Rights Commission, now was Nicoll's assistant. And Muskie was trying, still unsuccessfully, to lure George Mitchell down from Portland.

Nicoll's solution must have been tempting to Muskie. It amounted to a division of labors. Nicoll proposed that Bernhard come full time on the staff with responsibility for administration and political action. Nicoll would remain in charge of everything that dealt with substance. It seemed simple and what many people had recommended. But upon examination, it became more complicated. It was not clear, for instance, who would command— which meant that neither man would have authority over the other and therefore no firm directions could be set. It is possible to view substance, with its emphasis on policies, solutions to national problems and themes of the campaign as most important and therefore controlling; with Nicoll's decade-long habit of collecting power it seemed likely that he would continue to fight for control. On the other hand, his proposal would open things up. It would keep him on hand, doing what he did best and what Muskie needed. Ostensibly, at least, administration would be in Bernhard's hands, and while Muskie couldn't be sure that Bernhard would be better than Nicoll, he could hardly be worse. And most important of all, it would keep Nicoll happy and would save Muskie the pain of having to break the patterns of nearly twenty years and a lifetime emphasis on loyalty.

Late on the afternoon of Thursday, February 11, 1971, Muskie asked Bernhard to come to his Senate office. Once again they reviewed Nicoll's plan. Muskie asked Bernhard his opinion. Bernhard said he was dubious as to whether it would work, but he was willing to leave his firm and try. Muskie's office in the Old Senate Office Building then overlooked the grassy park that slopes down Capitol Hill to the city below. Muskie turned his big green leather chair and cocked it back, watching the trees fade in the wintry twilight, and after a while he said, "I just don't think it will work."

He turned back to the desk and sketched quickly what he wanted. Bernhard would take over the operation in full as staff director. Squier (and Dick Stewart of the Boston *Globe* who soon would become press secretary) would handle media. The emphasis would be taken off research and put on politics. They would bring in political operatives and a good speech writer who would deal with Bernhard. Nelson, until then Nicoll's assistant, would report directly to Bernhard. Mitchell would come in later. Nicoll would handle research, and while his lines to Muskie would remain open, he would take direction from Bernhard.

The effect, on paper at least, was to strip Nicoll and convert the staff into a real political operation. Muskie asked Bernhard and Nicoll to come to his home that night to review the new direction. He sent Bernhard back to the L Street office to describe

the plan to Nicoll. Nicoll was deeply angered. Still later that afternoon Bernhard called Muskie and told him they were in danger
of losing Nicoll completely.

Muskie's study is at the rear of his Washington home. It is a
smallish, well-furnished room with a sofa, easy chair, a chair with
the seal of Bates College, a desk, a small bar, bookcases and more
of the endless mementos that politicians acquire, originals of
political cartoons, an embossed copy of his acceptance speech to
the 1968 convention, a table made from a crosscut slab of a tree
that took root the year the Republic was formed. A deep window
overlooks a small grassy backyard. It is a comfortable room that
delights Muskie and it was here that Nicoll and Bernhard joined
him.

He gave them a drink and quietly began to outline the situation: how he saw the problems, what he considered everyone's
strong points, how he thought they could best be used and, therefore, what he wanted done. He was gracious but the effect was
obvious: it was not even a lateral move for Nicoll; it simply was a
demotion. It would have been comfortable if Nicoll had agreed,
but they were far down the painful road and he did not agree. He
too is strong and he fought. He reminded Muskie how long they
had been together, how hard he had worked, of the loyalty he had
given. He had committed himself to a pale freshman from a small
state; now that Muskie was his party's leading candidate for the
leading office in the world, new people were to take over and ride
the rest of the way. He asked Muskie to reconsider; he was willing to share the operation with Bernhard—he had suggested that
—but he deserved better than what Muskie offered. Muskie said
that he was sorry but that his decision was firm. Nicoll's face was
white. In that case, he said, he would leave the staff. If he no
longer had Muskie's confidence, if it was not apparent that he
could contribute, he preferred to drop it.

Muskie is a beautiful speaker when the mood is upon him
and for an audience of one he summoned the mood that night.
He swept Nicoll up in his vision of what could be. They had been
in politics together, he and Nicoll, since 1954, and they had al-

ways worked for the same thing—the opportunity to do things that need to be done. Now they had a chance at the ultimate platform, the greatest position in the world from which to do those things. There would not be another chance. They were in it together and he needed everyone—and everyone had to do what he did best. Administration was not Nicoll's forte, but he needed Nicoll's judgment and intelligence and insight and he wanted Nicoll to stay. Bernhard was surprised and impressed; his opinion of Muskie, he told friends later, went up that night.

Nicoll stayed. Berhard took control. For months the staff rattled and shook and then some order began to emerge. By definition, any political organization is haphazard, running behind, short of funds and lurching from crisis to crisis, and until the end, whatever the end, Muskie's will be no different. But at least things were moving, and mostly in one direction. True to form, Muskie now turned to Bernhard as the man with whom he would deal. Bernhard has a very jaunty air. To hell with that, he said— every staff man who had business with Muskie should see him directly. Muskie was in Maine. He grinned. "Okay, send them up," he said. Bob Schrum, a young, facile speech writer left John V. Lindsay's staff in New York to join Muskie. John English, New York national committeeman and a Kennedy stalwart, came to Muskie's political staff, as did Mark Shields, a skilled political organizer most recently on the staff of Governor John Gilligan of Ohio. Mitchell came down from Portland. Over Nicoll's objections, Bernhard slashed the research staff, and eventually all research was put in the Senate office under McEvoy, since so much of Muskie's research turns on legislation and committee work. Nicoll made the difficult transition and emerged in good spirits. He remains as special counsel to Muskie and, as he put it, "sort of chairman of the board," taking the long overview that is both vital and difficult in a political campaign, and his intellectual curiosity and rippling ideas are well exercised.

In retrospect, the move seems simple and inevitable, but it wasn't, nor was it a move that Muskie was prepared to make in 1969 and 1970. He was not ready until his perspective had shifted fully from that of a senator to that of a national candidate —until, in short, he had grown into the situation that had opened before him. It was not that the move proved him big but that the failure to have moved would have proved him small. But it was difficult, it caused him pain which any man would prefer to avoid, and it stands as evidence that he still is growing.

In terms of a Muskie Presidency, the staff story has both negative and positive sides. Delaying so long on a move that on the surface at least seems obvious relates to a pattern of caution and deliberation that had marked his whole career, particularly where personnel were involved. The most frequent criticism of his gubernatorial period was his slowness on appointments. Sometimes delay saved him from a bad appointment, but more often it gave him time for political opposition to develop against good appointments.

On the other hand, the staff matter can be seen in another frame, which is Muskie's unwillingness to immerse himself in the minutiae of his office. The staff facilities and the world-wide intelligence capacities of the executive branch would satisfy his constant longing for detailed information on which to make substantive decisions, but as for details of daily operations, a man has to decide whether to deal in those or in the broad sweep of policy directions. Sometimes minutiae are important and sometimes inattention to them builds crises and shapes policies by default. Nevertheless, a man must choose—he can hardly elect to deal with just the *important* minutiae—and the image of President Johnson following every raid while remaining blind to the reality of Vietnam does not argue for the efficacy of giving first priority to details. Muskie's attitudes might make trouble for him in the White House, but on balance his tendency to the broad overview and the sense for where things are going would be more of an asset than a liability.

The larger question of his capacity for growth is more significant to the sort of President he would be. There is no training course for the office and no one can say in advance how a man will respond to its pressures. "If Muskie gets to be President," Mike Mansfield once said, "he'll find out how difficult it is on the inside. No one understands that—no one—until they're there." As Majority Leader, Mansfield breakfasts frequently with President Nixon, as he did with President Johnson and President Kennedy, and he probably has as clear a view of the pressures as anyone not in the cockpit.

Surely any man who found himself in that cockpit would grow, though it is equally true that not all Presidents have grown enough. Muskie has shown himself capable of rising rapidly and surprisingly to many situations. He has come unerringly into a position not just of success but of commanding success in every situation that has opened to him. The fact that his manner of growth is unusual—that he responds to situations rather than to internal drives—affects the terms in which he is seen and the way that people react to him, but its only bearing on the sort of President he would be seems positive. The Presidency demands a capacity for growth beyond the expectations that any man has for himself or that others have for him, and over the years Muskie has demonstrated such a capacity. In the end, a man who simply expands to fill the situation in which he finds himself might make a better President than a man driven chiefly by the fires of his own ambition.

4

The Pleasures
of the Stump

When legitimate political situations bring Muskie into the lime-light—which happens more frequently as the political year quickens—he is very effective. His appeal to the mass of people who are drawn to him is clear when you see him in action, for in the flesh he is an attractive man. Tall, hair thick and lightly touched with gray, eyes a good blue, he is appealing in a rugged way. As his sense of national leadership and comfort in the role have grown, he has developed an increasingly commanding presence and seems more willing than ever to loosen his personal force in a controlled manner that avoids the ugly impact of anger and emerges as vitality and power. When he deals with questions he thinks silly or unfair on the network press shows, or when he handles a heckler in a hall, he appears formidable, a man not to be trifled with.

In most instances people respond personally to Muskie's speeches, partly because he so obviously enjoys speaking and interacts so clearly with his audience. He has some of the actor's capacity to project his words clearly through the room so that the tone and thus the mood is unchanged. He is rarely interrupted by applause; instead, the coughs, sighs, snores, moving chairs, clinking cups, rattling cellophane and ripping of struck matches that accompany most speeches are strangely absent. But, Muskie once said, "You feel the response. You can get more response from a thoughtful audience than from an applauding audience, which often just responds to the words and not the meaning; I think the greatest tribute to a speaker is to get his audience thinking."

Once he told an audience, "I never know when I appear exactly what I am likely to discuss. I try to get some sense of what is in your minds by reading what is in your faces. In one way or another, each of you speak to me even though you don't say a word to me. I get the same kind of communication from people all over the country."

Because he draws these speeches out of himself each time, it is an exhausting process. Once, recalling his own burst of anger at his friend George Mitchell in 1968 for which he ground out that reluctant apology, Muskie described the exhaustion. They had campaigned all day through a series of little Pennsylvania towns, had finished in the rain at a rally at Reading and then had gone to a Harrisburg hotel for dinner. Muskie assumed the day was over and was relaxing when Mitchell told him there was one more speech. "One more speech—and oh, God, I got angry. I had nothing left to give. I had poured it out all day, speech after speech—you know, when you start they say it will be just a wave-through, drive through the little town and wave to everyone. But when you actually get there, the people are out waiting and of course you have to stop and get out and someone hands you a microphone. Just a few words, they say, just say something nice to the crowd. But after all, they have come out to hear you, this is the only time they will hear you, this is likely to be the only personal contact they will have with the entire campaign, and so you give them a speech. Sure, you keep it short, but there has to be some substance, some bite to it, and this you have to pull out of yourself. It isn't written down. You don't know what you're going to say. You reach inside of yourself and pull it out. And after you've done that all day you are exhausted and drained." In the end, of course, he gave the scheduled speech.

Muskie's presence and his oratory come undiluted through television because his characteristics and his style harmonize with a medium that demands a cool manner. His calm voice, his restraint and his ability to cast large ideas in simple terms all fit the tube in the corner of the living room. The size of the television audience makes people overlook the basic fact of the medium, that it provides a one-to-one encounter between the man in front of the camera and the man in front of the set. This is the point on which television has destroyed so many political careers. A man who is hot and loud and bombastic in your own living room is too much—magnified passion is frightening. But even when he is soaring, Muskie's qualities taken all together fit television, probably for the same internalized reasons that his audiences in the hall respond with engrossed thought instead of counterpointing cheers. Filtered through television Muskie appears about as attractive and believable as he does in the flesh. Perhaps the most important thing it does for him, however, is to transmit his solidity of personality. Bob Squier has an engaging and probably accurate analogy of the camera's effect. "It really is a microscope," he said. "It reveals what a guy is, what his personality is. It bores into him. It shows you if he's not together, if he's not sure who he is, if he's not, well, an integrated personality. It's not just confidence—it goes much deeper than that. It really is a kind of a psychological thing. The camera seems to reveal—in ways I'm not sure anyone really can describe but which everyone seems to sense—the internal structures and strengths of a man."

It is just happy chance for Muskie that his qualities complement the medium. He didn't study it; he just started talking, and from the beginning it was good to him. Television came to Maine the year Muskie ran for governor and he used it because it was a cheap and novel way to reach people who ordinarily were not involved in politics. No one designed programs then. Muskie just bought fifteen minutes at a time, sat down and talked. Viewers had only one channel (the state's two stations did not overlap), and they were still so fascinated they would watch anything rather than turn it off. And so they saw Muskie, looking cool and easy and talking about real problems. The next morning they would see him at the mill gate and they would stand staring, transfixed, the romance of the electronic media realized in the flesh, and they would cry, "Hey! I saw you on television!" Muskie learned immediately that he was coming through clear and unhurt. He was not surprised because he didn't know how dangerous television could be. Since he started in confidence, he did not develop that suspicious, wary look that flits unconsciously over so many men's faces as they try to make of themselves what they hope the camera will find pleasing. The studio's sterile atmosphere, its great watching glass eye, its bloodless technicians bent to their dials—enough to make any man wonder if he is alone in an echo chamber—never had a chance to disturb Muskie. The immediate enthusiastic response of Maine people who were themselves still enthusiastic about the medium assured him the audience was out there listening, and he has been easy about it ever since.

It follows that Muskie is a strong campaigner, since a campaign gives him a structure for going to the people and doing things he enjoys. A campaign is exhausting and it is frustrating for all the things that must be left undone, but it also is a time of action, enthusiasm, momentum and resolution. It is a testing time before the ultimate temporal judge, a time when one is rewarded or punished, when one confronts one's enemies and wins or loses. If it is not quite a jousting tourney at Arthur's court, it shows that one of the attractions of politics still involves some old and bloody human satisfactions. A campaign provides the most legitimate platform possible for calling attention to oneself. All of Muskie's dislike for seizing the limelight vanishes, for the situation has reversed itself. To seek attention becomes proper and to fail to do so an affront, for it is the people's due to have their leaders appear and solicit their support. Though a campaign seems the height of disorder to the harried insiders, it actually offers a neat time frame with specific ground to be covered, both geographic and intellectual. A skillful man can strike a theme, develop it thoroughly and bring it into smooth cohesion as the polls open. It was the lack of this cohesion of theme and schedule that Muskie found so difficult after 1968 when he was seeking his footing as a Presidential candidate.

It is pleasant to go out and deal with people, to talk with them, listen to their problems and involve oneself in their lives. It is a relief from the dry substance of government. No one succeeds in politics unless he enjoys people, and it has been obvious since his boyhood that Muskie does, despite his shy and lonely temperament. Of course, in campaigning, he deals with them from a favored position: as the center of their attention. A novice who ran a losing campaign for Congress once observed, "Well, sure, I suppose it was exhausting, but being the center of everything, people listening to you, focused on you, hell, that was so stimulating that I hardly noticed the exhaustion."

Muskie comes to his campaigns tired and irritable, but almost immediately he begins to smooth out and soon he seems refreshed. He walks along streets and into shops, pursuing hands to shake. He goes to shopping centers, tours supermarkets, visits social clubs. He walks through little towns, knowing that word of his visit will spread and please people. He goes into radio stations to chat with disc jockeys on the air. He goes to mill gates at dawn to greet the changing shifts. He tours plants and meets men at their machines, and when he reaches some empty corner and looks around querulously for more hands to shake and people to greet, you realize he really likes this. It is an interesting point because the necessity for this somewhat mindless contact keeps many men of high intelligence out of elective politics. They can't stand the idea of killing a day in a shopping-center parking lot waving at people and shaking hands.

But the qualities Muskie brings to these encounters are intuitional rather than intellectual. Campaigning opens the door to the sort of oratory Muskie likes best. In normal times most speeches are on narrow subjects, given to narrow audiences. But in a campaign one appeals to an electorate so broad and diverse that except for occasional positioning speeches on overriding issues, one is free to roam about and talk to all kinds of people about things that concern all people.

It's no wonder, really, that Muskie makes his strongest political impression during campaigns and his weakest between them. Except for his localized campaign in Maine in 1970, he has been between campaigns since 1968 and thus has been trying to take leadership from a position that he sees as disadvantaged. In the approach to the battles of 1972, that particular disadvantage disappears. He has a solid platform. He is tougher. He is sharper and clearer in the image he projects. He is more willing to criticize, attack and even ridicule the policies if not the motives of his opponents. Increasingly, there is an air about him of both pleasure in and capacity for the fight. Under these conditions, the stylistic differences that have disturbed the politically aware probably become less noticeable. The substance of positions that Muskie takes in the focus of campaigning become more important than his positions in years past. The dichotomy of view in which Muskie is held never will disappear, for it is based on real differences, but in the pressure of campaigning it is likely to erode.

5

The Down-east Politician

Muskie's political attitudes—which are important long after stylistic differences are stripped away—came together in a single
dramatic year, from the middle of 1954 to the middle of 1955,
when he went from a political nonentity to a smashing success,
from a candidate without a chance to a governor who couldn't be
beaten. He slipped into real politics through the back door. He
long had been on the fringes and could have remained there forever; he was Democratic national committeeman, but Democrats
were the fringes in Maine. Years of an undistinguished small-
town law practice brought Muskie to this formative experience of
his life with very little personal baggage. And since his party had
collapsed and his own group had moved in as a thankless civic
duty, he carried equally little political baggage. There were no
albatrosses; he ran with no rules, no precedents, no rituals, no
sacred cows, no old retainers to be placated and—since he had
seen no chance of winning—nothing to lose.

The experience shaped him because while he was free, it

was obvious that there was little room for indulgence or mistake. He was introducing people to change that in the context of their lives was radical, and he had to find ways to make it acceptable. It was luck that he moved just when people were receptive (one of the basics of successful politics, Harry Truman once observed, is to be lucky), but Muskie's handling of the situation was not luck. He was skillful, showed abilities that no one had expected and emerged a pleasant surprise. He had won the election and now people would be watching to see if they had erred in deciding to trust a heretical Democrat. Maine is not an important state, nor is its governorship important in a national sense, but the effect of the experience on Muskie is important. It established and fixed his political attitudes. They have expanded as his range has expanded over the years, but their central themes remain the same. One sees them clearly in his Senate career, in his approach to the presidency and in the conflicting way in which people see him.

The Republicans held Maine in an iron grip for generations. Their candidates for governor regularly won by two-to-one margins without much pretense at campaigning and the office was handed around in the party as reward for service. They controlled the Legislature so completely that they did not let Democrats sit on important committees until 1955—in 1947, at the beginning of his political career, Muskie said that 85 percent of the legislation came from committees on which Democrats were not permitted. Republican local organization was active everywhere —the key to any party's success in a state legislature. The Democrats hardly had local organization and, at the time, they contested less than half the legislative seats, so that even if all Democrats running had won through some miracle, they still would not have been in control. Even today, Democrats don't contest every seat and the Legislature remains firmly in Republican hands. The Republicans care about the Legislature; they may surrender the governor's chair, but as an old Maine observer put it, "They'll fight like dogs for the Legislature, district by district, and they'll never give up." The reasons are simple enough: the Legislature writes the law that determines how free a run the money interests will have. And in Maine the money interests controlled the Republicans and the Republicans controlled the state. This is less true today, but only marginally so.

"They were controlled by the paper companies, the power companies, the businessmen who run things like sardine plants," Governor Curtis said recently. "They had an overflow labor force of people who had to work for very little and they were happy enough to keep it that way. The laws that passed were those that helped these plants. These were the people, for instance, who continually defeated the intrastate minimum wage in Maine even in the 1950s when the national Republican administration was extending the interstate minimum wage."

Writing in 1958, the political scientist Duane Lockard in his authoritative *New England State Politics* says flatly, "In few American states are the reins of government more openly or completely in the hands of a few leaders of economic interest groups than in Maine." Sophisticated economies that depend on stable, well-trained workers are much more likely to produce the balanced political climates that grow from the interplay of various more or less equal forces. In Maine, however, the combination of poverty and industries that use relatively unskilled and therefore easily replaceable labor give the economic interests free rein. As Lockard puts it, "The abundance of timber and water power has indirectly created Maine's Number One Political Problem: the manipulation of government by the overlords of the companies based on these resources. More than three-quarters of Maine is in woodland and most of that terrain is owned by a few timber companies and paper manufacturers." Developers of hydroelectric power, he said, "moved into politics not only to secure rights to water-power sites but also to protect their investment from rate cutters, competition and controls. These two groups, combined with the textile and shoe manufacturers, have done more than merely 'influence' Maine politics: 'control' is probably a more accurate term." Whole towns were (and still are) dominated by single plants which kept other plants out, by agreement or by pressure, and thus left the labor force dependent upon a single employer. The deposits of these giant firms controlled banks, which supported merchants who supported newspapers and radio stations. This interlocking at the local level corresponded to a certain interlocking at the board level among the giant firms themselves, which set intractable patterns for the state. State government controlled by a party that had no reason to be responsive to the people was a willing collaborator in the system.

The effect of such power, so confidently held, was to stifle the opposition party. Except in a few Democratic enclaves in towns like Waterville and Lewiston, a lawyer foolish enough to register as a Democrat couldn't expect many clients. A businessman soliciting credit and help from banks and suppliers did not inspire much confidence if he didn't even know the proper party. It wasn't personal and vicious; it was just that you hardly wanted a man to represent you or to handle your money if his judgment was demonstrably faulty and you knew that everyone of substance with whom he dealt would hold that view as if by instinct.

And then there was the social factor. All the best people— the town powers, the church elders, the social arbiters—were Republicans. When he took a friend to lunch recently at a country club in Portland, a Democrat observed placidly, "Twenty-five years ago, I couldn't have been a member here." Democrats still are not admitted to membership of the Portland Club, the leading city club there. The club fell into financial difficulty not long ago and considered admitting Democrats, but that was too bitter a pill and other means were found.

Under such self-reinforcing conditions, the stronger party got stronger and the weak weaker. All the action and the power were on the Republican side, and bright young men who saw themselves as tomorrow's shakers were not drawn to the Democrats. In most places running for office as a Democrat was an expensive, exhausting and somewhat ridiculous exercise in futility, and as a result the quality of Democratic candidates fell steadily, a decline that was hurried along every two years by a new disaster at the polls. That is the real reason that in 1964, when to the shock of everyone, including themselves, the Democrats rode Lyndon Johnson's coattails into control of the Maine Legislature, they did very little with their opportunity and were hustled back out of office two years later. The party's candidates simply were not of the caliber to take advantage of the opportunity. As the people of Maine observed the Democrats over the years, they saw little reason to abandon the Republicans. Through the 1940s and the early 1950s, Democrats turned more and more to vicious internal combat among small men for the small prestige of party control. This was the leadership that finally collapsed in exhaustion and disappeared as the 1954 political year approached.

Naturally when Muskie's little group took control, it could find no serious figure interested in running on the Democratic ticket, which, as we have seen, is why the governor's race fell eventually to Muskie. Candidates were found for the three congressional districts and the Senate seat (against Margaret Chase Smith) and the race began. No one expected to win and none did except Muskie. They ran as a beginning, not only because accepting control obligated them to produce a slate, but because they believed the Republicans were vulnerable and that a reorganized Democratic Party could ultimately make itself felt.

Muskie's first step was simple but radical for Maine: he took his campaign into Republican territory. Until then most Democrats had campaigned largely in Democratic areas where they were assured a warm if minority welcome. Dick McMahon, Muskie's old friend, a jolly, sentimental man of quick intelligence, was his campaign manager. Muskie had an old Lincoln sedan and with McMahon at the wheel they went all over the state on the narrow, slow roads, Muskie sunk as usual in silent abstraction, gazing at the Maine countryside. They started broke and things didn't get any better. McMahon tried to arrange their schedule so they could finish each night near a supporter who would give them a bed and breakfast. One night in Newport, Maine— McMahon likes to tell stories and he insists all his stories are true —they stopped at a diner and bought a package of cigarettes, two cups of coffee and a doughnut, which took the last of their money. They cut the doughnut in half.

All told, the five candidates spent a total of about nineteen thousand dollars in the entire campaign. The figure is ridiculous. At one point Tom Delahanty, who now is a justice of the Superior Court and at that time was running reluctantly for Congress in the Second District, met an old Boston politician who asked with professional interest how much money they had. The figure then was about fourteen thousand dollars. "Jesus Christ," the Bostonian said, "in a big Boston ward we spend that much for beer alone."

As the campaign opened they staged a rally for a handful of people in the square at Kittery and noticed that the blinds were drawn in most of the facing buildings. "God," someone whispered, "they don't even look at Democrats." But gradually Muskie began to make himself felt by going to people who rarely saw politicians or dealt with politics. Entrenched in their power, Republicans had fallen out of the habit of serious campaigning. Candidates relied on endorsements from party elders who formed a consensus which the people usually accepted. In the general election Democrats campaigned in their enclaves, and elsewhere the people placidly voted Republican, as in Hancock County, which for years consistently returned 13,000 Republican votes to 1,000 for the Democrats. So most Maine people were not used to seeing politicians in the flesh. Muskie bought a $28 bullhorn and drove unannounced into many little towns. McMahon would stop at the square, Muskie would hop out, raise a crowd with his bullhorn and start talking sense; it was a novel experience for most of the listeners and they paid attention. Every morning at dawn he was at a different mill gate shaking hands with the workers changing shifts. He walked streets shaking hands with pedestrians, went into stores and visited schools. He persuaded factory owners to let him tour their plants and he learned how to thread his way among the great machines with a minimum of interference and yet shake the hand of every man and woman there. Gradually his campaign began to move and he seemed to enjoy it. William McCarthy of Rumford, then a candidate for county attorney, now a Superior Court justice, remembers Muskie as "very outgoing as a candidate. As soon as we hit a town he'd say, 'Let's go meet people,' and he'd lead the parade. It embarrassed me to grab someone's hand and say, 'I'm Bill McCarthy, I'm running for county attorney,' I'd think who the hell cares, but Muskie seemed thrilled. 'They're liking us,' he'd say, 'I think they're liking us.' "

Years later, however, Muskie described his own sensations of those days. Speaking in Bangor, a center of Maine conservatism, he said, "One of the experiences I dreaded most [in 1954] was coming to Bangor and going from door to door, meeting people who were sure to be about ninety-nine percent Republican, to ask them for their votes." Then, significantly, he added, "But it turned out to be one of the most reassuring experiences I ever had. Because I found that if you really go out to meet people with a smile and a firm hand and a message, they welcome you . . ."

It was all new, the street tours and factory tours and hand-shaking at the mill gates and most of all the stunning new effect of television. The effect was to bypass the old channels of politics and thus to bypass the potent Republican organization. The new young Democrats had no organization, but they were reaching more and more new people. They appeared young and gay and exciting. People who normally were uninterested in politics suddenly found it interesting, an adventure in which they could participate with their votes. At the same time, of course, Maine people were ready to be shaken from their old ways. A generation of veterans brought to early maturity in war was ready to take control. The economic boom that was reshaping the nation was hardly touching Maine, and people saw prosperity everywhere but at home. The Republicans appeared oblivious to these forces (when they lost, as one of them said, "They couldn't understand it—it was like cursing God"). In fact, however, the old party had been weakened by serious internal fighting and by a scandal in 1952 involving state-operated liquor stores. Burton M. Cross, the incumbent governor running for reelection, pro-

jected a negative personality. He had a knack for alienating people, and when the intensity of Muskie's campaigning drove him
to the stump in self-defense he appeared awkward and cold, an
impression that television accentuated.

Still, while Muskie's approach to politics was new and exciting for Maine, his tone was reassuring. He took pains to appear a
reasonable and practical Maine man who well understood the
bounds of propriety. His theme was that Maine's economic stagnation grew from its political stagnation. The economic facts were
self-evident. Wages were low, recent wage increases the lowest in
New England, and new plant expenditures were down 70 percent
compared with 9 percent for New England as a whole. Maine's
population had been static for years. Since the state entered the
Union in 1820 (as the nonslave side of the Missouri Compromise)
its population had doubled while the nation's had increased
seventeen times. The eight Congressmen with which it had started
were down to three in 1954. On the other hand, the controlling
industries were profitable and comfortable with a docile labor
force, weak unions and a minimum of competition. There were
many issues—bad highways, deplorable eleemosynary institutions, a shaky higher education system, poor lower schools—and
most of them could be traced to economic failure.

"We had a lot of one-room schools in those days," Governor
Curtis said recently, "where the kids couldn't tell a basketball
from a pumpkin. Kids weren't exposed to variety and opportunity
and the tools with which to advance themselves. Maine kids had
a sort of inferiority sense because the situation led you to the
feeling that you couldn't be anything. Only a few went on to high
school, and those of us who did didn't talk about it much—the
other kids made you feel a snob. Going to college was very unusual. The thing was that the plants had an overflow work force
already and you had to scramble for a job. Either you left town
and went to college, went all the way, or you went to work in the
mill. Kids couldn't see going on to school—you could get the
same job in the mill after grammar school that you could after
high school."

The state government, which ostensibly represented everybody, was doing little to improve the situation. "We have some of the most Republican counties in America," Muskie said, "and what good does it do us?"

Still, it is not easy to make economic matters emotionally penetrating. To do so Muskie settled on a handle: the exodus of Maine's young people, whose departure to find better jobs (Muskie's own brother Eugene was already settled in California) was the basic cause of the state's static population. Why did they leave and never return? Why were they working in New York and Massachusetts and California? Why were your children and your grandchildren growing up out of your sight and knowledge, untouched by the life you cherished? Because they didn't like Maine? Didn't appreciate its beauty and its people? Oh, no. Night after night he soared on that point as mothers wept in the front rows in little Grange halls. Watching those tears one night, McMahon found himself thinking perhaps they did have a chance. "And in a minute, Jesus, I was crying myself. Of course, I'm a sentimental bastard, but still . . ."

The crowds got bigger, warmer, more enthusiastic. As a potato farmer in northern Maine said, "Nobody else ever took the trouble to come out here in the mud and listen to me and ask for my vote, and by God, you're going to get my vote." The remark was echoed around the state. Muskie's happy reflection of this enthusiasm enhanced the reaction and increased his momentum. He emerged a confident, clever candidate, and people brushed by the others in his group to shake his hand. He developed a flair for maneuver which he demonstrated the day he focused his long-standing challenge to Governor Cross to debate in public. The Democrats were meeting amidst the lobster pots on the town wharf at Rockland when they learned by chance that Cross was speaking uptown at a major Republican rally.

Muskie wrote a quick note reissuing his challenge: "I'll come to your platform or you come to mine." He had it delivered to Cross by hand and then anxiously awaited the answer, trying to delay his own speech. Delahanty, the Congressional candidate, was speaking and each time he reached a point that sounded like summation he heard Muskie whispering from the side, "Keep talking, keep talking." In fact, it was a ploy. Muskie would have destroyed Cross in a debate and both men knew it, so of course Cross was not going to debate. A clever politician would have found a solution or he would have ignored the challenge.

Instead, Cross answered the note with one of his own saying he believed no useful purpose would be served by debate. It was a foolish answer, which Muskie turned fully to his own advantage. He took the microphone and described the challenge and then read the governor's answer. "When we're talking about what will benefit the people of Maine and the governor says it will serve no useful purpose to debate, who is he representing?" he asked, waving the slip of paper, and down he went through his litany of issues, summing each with the cry, "Would no useful purpose be served by discussion of that?" Again it was a matter of finding a handle: its importance had little to do with Cross but exactly suited the legitimization of Muskie's positions. Newspapers gave the incident good coverage and the Portland *Press Herald,* the largest paper in Maine and strongly Republican, chastised Cross editorially, saying that Muskie's points demanded discussion. The incident was widely discussed in Maine; the editorial comment in the Republican press had the effect of establishing by imprimatur the significance of Muskie's charges and, conversely, of the failure of the Republicans to answer them.

The Democrats were moving, but they couldn't believe how much. A *Press Herald* reporter, Peter Damborg, caught the new wind so clearly that he wrote a story saying Muskie could win. His editors rebuked him for letting his feel for the crowds outrun his judgment and refused to print it; afterward—Maine people really *are* fair—the editors apologized to him publicly in a handsome editorial.

Muskie's own mood ranged violently up and down. On the night before election he told his brother-in-law, Howard Gray, "I won't win this time, but if I get a good vote it will give me courage to go out and try again." The next day he told another brother-in-law, Jack Gray, "Listen, I can win this one," and reeled off a set of figures to which Gray, sure he would lose, did not bother to listen.

On election night Muskie rented two rooms in the Elmwood Hotel in Waterville for six dollars apiece. A single reporter and a handful of friends appeared, but with the first returns the night went wild, for it was immediately clear that Muskie was cutting deeply into Republican territory. Hancock County, famous for that 13,000-to-1,000 margin, gave Muskie 3,000 votes. A community that always gave its twelve votes to the Republicans cast three for Muskie. When the Democratic centers came in, Muskie went into the lead and by 10:30 P.M. knew he had won. "When you win a big one you didn't expect to win, the first time," McMahon said, "oh, that's something. It never happens quite like that again and you never forget it and it never stops feeling good."

The hotel opened more rooms, which immediately filled with happy Democrats laughing, shouting, drinking whiskey, beating each other's backs and cheering each new figure and each new phone call of congratulations. At 1:45 A.M. Cross called Muskie to concede. The final count was not even close: Muskie 135,673; Cross, 113,298. Speaking to a crowd in Texas in 1968, Muskie recalled that night: "I never had an experience like that. If I win elections from now until the year 2000—this election, if we win it, wouldn't be nearly the exhilarating experience of that one. We won against hopeless odds. We won with almost no resources. We had had to literally walk that state from one end to the other. We had to talk to Republicans who had never even seen a live Democrat in their lives. We had to learn the political skills that none of us had ever developed. We had to do it against an establishment, against a machine, against a political organization which had had a century to entrench itself, and we did it."

Muskie's faith in going to the people springs from that campaign and has been reinforced by almost everything that has happened to him since. As he speaks around the country today, at a time when more and more people doubt their ability to cause change, he often remembers that experience. If you work hard, if you take the trouble to understand the fears and the hopes and the pressures under which people live, if you address yourself to them in those terms, you can make change. He did so in Maine, with Republican help and support, and he never forgets that. "The trick is," he said recently, "to keep people focused on the realities. If you ever let it get onto the basis that to support you they must be disloyal to their own, you're sunk. No, the thing is to talk about issues and realities, because they are not party matters. They are just matters of good sense."

The point also was essential to his success as governor. He faced overwhelming odds in the Legislature, which began its session the following January, on the day of his inaugural. Its ratio of Republicans to Democrats was 117 to 34 in the House and 27 to 6 in the Senate. Muskie could not even sustain his own veto over a party-line vote. If the Legislature chose—or more properly, if Muskie allowed the situation to arise—it could discard his program, write its own, pass it and then ram it through his veto with 16 votes to spare in demonstration of the governor's impotence. His only weapon was the support of the people who had elected him, and he set about immediately to consolidate that. Muskie continued to travel about the state, speaking at every opportunity and assuring everyone that he was a reasonable man. "I don't believe I'll have any trouble working with a Republican Legislature," he said. Then he reminded his audience that it was important to evaluate what the people had been saying on Election Day: they were saying they wanted change, and having said it, he wanted them to remember it.

Maurice Williams, a Republican, who became Muskie's administrative assistant said, "Maine had been run by such conservative people that when Muskie took over it was far behind in all sorts of things, in schools and institutions and the quality of its highways, and something had to be done. And Muskie had that touch, you know, to make people understand. He would tell them about mental hospitals where patients had been sleeping in the kitchens and the corridors for years. The teachers' colleges in those days—in what few dormitories we had, kids were stacked in tiers of threes, the light they studied by just a bulb hanging on a cord from the ceiling. But you have to make people see these things to understand them."

At the same time, however, Muskie was carefully making a basic Maine point. "If I try to reach for too much, I may not get anything." He said this to every reporter he met, and as he had expected, the newspapers soon were quoting it approvingly in editorials. It probably was reassuring: a wise man doesn't bite off more . . .

"Muskie's pragmatic style was developing then," McMahon said. "First isolate the problem, then devise a solution that he finds palatable as well as politically workable, and then figure out how to sell it."

The immediate problem was money to pay for Muskie's new plans, but again it was more a matter of appearances than of substance. Muskie had to prepare the state's budget for the next two years and have it ready a week after he was inaugurated. Estimated income for the period under current taxes was $68 million, and it would take all of that just to maintain current operations. Maine law forbids deficit financing; if spending bills unbalance the budget, new taxes must be passed immediately to correct it. To meet current operations and his own programs, Muskie would have to present a budget seriously out of balance, propose new taxes immediately and thereby appear the very spendthrift the Republicans already were warning against.

"The Democrats had the reputation of spenders," he once said, "and I could just hear the talk, 'Well, here's another Democrat, another New Dealer, a tax-and-spender, just can't wait to start throwing it around,' and that wasn't a very happy way to start a new administration." He didn't want the change he represented to be tarred immediately with that emotional negative. Muskie and his aides talked around and around the situation, often noting wistfully how easy it would be to offer a balanced budget that simply carried on as before, and one night Muskie said suddenly, "Well, why don't we do that? Why don't we keep the old budget and have a new budget too—you know, a supplemental budget?" There was a momentary silence and Muskie grinned. "What the hell *is* wrong with having two budgets?"

It was a beautiful political idea because it solved his problem in a stroke. He wasn't unwilling to spend, but he had to make spending understandable. Few people can fathom budgets anyway, and to present one $10 million or 18 percent out of balance, with new programs obscured in the forest of the old, would be to appear an unconscionable spender. But to offer a basic budget of $68 million that carried on in the same old way and then to offer a supplemental budget, with new things clearly marked and the taxes to pay for them clearly explained, was to make it all understandable. People know they must pay for what they want, and they had indicated they wanted change. Muskie believed in his programs; the supplemental budget made what he was doing clear and it also thrust the burden of proof onto the opposition, which would have to explain equally clearly if it was to refuse him. Again, he had taken the point out of normal political channels and put it before the people.

After his inaugural—as his budget and his other proposals were being debated—Muskie pushed much of the administrative side of running the state onto Williams and continued to travel and speak all over the state. He moved in more style, in a limousine driven by a state police officer, but his message was the same. He began giving radio talks and he learned to use the press conference as a tactical weapon. The Republican leadership, confident of its weight and numbers, had been inclined to ignore their new governor at first, but then, as Williams put it, legislators "started going home and hearing from their constituents," and they began to take Muskie more seriously. The Republican Party was not monolithic. There were the usual schisms, and while the leadership was in the hands of the industrialists there was a sizable bloc of rural legislators who called themselves "the little guys." They were financially conservative but more oriented to people than to business. So, Muskie found, there was room to maneuver.

The dominant figure on the Republican side was Robert N.

Haskell, president of the Senate. He was a big, solid, blond man a few years older than Muskie with a brilliant mind and an irascible nature. He was sometimes known as "Slide-rule Haskell," and was, as Don Nicoll once put it, "totally impatient with everyone not as smart as he, which was nearly everyone." He then was vice president of Bangor Hydro-Electric, one of the state's two largest utilities; today he is its president. His power in the Legislature was immense, for in addition to his native abilities, he held the keys: when a legislator really wanted something, Haskell was the man, and often the only man, who could work it out. He began as Muskie's chief antagonist and ended as a frequent ally, a point that neither he nor Muskie will admit to this day. But they were the powers, they were accommodators, and in time Haskell formed the habit of slipping into Muskie's office at the end of day for a drink and talk that remained private. Alton Lessard, a member of Muskie's original group, who then was a state senator and now is a justice of the Superior Court, once accused them to their faces of having become friends. "Hell," he said, "I think you guys are pals." They both got angry.

Two of his battles illustrate the political attitudes that were crystallizing under the pressure of action. The first was over his plan to start loosening the industrialists' grip on the state's economy. Muskie's attack was through the state's development program, which then aimed at tourism almost exclusively, instead of at more solid forms of growth. Whatever its benefits, the tourist industry produces a notoriously low standard of living for those who work in it. Democrats believed that beyond the obvious reasons, the state's economic interests found tourism useful for two purposes. First, it held in marginal summer jobs people who then were available for other marginal seasonal work, and then added to an overflow winter work force which maintained an employers' rather than an employees' market. Second, it is a tenet of faith among Democrats, though electric-power men dismiss the idea as nonsense, that the influx of summer visitors compensated for the normal seasonal lag in power demand and allowed the utilities to use their generating equipment at a profitably high percentage of capacity the year around.

The point of Muskie's attack was the twelve-member Maine Development Commission, which operated independently of the governor and was rigidly controlled by its chairman, Harold F. Schnurle, who also happened to be a vice president of and chief lobbyist for the Central Maine Power Company, the state's largest utility. Schnurle was passionately devoted to the free enterprise system; the commission focused on tourism instead of industrial development because he believed the place for business development was in business, not in a state agency. His company happened to have a development department that was expected to assist any industry wanting to locate in Maine. Schnurle seems to have felt that that was entirely adequate, but even more important, proper.

Muskie approached the problem obliquely. He prepared a bill which would create a new department of state government responsible to the governor which would devote itself to real industrial and economic development. His intent was to bypass Schnurle; the bill left the commission intact and limited its interests to tourism, which, Muskie observed, was all it had been doing anyway.

When the Democrats introduced the bill, Schnurle exploded. He denounced the bill, insisted the commission was doing everything necessary and said that a new department would serve only to expand the bureaucracy and extend government still further into that sanctified realm in which it had no place, private business. Haskell condemned Muskie's plan as a matter of routine and said he saw no chance of the Legislature passing it. "It quickly became a hell of a fight," said Delahanty, "because Schnurle really had tremendous influence, and anyway, business was just petrified. It had visions of TVA and everything." McMahon, whom Muskie had named to the Public Utilities Commission, said bluntly, "Listen, when you talked economic development you were walking right on the toes of power and paper. They controlled the labor market and they didn't want any competition."

But Muskie was everywhere, rattling off figures that demonstrated Maine's failure to keep economic pace with the country. One can see such growth as a mixed blessing today, but then the liabilities of economic boom were still hidden and its benefits seemed obvious. Muskie's case was thoroughly prepared and people began to listen to the figures which he presented in a thoughtful, evidential way. It didn't sound like an attack, and of course there was no question of personalities. The governor was very kind to the commission—its failures were not its fault, he explained solemnly, for the science of attracting modern industry is complicated and requires experts, the very sort of men whom his department would attract.

Muskie was invited to the sacrosanct Portland Club—where he could not be a member—and he spoke for ninety minutes on his plan. Support began to build in the newspapers and a tendency to chide Republicans for "obstructionism" crept into editorials. A few Republican legislators were drawn to Muskie's plan and threatened to bolt. Schnurle's autocratic manner had irritated his fellow commissioners and under the pressure three of them broke with him and declared for Muskie's bill.

The effect of this increasingly serious discussion of Muskie's proposal was to certify the need for something new. Once this was established, the Republicans were in disarray, for they had no alternative plan and their negative case that they would just as soon go on as always seemed intolerably weak. They caucused for two hours and emerged with nothing decided, looking rattled. In his study of the period, Lockard noted that "Republicans were told that failure to pass the bill was handing the Democrats the next election on a platter. One Republican predicted that the party would be blamed for everything from the departure of a textile mill to the death of a chicken in Aroostook County."

Something had to be done and Haskell did it. He surrendered. At the same time, he arranged a little advantage for himself. There was no love lost between Haskell and Schnurle, nor between their companies which together dominated the Maine power market, though their trade areas did not overlap. Haskell went down to the Portland Club to speak. He praised Muskie's sincerity, praised the commission's work and offered a substitute motion that not only gave Muskie everything he wanted but destroyed the commission as well. He agreed to the new department under the governor, but instead of leaving the commission intact, he proposed incorporating it into the new department and keeping the commissioners in a purely *advisory* role. The result was not to circumvent Schnurle but to dump him. Lockard noted that "the Republican leadership had conceded," and though Muskie treated it as a compromise toward which he allowed himself to be drawn slowly, it was an obvious victory, gained by taking his case to the people and cutting the ground from under the Republicans.

The second battle that illustrated Muskie's firming political attitudes took place at the end of the six-month legislative session when his $10 million supplemental budget came to a showdown. In his budget message Muskie had proposed raising the $10 million with an income tax, which then was regarded as heresy in Maine. Failing that, he proposed an increase in the sales tax with a list of basic necessities exempted in order to lower the tax burden on the poor.

On the spending side of the budget, Muskie had included $4 million to begin a long-range-funded building program. At that time Maine still erected its public buildings on whatever surplus there happened to be at the end of the budget period—which was one reason for the disastrous state of its institutions. The other $6 million covered a variety of programs.

The Appropriations Committee passed the $68 million basic budget readily. In the supplemental budget, it knocked out the $4 million building fund and pared out another $1 million, leaving Muskie with $5 million for his several programs. Except for a sensible building system, this gave him most of what he wanted. The committee rejected his income tax proposal instantly and for his sales tax increase proposal it substituted a series of patchwork taxes it said would add $6 million to Maine's income. The extra million was meant to fund some of the local or specialized bills that stack up awaiting passage at the end of any legislative session. These bills are small in an overall sense but they often are of great importance to individual legislators because they represent specific achievement which can determine whether the legislator is going to be reelected. This fact was the lever around which Muskie turned the fight.

He called a joint session of the Legislature and gave a long address pleading the good sense of his program. Though the legislators paid him scant attention, the speech provided a superb and well-covered format for making his case to the public. Again public support for his position began to grow. A Republican newspaper suggested that "the Republican Party in the Legislature is more intent on thwarting Gov. Muskie than it is on solving the state's budgetary and taxation problems." Gradually, once more, the Republicans were being made to seem the villains. Again there was defection in the Republican ranks, but this time the leadership rammed through its version of the supplemental budget and tax proposal and sent it to Muskie to accept or to veto.

The situation posed interesting political problems. The Legislature's budget was unsoundly financed and it whittled down his plans. On the other hand, it gave Muskie the bulk of what he wanted, and the opposition was looking more than ever like dogs in the manger. If he vetoed the bill the Republicans could override him, which would be costly to them but more so to him. He had five days to think it over before the bill would become law without his signature.

On the fourth day, Muskie called a press conference and announced that Raymond Mudge, Commissioner of Finance and the state's senior budget officer, had studied the tax bill and believed that it could not possibly produce the $1 million extra which the Legislature anticipated. He saw a surplus of a mere nine thousand dollars. If the commissioner's estimate was accurate, it doomed all those little bills on which so many legislators were counting.

The fact was, however, that Mudge was a famous old conservative whose estimates of income always were drastically low. He always calculated the worst and counted on it happening. Muskie knew this; he simply relied on Mudge's estimate because it was useful to do so. The Republican leadership knew it too, which is why they felt safe in ignoring his estimate. But Mudge was their appointee, a carry-over from previous administrations and a party stalwart, and they could hardly repudiate him publicly.

At 10:15 P.M., before the midnight deadline, Muskie called in the press to announce that he would not veto the bill but would let it pass without his signature. To veto it, he said, might endanger what it did provide, which amounted to success for much of his program. Its taxing plan, however, was "narrow and unfair . . . [and] I cannot now in good conscience give formal approval to it." He was, in other words, taking credit for the appropriations while disavowing the patchwork taxes.

The session drew to a close in great tension, for the local bills remained unpassed and Muskie insisted on standing on Mudge's estimate of the money that would be available for them, an estimate that Mudge further refined to exactly $9,387. The Republican leadership met and assembled a list of Republican bills it intended to pass despite Mudge. Their total spending came to $777,000, and Muskie called another press conference.

It was an engaging situation. Muskie, determined to show the Republicans as big-time spenders, insisted on relying on Mudge's figures. The Republicans, knowing Mudge, insisted on passing their bills. Thus the public saw a Democrat standing for fiscal righteousness and Republicans throwing away the best advice of their own expert to plunge into further spending. Even the Portland *Press Herald* talked ominously of the judgment that would be made by the people "who have expressed a desire for additional services and a willingness to pay the freight through new taxation."

At showdown, however, the matter was dangerous. The Republicans were going ahead, and while Muskie's veto would have given them trouble, in the end they would drive their bills through. Having another set of measures rammed past him might replace Muskie's image of righteousness with one of helplessness. At the crucial moment he met with the Republican leadership and offered them a deal, and the fact that they took it showed they still had not grasped the implications of going to the people. They had operated internally too long, while Muskie of necessity always had an eye cocked out the window. The arrangement, which Muskie announced immediately at a hasty press conference, was that he would not veto the bills if the Republicans would pass a resolution accepting full responsibility for raising the estimate of income above that of the state's budget officer and thus take the blame for any shortages that might result.

Of course it was a matter of appearance rather than substance. There was little reason to think the Republican estimates were too high. All the Legislature's resolution said was that it believed its own estimates to be accurate, which was obvious anyway. But by then the central point was well anchored in people's minds. News stories reported that the Republican leaders had agreed to take the blame for this rash of last-minute spending and again the old canard of the Democratic spenders had been reversed. There is more to it, however, than mere image or who won or political trickery. If Muskie was to start the state on the way to change, he had to demonstrate his own soundness and responsibility. Mere election was not enough: the people had to see him in action and find him trustworthy before he could hope to move them. Just the same, the battle had been satisfying and it brought out the political brawler in McMahon: "Oh, it was great. They had the power and they thought they could sack him up like a ham, but Muskie whipped them flat and by the end of that first session they knew it and next time around they were as nice as could be."

He was reelected in 1956 by almost 60 percent, and ever since there has been two-party government in Maine. In the second session, to put funding on a sounder basis, Muskie got his sales tax increase with its exemptions. He reorganized the system for dealing with highways, always a problem in a state with violent weather and a ratio of land area to population higher than, for instance, the state of Texas. Highways also have become an increasingly dubious blessing in modern America—so few virtues are holding—but in a rural state without cities they mean a great deal in terms of going to work, to market and to school. Muskie fought for and got an independent study of Maine government, which recommended many of the reforms he had urged; they didn't all come to pass, but the effect of the study was to remove the issues from partisan contention. He developed a new formula for aiding education that started wholesale improvement in lower education, and at the same time he began to revitalize the University of Maine and the state college system. The trend has continued ever since; the most recent figures show that state subsidies to secondary education have increased almost eight times and state spending on higher education has increased more than nine times since the year Muskie was elected—and this in the face of a population that has remained static. In that second session, Muskie got the building authority he lost the first time. The authority provides continuity of funding and therefore of planning as well as architectural and quality overview unknown in the past.

One day not long ago McMahon was driving Muskie past the state capitol when on impulse he turned in. "I want you to see what you've done," he said. "You just don't know all you got done." Muskie, sitting slumped in the seat, looking up at the bright new buildings, grinned and said, "Just call me Muskie the Builder."

The attitudes that Muskie developed in Maine have never really varied; grown, expanded, adapted to new circumstances and opportunities, certainly, but the basic ideas hold. His manner probably caused the trouble when he came to the Senate and clashed with Lyndon Johnson, but his attitudes determined his position. As we have seen, Johnson's compromise on Rule 22 was to switch from the two-thirds vote then required to stop debate and break a filibuster to two-thirds of those present and voting, a very modest change; the liberals insisted on a simple majority cutoff. Muskie went with the liberals against Johnson, but he wasn't happy about it. Years later he remarked, "I thought the whole thing was a mistake. I suggested then and I still think that we could have won a three-fifths cutoff. That's the difference between sixty and sixty-seven votes and anyone who has ever tried to round up an extra seven votes on a tight issue knows what an immense margin that can be. I was a brand-new freshman then and no one was listening to me, but I think events have proved me right. The change to two-thirds of those present and voting has made little real difference in the way the Senate operates, and we've been trying ever since to get further change. We had the momentum for real change then, but the leaders of the movement wanted it all, and all was too much at the time."

When the Senate convened in January 1971, liberals fought another long and unsuccessful battle to modify Rule 22—this time to three-fifths. There are things to be said, a friend remarked to Muskie at the time, for the half-a-loaf concept. "Well," Muskie said, "I don't really see it as half a loaf. I see it as getting a start on the whole loaf. You keep right on fighting for what you want —you never give up on that. But in the meantime, if you want to make things work, you've got to get them through and a lot of times you've got to do some giving to get. If every step you make is in the right direction, you'll get there eventually and things will be getting better as you go. That's what the whole thing is about, you know. You can talk about crusades and causes and so forth all you like, but what we're really trying to do is to make people's lives better, and you just keep on working on that."

Muskie is a pragmatist and an idealist, each justifying the other and making it workable, since neither is worth much alone. It is this quality that allows him, the working politician, to say creditably to a group of editors, "The quality of political dialogue in American election campaigns is a disgrace to the Republic."

This was the speech in which he observed tartly that freedom of the press didn't mean freedom for "the news media to decide what is truth, but the right of a free people to have access to the truth," but his central thrust was that politicians and press are equally guilty—the politician plays dirty for headlines and the dirtier the campaign the more headlines he gets. Before giving the speech, Muskie showed it to Hal Pachios, who was a White House aid in the Johnson administration. Muskie was irritated when Pachios said, "Well, you know, it's very nice, it's a fine idea, but it won't really work. You can't really establish an uplifted dialogue among politicians in an adversary situation. It would be great if you could, but the system won't let you."

"What do you mean, the system?" Muskie asked.

"Well, the way things are in politics—you can't separate the way you'd like it to be from emotion, anger, greed, human fallibility."

"You call that the system?" Muskie cried. "That's not the system. The Constitution, the Declaration of Independence, that's the system. What you're talking about is just what people have made of it."

"I know," Pachios said, "but just the same, the way things are more or less requires Agnew, for instance, to maintain some kind of partisan rhetoric—"

"They are all free men," Muskie interrupted angrily. "They can make what they want out of it. Is it your idea, for God's sake, that the American system requires Spiro Agnew to go around calling me a son of a bitch?"

When the flag, that symbol so fraught with ironic new significance, appeared on the lapels of liberal candidates in the 1970 elections, someone asked Muskie if he thought the party was moving to the right. Maybe, Muskie said, but he added that the question usually arose around issues and he believes it a mistake to view issues in ideological terms. "Safety, you know, your own personal security, which means crime and your chance of getting mugged or raped or your house broken into, that is not a fringe issue. It is central to everyone's concern and if you're in politics you've got to deal with it. Now it's possible to deal with it from one side of the spectrum or the other, obviously, but it serves no useful purpose to put it on that basis because finally, the act of dealing with it is not an ideological matter, it's a practical necessity."

Muskie doesn't think code words really work, no matter their fatal attraction for so many politicians. They are a substitute for the hard work of making reality plain, and in the end "the apocalyptic statement just doesn't sell. The people don't buy the devil-and-the-saint theory of politics. They see us on TV and they know we aren't all devil or all saint. It just doesn't work."

Dividing people by exacerbating their fears isn't practical, Muskie thinks; it makes much more sense to bring them together. "You've got to win elections to change things you don't like," he told an angry, militant crowd in New Haven one night. "The only way we have ever achieved constructive change in the interests of broad masses of people is to put together majorities, the right kind of majorities, people who can identify their common values and their common interests." That's what it takes to make change. "No group in this country, no minority, is strong enough by itself to build a country to its own specifications." So if you want change, "You've got to develop the skills and the talents and the organizational ability and the persuasive power to convince other people to follow you . . . All my life has been devoted to that kind of political activity and I've seen it work, I've seen the system, government, government policy respond . . . In a period of change, a time of creating new institutions, of course you'll have imperfections. And you know, blueprints or legislation or new ideas aren't self-executing. They depend on the willingness of people to support them and to accommodate to each other and to different points of view."

So, Muskie said another time, "The activist cannot be a perfectionist. He's got to be a realist. And he ought to be an idealist. So if you have the three, the activist, the realist, the idealist, then you've got some hopes of moving to your objectives, whatever the imperfections of the means that you may develop at any given moment."

Another time, he said, "I'm willing to fight, but the question is when. You have to pick these battles, you have to pick the times when you have the troops and the issues are important. You should be willing to fight losing battles too, but you shouldn't make this a habit. You should compromise, but you shouldn't compromise until you have nothing left. Your whole position has to be balanced."

Muskie started a small revolution in Maine ("He made the change from standstill to go-ahead," Williams said) and it has been going on ever since. "In those fights in Maine," Muskie said, "I shaped the issues and I prepared my positions very carefully and I took some strategic defeats. But every time I lost, I won; I lost, but I had shaped it so that there was a clear image in the public mind of what was at stake. There was plenty of fighting and I won with the public. But you know, I worked with the Republican Legislature, too. I didn't really veto many bills, but I used another device. I'm not even sure if it was constitutional, but it worked. If a bill came to my desk and I found some good in it, I would call in the Republican leaders and I'd tell them, Now, if you'll take this out and that out, I'll pass it through, and if you don't, I'll veto it. Well, of course, they could override my veto, but that took hard party-line discipline and they couldn't do that every day. And a lot of times they'd go back into conference and produce a bill that made more sense. I guess we saved maybe a hundred bills that way and we could have made each one a battleground. Now, in my second term as governor, I got eighty-five to ninety percent of my program through the Legislature. So which is the better way? I could have fought all the time and gotten very little done. What is really important? I say it's to get things done."

Muskie likes politics. He is a professional and he enjoys the plain mechanics of his profession. All of its ingredients make the whole, of course—the art of maneuver, the pleasures of solving puzzles when the terms are in constant flux, the ego-satisfying matter of serving your country and your fellows, the plain pleasure of success itself. Politics does appear to serve Muskie as a structured release from shyness, but the quickest glance across the span of his life shows that nothing else ever really appealed to him or drew him. On the other hand, he has a high capacity for self-pity and he enjoys complaining about how hard he works and how little help he gets. He was doing so one day when one of those straightforward Maine shopkeepers asked him why he didn't quit. "I guess I would," he said with an inward look that seemed faintly surprised, "if I didn't really like it."

His Republican friend in Waterville who wants to remain anonymous said, "Listen, every time Muskie sees me he says, 'Ah, you lucky bastard, taking it easy, living the good life.' He gets to remembering drinking boilermakers and cruising off Boothbay and ice fishing—but if he found himself back here in a law office, he'd last about three days. His soulfood is the appreciation of lots of people and how they show that. He needs that—he really needs it. Nothing brings him out like a big group of people, listening to him, showing it in their faces. All of us need a sense of public acceptance, you know, and Muskie needs it more than most. He needs the cheering crowds, and what's more, he needs to earn it. That's part of the addiction of politics—I've met many people who have left politics and who are morose and low, absolutely unfulfilled. Three days without some form of food for the addiction would bother Ed more than most men in politics. And this food, you know, is not just the crowds and the tinsel, but the basic knowledge that you are important and that you are doing something that is significant and worthwhile. He's just a political creature."

When you mix the more standard kinds of ego with the ego of idealism you come straight to politics. "Government is our only collective instrument," Muskie once observed to some conservative recalcitrant, "and when you cut back its work you begin to cut back the quality of people's lives. It relates directly to how we all live, and very directly indeed to how a few live—the people in need of help, hospital help, for instance, or welfare. And when you reduce the level of that help you begin literally to destroy lives."

Such a view, filtered through the economic realities of a state like Maine, imposes a certain discipline. When Muskie went to the Senate, his interests ran to a continuation of the economic improvements he had worked for as governor. He fitted naturally into things like the Area Redevelopment Act, the Accelerated Public Works Program, the Manpower Retraining Act, all of which had specific implications for Maine. His attitude toward foreign trade grew directly from the tension that still exists in Maine today: oil import quotas keep fuel prices artificially high, which is hard on individuals and inhibits industry; unrestricted imports of shoes and textiles have been battering Maine industry and therefore Maine working conditions for years. Muskie introduced his Orderly Marketing Act, which would have authorized the Secretary of State to intercede in situations in which goods are produced at wages and working conditions substantially below those of the United States. The bill never passed, though Muskie enjoys somewhat ironically the fact that the phrase "orderly marketing concept" has crept into the language.

He developed an interest in hydroelectric power keyed to Maine's chronic power shortages. In 1959 he spent thirty days in Siberia studying Soviet water projects. He fought a long battle for a hydroelectric project in the Maine wilderness, a dam long planned and very popular with the people of Maine. This was another of those situations, as some wit once put it, admitting Muskie to the Order of the Cellophane Wall—where when the time of crisis came, he shall be stood against it and shot at from both sides. Naturally private power interests in Maine fought his dam project, but when conservationists awakened to the fact that the dam would flood a big segment of unspoiled wilderness, they opened fire from the opposite side. Power interests long have blocked the dam in the House and Muskie doesn't talk much about it now. "I think it makes people mad," he said. "They want it, we talk about it, they get their hopes up and then again, nothing happens—no wonder they don't believe us much any more."

Things are better in Maine today than they were in the 1950s, but there are still many people leading lives that are not exactly flush. During his 1970 campaign Muskie visited a marginal shoe factory at Dexter and for the newcomer who was with him it was a startling experience. Hundreds of men and women, each responsible for some part of a variety of shoes, were at machines that clattered and roared beneath low ceilings. The light was dim and the air heavy with the acrid smell of dyes and new tanned leather. Machines stamped out the parts and other machines sewed them together. Machines glued and shaped the finished product, buffed it, packed it. Pay was by the piece and the people worked at great speed, their bodies moving in strange, jerky rhythms: one hand guiding a piece through as the other snatched up the next; the great blades, shears, stamps, presses and needles rising and falling amid the flashing fingers. The work is sought after; if you are slow, someone awaits your job. Each man worked until the political party was upon him, stopped, smiled, shook hands and fell back against his machine. Politics had cost him a nickel.

Sometimes you have to see these things—these marginal factories or the coal mines in West Virginia or the melon rows in Texas—but when the newcomer commented on this somewhat floridly, Muskie scowled and began to discuss the fact—rather overlooked in some liberal circles, he thought—that a hell of a lot of people in this country work hard for little pay and manage to get along. Factory and mill work is sought after in Maine, he said, by people whose expectations from their work run less to psychic satisfactions than to food and shelter for their families. At least in Maine they have beautiful surroundings and when they leave work they can hunt, fish, walk in the woods—how about those in equally grim mills in the city or those trapped in the ghetto with no way out and no work? "These are the goddamned realities, you know," he snapped.

Such attitudes, from such an environment, led Muskie naturally into things that, as he once observed to a crowd in New York, "don't sound very glamorous, things that require tough, tedious, nuts-and-bolts work. But that is the only way to make the system work for people, and that, after all, is the real meaning of American politics."

The remark nicely sums his position in intergovernmental relations. Banished to a minor committee, Government Operations, Muskie took on the work that led to his sponsorship of and membership on the Advisory Commission on Intergovernmental Relations and then the chairmanship of a subcommittee on the matter. It was for many years a subject of such towering ennui that others were glad to leave it to him, though it actually is one of those places that the most tedious of government mechanisms mesh with the lives of the governed, and this appears to be its real appeal to Muskie. "It does seem an idea whose day is slow in coming," he said a little wistfully some time ago, "but still, it has a persistent life and that is probably because it really is a fundamental area—it turns on the need to rebuild the American system. It deals with our ability to get things done in this country. Our system is based on fragmented authority, so that there is never too much in the hands of anyone, but this vastly complicates the process of dealing with problems, and this is more true today than ever. The point is the balance, you see, to maintain that fragmentation so that power cannot be assembled to destroy freedom, but at the same time to organize it so as to be effective. That's the stress of the last two hundred years and we're still working on it."

After years of grubbing with nuts-and-bolts mechanisms, such is the wheel of legislative fortune that Muskie emerges as the ranking expert and chief antagonist of President Nixon on one of the great issues of the day: revenue sharing. Early in 1971 Muskie started a political furor by telling a national meeting of mayors that he opposed the President's revenue-sharing bill and intended to introduce a better one of his own. The mayors, desperate for money as their cities stumble toward bankruptcy and collapse, heard the first part of the message and were angry. They needed money, the President was offering it and they weren't interested in quibbling over details. But in a couple of months

Muskie introduced his promised bill. It was clearly superior to the administration's bill, and though it has not been resolved at this writing it is worth examining in some detail, as much for what it says about Muskie's legislative mind as for what it is as a great current issue.

The basic fact is that America's cities face collapse. Lack of money is the immediate symptom, but the cause is twofold. First, we operate a form of government which encourages endless independent local subdivisions nothing at all like the original series of independent towns from which the system grew. Second, relatively affluent middle-class people are abandoning cities, taking refuge in the subdivisions and refusing to take any responsibility for what they've left behind. We won't solve the city problem until we accept this responsibility collectively and permit a massive reallocation of our resources, ranging not only from military hardware to cities but from suburbs to cities.

One of the central differences between the administration's revenue-sharing bill and Muskie's is that his starts paving the way for that reallocation of resources. To develop evidence as well as a political climate for his bill, Muskie held extensive hearings at which mayors appeared and poured out their anguish. This is how Muskie summed the problem when he himself testified before the House Ways and Means Committee: "In Cleveland, for example, there will be no city-run recreation centers this summer. And that city has had to fire 1,500 public health doctors and nurses, garbage collectors and recreation directors. In Newark, of 20,000 drug addicts, only seven percent are in treatment. In New Orleans, crime was up 43 percent last year and visits to VD clinics up 32 percent, but the numbers of police and health workers, for lack of funds, remained the same. In Pittsburgh, the city government cannot afford to buy new police patrol cars or build new firehouses. In New York, Newark, Detroit, Philadelphia and Atlanta, to name just a few, city workers face the prospect of being laid off within just a few months if no new revenue is found."

Furthermore, he added, the capacities of the cities to raise more funds in their usual fashion is exhausted, for the well-to-do have left the cities in the hands of the poor. "In Baltimore, for instance, only one out of six residents has a taxable income of more than $3,000 a year. In Newark, property taxes are so high they are no longer just regressive, they are confiscatory. Buildings in that city are being abandoned so fast that a nine percent increase in the property tax rate this year resulted in a three percent decrease in revenue from that tax. In short, our cities have reached the end of the line." If the trend continues, Muskie had told the mayors, ". . . if we fail to provide the public services people need in urban America, if we allow worn and dilapidated neighborhoods to go unredeemed, if we stand passively by while cities breed crime and deprivation and despair, then we will become two societies—the suburban affluent and the urban poor, each fearful and suspicious of the other, each bitter and hostile toward the other."

The federal government is by far the most efficient collector of tax monies but most of the immediate services people expect from government are provided at the city level. The obvious answer is to funnel some of that federal money back to the local level, though there are other areas also worth considering. In that same speech to the mayors, Muskie urged the "federalization of welfare, which is another version of revenue sharing, and a good one . . ." which "even under the present inadequate [welfare] system would relieve the states and cities of $7.5 billion in welfare costs they will spend this year. That figure is expected to climb in the next fiscal year above $9.5 billion. But even more important, federalization of welfare can give us the opportunity to reform and to humanize our archaic welfare system, under which payment levels vary from state to state and are inadequate for all. It can give us the opportunity to improve the lot of 9 million persons who presently receive some form of welfare assistance, and of millions of others who do not but should. Federal assumption of welfare costs should include welfare reform. It should provide for decent minimum annual income for every family receiving welfare assistance."

Much of the states' problem, Muskie said on the Senate floor, grows from the fact that states have not "effectively utilized the most lucrative source of tax revenue—the income tax. Ever since the federal income tax was enacted the discrepancy between the revenue raising capacity of the federal government and state and local government has grown. Income taxes provide the single greatest portion of the revenue raised by government. And in 1969, 91.1 percent of all income taxes in the U.S. were collected by the federal government. The income tax is lucrative because its returns grow automatically as the economy expands. Every time the economy expands one percent, federal income tax revenues increase 1.5 percent."

Just the same, there is bitter taxpayer resistance to the state and local income tax. Only nine states still have no income tax, but few use the system to its most efficient potential, often because the political results are so painful. Maine introduced an income tax which brought Governor Kenneth M. Curtis to within a hair of defeat in the 1970 elections. In Connecticut, people reacted so violently to a new income tax that the Legislature went right back into session and canceled it.

Muskie's revenue-sharing bill attacks this attitude by providing a mechanism to make state income taxes more palatable and easier to pass. Both bills, Muskie's and the administration's, propose a fund of $5 billion a year to be returned to state and local government, based on 1.3 percent of the total taxable income reported on federal tax returns (which means that as that future grows, so will the return to the states). To that basic fund, however, Muskie's bill adds an extra $1 billion, to be paid to each state on a ratio of 10 percent of whatever it raises through its own income tax. The purpose of the mechanism, of course, is to give local officials a handle to make this most efficient form of taxation attractive to their people. Look at the money we'll gain from Washington with such a tax, and which we'll lose without such a tax—and which will go instead to our neighbors. It is a version of the carrot that federal bills often have dangled before local people. Referring to this useful extra billion, Muskie ob-

served tartly on the Senate floor that "these additional funds—
and more funds for other programs directed at the needs of our
people—can . . . easily be made available by reducing wasteful
expenditures for extravagant military hardware that do nothing to
add to our national defense, or by ending our involvement in that
costly and fruitless war in Southeast Asia."

Muskie's bill cranks relative need into the formula for the
money's distribution. The administration bill would distribute the
money in ratio to a community's tax effort, which means that
well-to-do communities that can afford to tax themselves would
get more help, that Commerce, Calif., would get four times as
much per capita as Los Angeles, that Highland Park would get
2.5 times as much per capita as Detroit. The need factor in
Muskie's bill is calculated on the number of people a city has on
welfare and the number of its families that earn less than three
thousand dollars a year. To guard against funds being used to
perpetuate discrimination, Muskie's bill includes a specific
mechanism under which anyone can sue a government unit which
he feels is using the money it receives in discriminatory fashion.
The administration bill simply relies, as Muskie put it, "on the
inclination of officials in Washington to enforce civil rights laws."

Defending the practicality of his legislation, the summation
of Muskie's speech to the mayors reflects his capacity for seeing
large vistas out of the nuts and bolts of government. "I believe,"
he said, "no matter how long it may take or how much money, we
must not lose sight of the ultimate goal—where we have cities of
lively promise, of beauty, of spaciousness, where men and women
are truly free to determine how they will live. The freedom to
escape to the suburbs is not a real choice. People will live in the
cities if they are places which bring out the best in man and not
the worst . . . if they are places of confidence and not of uncer-
tainty."

Muskie is a liberal by philosophy and a centrist by position.
He voted to cut the military budget and was against the ABM and
the SST. He opposed the nominations of Haynsworth and Cars-
well to the Supreme Court and of Butz to the Department of

Agriculture. He opposes oil import quotas. He spoke out against the atomic test at Cannikan. He supports public-interest law firms, OEO legal services and many other actions designed to give people a greater voice in their institutions. His record is absolutely clear on civil rights and civil liberties. He denounced the District of Columbia crime bill as "repression." He would limit the term of the directorship of the FBI. He is a co-sponsor of national health insurance. He is an old toiler in the vineyards of housing, job training, better schools and public service programs. He is for broad tax reform and election reform. He denounced the administration's attempt to suppress the Pentagon Papers and characteristically made the most sensible proposal offered by anyone on any side of the entire controversy; he went to the heart of the matter—the fact that classification serves as a device to hide official responsibility—and proposed an independent board to review documents regularly and remove classifications no longer required by national security.

Muskie's liberalism is plainly practical. He is impatient with doctrinaire positions because he thinks that moderate positions work, positions that recognize the self-interests—"the self-interests, mind you, not the selfishness"—of all kinds of people. "I think I've been pretty effective in the Senate," he said once. "I've moved some pretty startling legislation. We passed a law that says in effect that if the automobile manufacturers can't produce a clean engine by 1975, they stop producing cars. Now, that's a pretty damned drastic law, don't you think? One reason the Senate is willing to rely on what our subcommittee brings out—and we've never had a proposed piece of legislation turned down and many times we have co-sponsors who are in themselves a majority or nearly so—is because it knows, it has learned over the years, that we are solid and responsible and that we do pay attention to the rightful claims of every side. And so when we come in with a bill that has immense opposition from the largest industry in the world, the Senate passes it."

The philosophic centrist—centered between extremes, balancing holdfast against go-ahead—is likely to be pinned motionless to the board between move and countermove. With Muskie the question is quite the opposite: what is the best footing from which to go ahead? In a sense it returns him to the clash of style that plagues him with the politically aware. One style of liberalism is to fight for it all at once, denounce those who resist, emerge triumphantly bloody and settle for an inch or two of progress. The other style is to sit down and negotiate the inch and start immediately on the next inch. Both styles are valid, they complement each other and they may well depend upon each other.

Muskie has great respect for those who fight on the leading edges. "I don't think there's any doubt," he once said, "that the quality of the center depends in part on the quality of the extremes." Flamboyant attacks that produce violent resistance lead men who otherwise might not have changed at all to turn with relief and pleasure to the substantial but less frightening change that Muskie proposes. The other side of that coin, of course, is that the violent attack could never exploit its opening, never capitalize on its momentum, without the rational, tough-minded probing, the grasp of detail and mechanism, provided by the man who operates on the basis of getting things done. Still, the latter position is not nearly so exciting.

The practical man is likely to be impatient with the rhetorical demand for change that outruns what people can adjust to and understand. Muskie's political philosophy certainly would include the fundamental idea that in a democracy, decision must be made from the broadest possible base. People can make such decisions only if they understand their terms, Muskie once said, and "so it is important to give them the facts. Government policy has a role in this process, for in effect it shapes with its presentation of information how people make these decisions. Now, for instance, we are a pollutant-producing society, a consumer society. How can you force individuals to reduce their consumption, which is the inevitable sense of what is out ahead. By government edict? In a free society you can hardly do that. You can only illuminate, educate, lead, persuade. How far you are going to go in taking the options from the individual citizen is the real question. The difference between family planning, for instance, and limiting the number of children one may have is quite a difference. People get all mixed up in these matters, you know. They complain of the abuse of government authority in some area that affects them, and at the same time they complain because government is not managing life in some other area of their interests. But the point is that our function is to show them what must be, to give them the facts and then count on them to make the rational decisions. That's what a free society is."

One makes progress by putting together majorities and winning elections, and majorities come from easing fears and leading people. With such attitudes, of course Muskie is a compromiser. He believes, with others who are effective in politics, that compromise is a sound basis for going forward; it is an art he has practiced for years. The problem is the ugly connotations the word has taken. There are always foolish or bad or dishonest compromises, but what really has given the concept its bad name is the use of the term to cover abject surrender. As a practitioner of the art, Muskie suffers from the general distaste the word produces in many people.

But in reality, the only valid question is how effective one is in compromise. A stupid or fearful man compromises too much, a rigid or arrogant man too little. How much is enough? Who decides? By what criteria? There is no answer. How high is high? Muskie's career in government (as opposed to his image of leadership on issues) has been eminently successful, so obviously he has made more good than bad compromises. But it also is true that his feeling for practicality and for working things out and his tendency to follow the parameters in which he finds himself have led him into failure. The use of compromise is central to his career in government, and it provides a workable, convenient frame in which to examine the area of his great success and of his great failure.

Muskie's great success and the capstone of his legislative career is the body of legislation that deals with pollution of the environment, particularly of air and water. Concern for the environment has become such a vital subject today—seen as it is on the one hand as a matter of survival, and on the other as a philosophic test of one's values—that it is difficult to remember how little attention it drew a mere decade ago. People who were actively interested called themselves conservationists and thought in terms of preserving unspoiled wild places and wildlife. This thrust of the movement was so strong that conservation was hardly seen to have an urban bearing. Air pollution was a Los Angeles problem; the disaster at Donora, Pa., in 1948 and the London inversion in 1952 were seen as aberrations. Only professionals noticed that solid waste was becoming, literally, a monumental problem, and noise pollution was unrecognized if not unheard. Water pollution was better understood because it was more advanced, but the focus had grown very slowly from the initial concern with floating objects that might imperil navigation.

Indeed, the magnitude of the subject was so unclear in early 1963 when Pat McNamara of Michigan, then the new chairman of Public Works, formed the subcommittee on air and water pollution and made Muskie its chairman, that he also made it a temporary special subcommittee. McNamara disliked the proliferation of government institutions and he simply was not persuaded that pollution would be a continuing problem. Ron Linton, then staff director of Public Works and now a Washington environmental consultant who was instrumental in the subcommittee's formation, remembers that people then did not even consider the environment as a whole. He started a clipping service that year and found the material easily manageable. The commercial press showed some focus on water problems, little on air except in Los Angeles and nothing on solid waste or noise. The technical specialty publications were heavy on water, moderate on air, light on solid waste and only vaguely aware of noise as a problem.

At that time, of course, even the most prescient had no way of anticipating the country's extraordinary economic acceleration which made the problem suddenly acute, bringing the long abuse of the environment abruptly to the saturation point and shifting the focus from esthetics and decency to the literal survival of man. The linkage between the unprecedented near doubling of the gross national product in a single decade and the consequent destruction of the environment is often overlooked, but it is one of the great dislocations of our times. The idea that what the American ethic long has seen as both virtuous and successful should suddenly backfire is intensely disquieting to people who find radical shifts in thinking difficult. The facts have become undeniable, but the implications are no less shattering.

The pollution legislation already in existence was minimal when the Senate subcommittee was formed. The members were starting from near zero and they intended to pass two pieces of legislation that would be crucial in laying the groundwork for the future: the Clean Air Act of 1963 and the Water Quality Act of 1963. They began with public hearings to gather information. There was no such thing then as the massive citizens' lobby that today has become the fundamental pressure point on pollution control. It was hard even to get press coverage and it was difficult to find witnesses beyond those already polarized and intemperate. The issue, of course, was regulation: first the setting of standards and then their enforcement. Industry's reaction was fear and resistance. "They thought we were fanatics," Linton said, "that we wanted to see rabbits running in the streets." If there must be standards, industry's position was that they should be minimal with ample loopholes to cover every unusual situation.

On the other side were the ardent conservationists whom businessmen dismissed as "bird watchers," various civic groups and the first alarmed scientists, most of whom had little understanding of the economics involved and were for rigid standards. And caught in the middle was local government, already squeezed by a failing tax base and a rising sewage problem. The people as a whole were still silent, represented in effect by the committee itself. Industry's fears were self-serving and profit-oriented, but standards that might close plants and thereby further erode a town's tax base and throw its citizens out of work had to be of concern to mayors and the presidents of union locals. The point is not that economic factors should override, but that they are so important that compelling evidence is necessary to persuade those involved that they should be set aside. The argument in this field that is based, or appears to be based, on esthetics fails.

The importance of the subcommittee hearings and the legislative process was that they shook all these arguments into the open, examined them, amassed evidence and gradually emerged with consensus views that could pass into law. Thus the committee's initial function was to educate people to the dangers ahead and develop a constituency without which it could pass no serious legislation. A bill that made real change surely would crunch a whole variety of toes in the process and the owners of those toes would be applying their own political pressure. The committee had to have a countervailing pressure to be effective. The building of a constituency began with the hearings, which went on year after year. Scientists were becoming alarmed and vocal, and the hearings gave them a dignified, certified and well-publicized platform. The committee traveled, holding hearings in cities across the country, so that local people heard local problems aired and felt the impact of a Senate hearing, which is much greater in, say, St. Louis, than in Washington. Muskie also became a pollution evangelist, traveling about the country and speaking almost exclusively on pollution problems. The committee eventually produced two educational films (for which Muskie made the closing statements), called "Troubled Waters" and "Ill Winds"; they are still being shown today.

By 1966 there was a deluge of material in the press. Expert information poured into the committee. Scientists were recognizing ever more fully the problem's magnitude and its threat to the future, and they found increasingly dramatic ways to make their insights understandable and gripping to laymen. Most of all the terrible evidence of brown skies and dying lakes and soapy streams and rivers that caught fire forced their way into everyone's consciousness. The citizens' lobby developed muscle, and people lay down in front of bulldozers and filed lawsuits to block new plant construction. The National League of Cities prepared state-by-state studies of the actual backlog of need to repair specific damage from pollution. This not only documented the problem in terms of dollar magnitude but also showed each legislator the extent to which his state or district suffered and thus how directly his own interests were involved. So the constituency grew, and while the chief impetus obviously was the awful growth of pollution itself, some credit must go to the educational process which the committee conducted.

In retrospect, however, there is little of the excitement in those years that one associates with the beginning of great ideas. It was a slow, exploratory, building time, the hearings piling up ever-greater and more damning bodies of evidence, the legislation paving the way block by block to establish the precedents of government control. The right to set standards, impose conditions and order changes had to be asserted in the form of legislation and fought through the subcommittee, the parent committee, on the floor of the Senate and in conference with the House. Once established they became routine, the basis on which bureaucratic bodies built, but it all started with establishing, justifying and fighting for the original concept.

"That is the key to what follows," Linton said, "and the derivation is by no means clear to most people. Take the two acts of 1965, in air and water, for instance. The virtue of the 1965 air act was that it got the public policy adopted that the federal government had the right to regulate auto emissions. I don't know how much good the actual regulations did—they were applicable to 1968 cars—but they certainly paved the way for the 1970 act which will make a real difference in air pollution. In water, prior to 1965 the federal policy to enhance the quality of the nation's waters simply did not exist. Now, in fact, we have not enhanced it—we haven't even kept up with the degradation —but if we had not done what we did in 1965, we would still be fighting the issue. The real thing that Muskie did in those years was to set policy. Now the argument is not whether we should do things, but how we should get them done and that is a critical difference."

In the 1966 water act the committee turned to the increasingly critical shortages of sewage-treatment plants about the country. The Johnson administration, already feeling the economic pinch of the build-up in Vietnam, proposed grants of $50 million for one year to help localities build new sewage-treatment plants. But Muskie believed the problem was critical and he introduced a bill authorizing grants of $6 billion over the following six years, 120 times the scale of the administration plan. The fight that followed established permanently the concept of massive federal aid to local sewage-treatment facilities. Muskie saw his bill intact through committee and the Senate; in conference with the House, the grant authorization was scaled down to $3.55 billion over five years. This was just half the battle. Bills authorize various spending sums in the abstract without any clear idea of whether the Appropriations Committee will see fit at the end of the session actually to appropriate the authorized funds. Eventually Muskie's bill worked its way to the Public Works Appropriations Subcommittee, chaired by Allen J. Ellender of Louisiana. Ellender does not feel the problems of pollution as keenly as does Muskie, and his funding of the bill reflected that fact as well as the increasing budgetary pressure of the adventure in Vietnam. In the second year, for instance, fiscal 1968, the authorization was $450 million and the actual appropriation was $203 million. In fiscal 1969 the authorization rose to $700 million but the appropriation was $214 million. Each year Muskie and his staff appeared before Ellender and the committee to present elaborate evidence and argue for fuller funding of the original authorization. And they were persuasive, for the percentage of appropriation to authorization continued to rise. In fiscal 1970 the authorization was $1 billion and the appropriation rose to $800 million. In the fourth and final year of the bill's life, with the authorization at $1.25 billion, the Appropriations Subcommittee burst its buttons and appropriated an even $1 billion. While this was still short of the authorized figure by 20 percent, Muskie and all of his staff took it as victory, the reward for perseverance in the long fight.

Obviously compromise is central to bills that are developed in a new and unusual field, one in which the changes demanded have huge economic implications for those who must make them. This is the more true because pollution is one of the few legislative subjects in modern times that did not have its real impetus in in the White House and thus operated without the White House's power for massing support. Pollution control advocates were forced to move step by step to build their constituency. But as the pressure grew and more and more people understood the need, it became better business for industry to accept the change, not only from a public relations viewpoint but because the technology to make the change workable was being developed.

The question remains, therefore, how much compromise is good compromise? On a 1968 water pollution bill, for instance, Muskie refused a compromise his opponents were sure he would take. The Senate bill included tough provisions to establish responsibility for cleaning up oil spills. The House passed a different bill, and in the conference that followed, oilmen's views prevailed with enough House members to cause them to reject the Senate bill. The move came while Muskie was on the 1968 campaign trail and they obviously believed they held the advantage. Muskie could hardly stop campaigning to come back and fight for the bill, and they guessed he would take a weak bill rather than take responsibility for losing a bill in the midst of a campaign. But they were wrong. Muskie was in the air on the *Downeast Yankee* when the proposal was phoned to him and his reaction was immediate: Let the bill die. The following January, offshore oil wells in the Santa Barbara channel blew out; oil soaked Santa Barbara's magnificent beaches, and the momentum was generated for a much stronger bill, which eventually passed as the 1970 Water Quality Act.

Compromise really is at the root of the attack which a task force sponsored by Ralph Nader, launched at Muskie in mid-1970. The study by the Center for Responsive Law, made under Nader's auspices and captained by a young attorney, John

Esposito, dealt overall with the failure of the air pollution control effort in America. The truth of this failure can be seen by anyone who bothers to look out his window in almost any city when an inversion occurs, but the conclusions the report drew were more subject to interpretation. It focused its attack on Muskie's 1967 Air Quality Act, which it called "disastrous" and "a license to pollute," and on Muskie, whom it accused of collusion with industry powers in writing the bill and whom it described as "an extremely astute politician who by temperament avoids conflict and unfavorable odds." It added that Muskie "has never seemed inclined, politically or temperamentally, toward taking a tough stand toward private industry." It announced resoundingly that Muskie "has failed the nation in the field of air pollution control legislation." At a press conference in which he introduced the report, Nader remarked that if Muskie could not find time to run for the Presidency and care for pollution legislation he should choose one or the other. All in all, it was a very splashy performance, the more so because while the politically aware find the subject boring, they have always accepted Muskie's preeminence in the anti-pollution fight. Naturally the report angered Muskie, though he permitted himself no more display than a grim expression when he discussed the matter.

Much of the report's attack on the 1967 bill revolved around the difference between setting national emission standards which the administration wanted, or area air-quality standards which Muskie wanted and got. The difference is highly technical and disputatious with good arguments on each side and it is enough to see that it was hardly the clear clash between vice and virtue that the Nader report described.

When Muskie protested the attack, Esposito responded by saying, "Our general conclusion was that the federal air pollution effort has failed," and though the statement ignores the cumulative factor in legislation and the effect of the fantastic growth of a polluting society in the last decade, still its substance certainly is true. In both water and air pollution, promise has run far ahead of payment; appropriations committees have cut the spending and the executive branch—under both Johnson and Nixon—has refused to spend all that was appropriated. Agencies ordered to execute the laws have been staffed as low as half their authorized strength. It is quite true that polluting plants had not been shut down at the time of Nader's attack and few have been since, nor did the emissions controls ordered for 1968 autos prove very effective.

The day after Nader's attack Muskie called a press conference in which he discussed interminably the technicalities of air pollution control standards, soaring far over the heads of most of the reporters. Only reporters with technical backgrounds could follow him, and as a result he failed to answer Nader effectively, though Nader's charges certainly were answerable. At one point, however, he did break into a statement that was widely quoted because it was the only emotional, human thing he said that day that made clear sense in lay terms and it did go truly if somewhat indirectly to the nub of the question. Breaking off suddenly from some figure-laden comment, Muskie said, "Our way of being tough in my part of the country is to do so without name-calling or recrimination but to develop clear ideas of what we stand for and to press for them as hard and as effectively as we can. We think there are ways to be tough that are sometimes silent, that are sometimes restrained. I can't be something I'm not. I can't change the way I am. I come from my region. I reflect its attitudes. That doesn't mean we don't get things done. We do."

Then, ever reflective, his mind cut suddenly to the basic point: "We happen to live in a time of confrontation. I understand, of course, the deep-seated unrest and discontent that are responsible for that confrontation. So confrontation serves a useful purpose, I suppose, as an outlet, as an escape valve. But in order to really make this society work, at some point we're going to have to move across the lines of confrontation and reach agreements and get results that would improve our country. To do it needs toughness, it needs courage, but it also requires effectiveness. And these are the qualities which I understand and which my people understand in my part of the country."

The Nader attack had little effect on Muskie. Few people were likely to accept the idea that Muskie was in industry's pocket. Overall, however, the probable reason the report did not damage Muskie and also did not discredit itself or damage Nader is that both Muskie and Nader ultimately are right. They just approach the question from opposite sides. Muskie's approach of building legislation piece by piece implies working within possibility, of compromising, of developing the case carefully and getting things done. Bills that Nader would have endorsed would not have passed in 1967 and Muskie doesn't think that is effective. On the other hand, Nader's approach, which might be described as deciding what's needed and what's right and then fighting a long losing battle until he wins, can hardly be called ineffective in view of his extraordinary impact and record of success since he emerged a few years ago as a lonely crusader against the auto industry. Probably both the Muskies and the Naders are necessary to each other's success; the quality of the center does depend on the quality of the extremes. Many people think Nader's report was purposely provocative. "He's got great guts," Linton said admiringly. Perhaps Nader spurred Muskie to his greater successes; more likely, Nader's attack helped expand the constituency and in effect helped push Muskie's next bills.

Finally, however, Nader's attack simply was swallowed in the immense bills that Muskie soon presented. They are the strongest anti-pollution legislation ever written in American government, and least of all are they based on compromise. This is partly because the constituency to support them has been built, partly because they are so obviously needed, partly because Muskie now carries more national weight. These bills demonstrate his current version of getting things done, but the method is different only in degree; if his bills were not logical progressions from what had gone before, he couldn't get them through; they are the result of a decade of work. The Clean Air Amendments of 1970 and the Federal Water Pollution Control Act Amendments of 1971, which passed the Senate but at this writing is under serious attack by the Nixon administration, suggest for the first time that pollution problems are solvable and that the time may be coming in a decade or so when we no longer will have to live in our own slime. It is interesting in reading such bills to feel a loosening of the sense of despair that has so long been our companion, the feeling that we cannot or will not save ourselves. Perhaps we will.

The air bill of 1970 demands the production of a virtually clean automobile engine by 1975. Compared with a car with no emission controls, it demands a 97 percent reduction of hydrocarbons, 96 percent reduction of carbon monoxide and 90 percent reduction of nitrogen oxide. These are goals which the industry said it would be most difficult to meet by the 1980 deadline the Nixon administration proposed. The technology necessary to achieve them does not yet exist. "I know it doesn't exist," Muskie once snapped. "If it did, I'd demand it now." The bill is explicit on this point, noting that "standards should be a function of the degree of control required, not the degree of technology available today." In other words, the criteria were the health requirements of people rather than the economic dislocation that may follow. The bill also orders cities to establish health-oriented pollution standards and then take whatever action is necessary—including the possibility of limiting traffic—to enforce them. This legislation, Muskie said in his opening statement on the Senate floor, "provides the Senate with a moment of truth: a time to decide whether or not we are willing to let our lives continue to be endangered by the wasteful practices of an affluent society."

Robert P. Griffin of Michigan, Muskie's Republican antagonist on the bill, described it as "holding a gun at the head of the American automobile industry in a very dangerous game of economic roulette." Griffin went on to give a succinct picture of the power that Muskie was challenging: "800,000 Americans are directly dependent upon the automobile industry for their livelihoods and more than 14 million other jobs are dependent upon its products—in all, 28 percent of all private nonfarm employment in the United States. Expenditures for automotive transportation account for more than 16 percent of our gross national product. Even a slight dip in auto sales . . . sends shock waves through the financial community."

It is a formidable force, but on the other hand, Muskie had been prodding the auto industry since 1964. He held hearings in Detroit. He visited the plants and talked to the engineers. "I will say in frankness," he told the Senate, "that the industry has never, during all those years, shown any sense of urgency about anything except the preservation of the internal combustion engine . . ." Once in those years an auto-company president—Muskie has never said which company—lingered behind in Muskie's office after a meeting. They were chatting and Muskie said, "Come on now, how far are you—really—from a clean engine?" The man grinned, held thumb and forefinger an eighth of an inch apart and said, "You can't put this in the record, but we're that close." But when it became obvious that Muskie intended to impose an absolute deadline, friendly attitudes evaporated.

The presidents of Ford and General Motors and a vice president of Chrysler, who believed Muskie had been led astray by the young and fiery staff of the subcommittee, arranged a meeting in which they obviously intended to set Muskie straight. Instead they sat largely in silence and took a savage lecture, in which he told them bluntly, "You have never dealt openly with this committee." No transcript of the meeting was kept, but in effect, pounding his long forefinger on the table before him, Muskie told them, God-dammit, you people have been stalling and dragging your feet and telling us it couldn't be done for years, and all the while you've been spending billions on model changes and millions on advertising—now we're going to tell you that you're going to *have* to produce a clean engine!

The real impetus to the committee was the generally neglected point that a car lives an average ten years. Even under this bill, the last polluting cars won't fade away until 1985—and to wait until 1990, if the Congress had followed the administration's proposal, was just too much. "The used car is the real problem," Muskie told a group in Maine. "We say in this bill that within three years of when standards are set, cities must reduce pollutant levels to those levels which are consistent with public health. The big violator is the used car; how are cities going to do that? They are going to have to restrict the extent to which cars are used in cities, people going to work, people getting out of the ghetto—and that's another problem in itself. We want to correct poverty. The way you help poor people is with jobs and the way they get to jobs is by car and those cars are likely to be old. So what then? Are the American people ready to limit their transportation? They don't even know as yet that they are being asked."

By forcing the deadline for the clean engine, toward which the industry already is making good progress, Muskie put the auto makers in the same political position he put the Republicans years before in Maine: if they were to have to come back to Congress and insist that they couldn't meet the deadline, the burden would be on them to explain why not and to demonstrate what they had done and how they allocate their resources. In the present climate, that would not be a comfortable discussion for the richest corporations in the world.

At the same time, however, Muskie also was setting up some interesting opposite political risks. Ruminating about this one night when the bill was still in committee, he observed, "But the other side of the coin, you know, is that no one *knows* whether such a machine can be developed. Suppose it can't. It's fine to be sure the industry can produce—and I'm really sure that it can—but let's consider what happens if it can't. As the law is written, it means that auto production would have to stop. And imagine the economic effect of that! Imagine all the tire workers, oil workers, auto dealers' employees, steelworkers, glassworkers, machinists, filling station operators, to say nothing of the auto workers themselves, who'd be out of jobs and out of business. Now, that would be a catastrophe. Well, of course, it wouldn't come to that, but that's just the point—if a year before the deadline, it became clear that it really couldn't be met, really clear beyond question, we'd have to repeal the law that stupid Muskie got us to pass, the sucker bill that he assured us would press the auto companies to action. And then, all aside from any private political consequences, what would be the political consequences on other similar legislation, on future legislation, on the whole question of how we're going to adjust our lives to the inevitable realities that are coming? A record of failure, of having to back down, is no way to establish a precedent of moving forward. And it's already so hard to move people along these paths, to make them understand and to lead them to action, that having to back away and admit we'd gone too far too fast would put in question all the other demands which must be made on people more and more frequently in the future if we are to resolve these environmental questions and make sure that we start paying the real costs of progress as we go along."

The clean engine was the most noticeable feature of the air bill of 1970, but it carried a variety of other provisions toward achieving "in the next five years" its goal "that all Americans in all parts of the Nation should have clean air to breathe, air that will have no adverse effect on their health." One of the most important of these was the requirement that henceforth new stationary plants—manufacturing and power-generating—be built to include the latest and best (instead of the most practical or most economical) emissions-control technology. "If the gross national product really is going to double or triple by the year 2000," Muskie once said, "then the important thing is to see that where we go from here isn't allowed to compound the disaster. Then we can get started on cleaning up the disaster we've already got." The bill establishes procedures for setting national ambient air quality standards based on public health needs, provides heavy civil and criminal penalties for disobedience, allows citizens to file suit to enforce standards, provides nearly a half-million dollars in research funds, spells out implementation plans and provides testing plans to make sure that the clean auto engine stays clean.

The Federal Water Pollution Control Act Amendments of 1971 was a longer-range and even stronger bill that passed the Senate but produced violent political reaction. The bill was based on the committee's conclusion "that the national effort to abate and control water pollution is inadequate in every vital aspect." It noted that major waterways near industrial and urban areas are "unfit for any purpose," that rivers are severely polluting coastal areas and the sea, that lakes and confined waterways are aging rapidly and that "the use of any river, lake, stream or ocean as a waste treatment system is unacceptable." It established as national policy, among other things, that the discharge of pollutants into navigable waters be ended by 1985 and that water quality adequate for the propagation of fish, shellfish, wildlife and recreation be achieved by 1981. This is a policy objective, Muskie noted in his statement on the floor, and "is not locked in concrete. It is not enforceable. It simply establishes what the committee thinks ought to be done on the basis of present knowledge." But, he added, restating the theme that runs through the body of pollution legislation, the committee "recognizes the absolute requirement that goals be set, that a sound program be developed, that deadlines be established and that a single set of requirements for each pollutant be established for a sufficient period of time so that communities and industries can plan for their needs over an extended period and can make sound decisions to carry out their plans."

This bill also is based less on compromise than any water pollution legislation ever written in America, for while its general goals are unenforceable, the mechanisms by which it hopes to achieve those goals are both enforceable and very tough. They take head-on the two great sources of water pollution that are controllable, the discharge from industrial plants and from municipal sewage plants (there's no way yet to control agricultural runoff). And they deal directly and explicitly with that political bugbear, the marginal plant which will close rather than correct its pollution problem. Furthermore, as the air bill of 1970 challenged the auto industry, so the water bill of 1971 challenges the great industries of the nation, the pulp and paper industry in Maine and elsewhere, the steel mills and other metal mills and all the other industries which as a matter of course pump public water through their processes, use it and pump it out again carrying waste debris. The key factor is that it serves notice on them all and gives them time—a full ten years—to make their adjustments.

First it changes the enforcement mechanism from the overall maintenance of water-quality standards now used to setting specific effluent limits. The water-quality-standards system has not worked because of the difficulty, among several reasons, of establishing a causative link between deteriorating general quality and the specific effluent flow of offending plants, both industrial and those processing municipal sewage. Under the new system, Muskie noted, the enforcing officer can require of a plant "the best control technology; he need not search for a precise link between pollution and water quality."

Next, the bill directs the administrator of the Environmental Protection Agency to set up a two-phase program. The first phase, to be implemented by 1976, requires all industrial pollution sources to use the best *practicable* technology to treat the effluent they discharge. Under this phase, communities will be required to have construction programs started by mid-1974 for plants for secondary treatment of sewage. The second phase, to be implemented by 1981, requires both communities and industries to treat their effluent with the best *available* technology when the goal of no-discharge cannot be attained.

To help communities meet those deadlines, the bill provides $14 billion over the next four years to build secondary sewage-treatment plants. The minimum federal grant will pay 60 percent of the cost; if the state contributes 10 percent—that carrot again—the federal share will rise to 70 percent, leaving only 20 percent to the community itself.

Sewage treatment is an acute problem. In 1968 about 75 percent of the American people were served by sewers; of these, about 60 percent were served by a plant giving secondary treatment, about 30 percent by a plant giving only primary treatment and the wastes of the rest went directly into the receiving waters. Even these figures understate the problem, however, for rapid population growth in urban centers is seriously overloading many secondary plants, which pump their overflow into the streams largely untreated. What's more, many communities with secondary plants have combined sanitary and storm sewers, which guarantees a raw sewage overflow every time it rains.

The effect of the bill is to do what everyone has known had to be done. It will mean great dislocation for some plants and their stockholders, their workers and their towns. The first deadline will close the truly marginal plants and the second deadline will close more. Those that survive will do so by making expensive changes. But the political counter pressure that builds around arbitrary, sudden moves will not develop, for this is a reasonable schedule that gives everyone time to adjust and plan ahead. If you know what's coming for a decade and know it is necessary, there is not much political outrage to focus against it. Should it have been done earlier? Of course. Could it have passed earlier? Probably not. But it *did* pass the Senate this time and that it developed a workable mechanism for what's necessary means that ultimately it will prevail. And the decade of grace? We have been digging the environmental pit in which we find ourselves since the Industrial Revolution began; perhaps a decade is about right to dig ourselves out.

The pejorative connotation of compromise, Muskie believes, is "oh, completely a false issue. Compromise and timing are still two important political tools, and anybody who ignores them just isn't going to get anything done. Oh, sure, my judgment isn't infallible. It's always conceivable that you're giving away something you don't need to give. Unless the other side in a compromise feels it's gotten something, you don't get compromise. So by definition . . . still, you know, we spent five months in conference with the House on one of the water-pollution bills, one of the longest conferences I can remember—would we have gotten more if we'd stayed ten months? How can you answer how high is up? On the Model Cities legislation, that was dead until I picked it up—well, did I go as far as I could have gone? At least I breathed some life into something that was dead."

Occasionally someone suggests that because Muskie often

gets unanimous Senate approval, his bills may be soft. "Well, let's take that deadline we set for automobiles. No one voted against it, even though the automobile industry had a very articulate spokesman in Senator Griffin. In other words, the way we operate is to build the support within the committee and take the time to get unanimous reports out, not by giving things away but by building the case, mobilizing public opinion behind it so that when we get ready to go, we go with maximum political strength. But anyone who argues seriously that we could have set a deadline earlier than 1975 just isn't . . . So what did we give away?"

There are, however, a series of compromises—or actions which can usefully be seen in the framework of compromise—which have caused Muskie trouble, particularly as his national candidacy has grown. The first is worth mentioning largely because his opponents will be mentioning it, though it hardly qualifies as an issue. It concerns a proposal to build an oil refinery near Machiasport, in Washington County, Maine, an area famous for its beautiful coast, its poverty, its dour weather and its deep harbors. Its harbors are attractive for the huge deep-draft tankers the oil industry is using; its weather, both fog and storms, would make their approach dangerous. Its poverty makes anything attractive that would produce jobs and add to its tax base, but its beauty makes its people the more fearful of anything that might damage it.

A great volume of oil now comes to Portland by tanker for transshipment by pipeline to Canada, where it is sold for considerably less than in Maine. The refinery first was proposed for Portland, and because of the tanker traffic already coming to that city, Muskie was dubious. Then, when the plan shifted for a refinery in one of the deep-water ports to the north, his early reaction was one of approval, though no decision was required of him since it was not a federal matter. Furthermore, the refinery remained a proposal rather than a plan because it turned on its owners being able to avoid in one way or another the oil import quota problem. To this issue both the Johnson and Nixon administrations remained deaf.

Muskie's initial reaction clearly was based on his old economic orientation that grew from his time as governor and continued in his early Senate career. A refinery meant industry, which means jobs in a consistently depressed area—unemployment normally runs above 20 percent in Washington County—which he had long been trying to help. Gradually a controversy arose in Washington County with local people more or less balanced on both sides. One side wanted the refinery for the jobs it might produce and the auxiliary industry that might follow it; the other, made up of conservationists and people who lived by the slowly failing lobstering and fishing industries, believed the refinery and the delivering tankers surely would befoul the waters. This view was greatly encouraged by the wreck of the tanker *Torrey Canyon* and the Santa Barbara incident.

Suddenly oil spills and oil damage to coastal ecology became apparent and soon Muskie was writing national legislation on the subject. Naturally he began to take second looks at the Machiasport proposal. Eventually he held a subcommittee hearing there and took two days of testimony, which persuaded him that the industry had no way to protect the ecology and he came out against the refinery.

Typically, he came slowly to the decision. "It's really a global dilemma," he told a Maine crowd one night. "This planet can't get along without oil, unless you want to repeal civilization. There's no other lubricant and there's really no other fuel that can replace it. The only possible substitute is nuclear energy, which is an environmental hazard perhaps even greater than oil. We tend to neglect the radiation hazard because we think all that's under control, but it isn't so. So fuel and lubricants, we can't do without them and yet they're one of the great potential despoilers. Of course, it's easy to say let's not take any risks. The real challenge is when you do say yes. Because unless you learn the circumstances when you can say yes to economic growth, you will force a lot of people to go on welfare, you will impose lifelong poverty on a lot of disadvantaged people who can climb out of it only to the extent that we achieve economic growth . . ."

Committed environmentalists felt that Muskie's appreciation of both sides of the Machiasport situation betrayed the environmental vigor he was displaying nationally. It was the sort of political situation that often arises and is worth detailing only because he is standing for the Presidency.

Another Maine incident is worth noting for the same reason. John P. Jabar, an attorney who worked part time in Muskie's Waterville office helping constituents arrange loans from the Small Business Administration, was himself connected with corporations that received two government or government-backed loans with which to build nursing homes. One loan was for $345,000 with the SBA, and the other was for $415,000, backed by the Federal Housing Administration. All was in order with the loans, and while it was ethically questionable for an employee in Muskie's office to arrange loans for himself, it was not illegal.

There has never been any evidence offered that Muskie himself was involved in the loans or the nursing homes or that he stood to gain in any way or that he even knew about them, but inevitably it exposed him to the implication that he profited by virtue of his office, an implication that he otherwise has scrupulously avoided. The situation was made more difficult by the fact that Jabar's partner was Paul J. Mitchell, older brother of the head of Muskie's political operation, George Mitchell. Further, the head of SBA in Maine at the time was Maurice Williams of Muskie's gubernatorial staff, and the head of FHA was and still is his old friend and 1954 campaign manager, Dick McMahon. Congressman H. R. Gross of Iowa and Senator John R. Williams of Delaware both called attention to the transaction and Muskie issued a long statement of explanation. He was angry, but characteristically he only gave Jabar a tongue-lashing and ordered him to divest himself of his interests. On the night Muskie was nominated for the Vice Presidency, Don Nicoll phoned McMahon. Is Jabar clear, he asked? McMahon said no. The next day Jabar was fired.

In another Maine situation, however, one that involved the continued defiling of a brook known as the Prestile Stream,

Muskie's feelings for compromise as a normal pattern of operations did lead him onto seriously questionable ground. In a literal and technical sense he played only a modest part in the stream's fate, but in a moral sense his part becomes much larger because he then knew as much about the problem of water pollution as anyone in America and was at the very moment passing laws to correct nationally the sort of thing that was happening locally on the Prestile.

The story begins with the weak economy of Aroostook County, the huge northernmost tier of Maine that relies almost entirely on the single crop of potatoes. Potatoes are unsubsidized and unstable, and they produce a boom or bust economy. In the late 1950s and early 1960s there were nine bust years in a row and the Aroostook economy was shaky. The great dream had always been a second crop. The possibility of achieving the dream arose when the United States severed relations with Cuba and stopped importing Cuban sugar, which had supplied about a third of the U.S. sugar market. Since sugar is a controlled crop, the government had to delegate that share of the market. The domestic sugar-beet industry wanted part of it and the government agreed to make six allotments of 33,000 acres each for the production of sugar beets.

The details of the complicated allotment mechanism are not important here, but the point is that without the allotment, raising sugar beets is not economically feasible. Sugar beets are one of the few crops that are compatible with potatoes. The two are grown successfully in rotation in places like the Red River Valley in Minnesota. Since the controls make sugar beets very stable and the potato market is wide open, the two also make a good economic balance. It seemed a natural second crop for Aroostook. Maine's application for an allotment would be considered only if there was a refinery there to process the sugar and if all the financing for it was complete. A committee headed by the presidents of Aroostook's biggest bank and of the Bangor and Aroostook Railroad persuaded the Great Western Sugar Co. of Denver, the largest sugar-beet processor in the country, to agree to build the refinery. A complicated financial package was assembled. The state, through the Maine Industrial Building Authority (another of the agencies which Muskie's revitalization of Maine produced) would guarantee bank loans of $8 million and take a first mortgage. The federal government would loan $6 million through the Area Redevelopment Administration and take a second mortgage. Under the rules local people had to put up 15 percent for third mortgages and Great Western would put up the rest, for a total well over $20 million. With all this in place the Maine application, one of some forty from twenty-four states, received one of the six allotments. Politically speaking, the application was bipartisan: Maine's Republican governor, its three Republican congressmen, its Republican senator and Muskie were all eager proponents of the plan.

The allotment was granted in early 1964. Great Western arrived with engineers, began planning its refinery and planted five hundred test acres of sugar beets. To its dismay, there was a very poor yield. Maine people said the Coloradoans insisted on doing things as they were done in Colorado and that wouldn't work in Maine, but the question of how well sugar beets can do in Maine has not been resolved to this day. At any rate, Great Western's disappointment over the yield was so great that it decided to pull out. Maine's hopes for a second crop were rapidly disappearing.

At this point there enters a man named Vahlsing who is known universally by his first name, Freddie. He is a businessman of immense energy and unshakable optimism whose father had expanded his business from a vegetable pushcart to a food-growing and processing empire. His son Freddie, who hurtled about the country at the controls of his own airplane, was very successfully expanding it some more. He is an exuberant man, a back-slapper who seems to love attention and often is found around the fringes of politics. Though he has headquarters in New Jersey and operates nationally, the family enterprise had been buying and shipping potatoes in Aroostook County since 1928. In 1961, with an ARA loan, Vahlsing built a potato-processing plant to produce frozen French fries in Easton, Maine, on the head of the Prestile Stream, and in 1963 he enlarged the plant.

The Prestile is a tiny stream; in the summer one can step across it, for there are places where it is literally a yard wide and a foot deep. It runs about twenty miles in Maine, passes the town of Mars Hill, crosses the Canadian border and empties into the St. John River. There is a myth that until Vahlsing appeared it was a fine trout stream, pure as snow water. It must have been once and it still is beautiful, but a series of plants that made starch from scrub potatoes had discharged into it so heavily during the 1950s that even then it was the equivalent of an open sewer. In the late 1950s, however, the state began shutting down the starch plants. It forced Mars Hill to build a sewage-treatment plant. The state had developed a water-classification system, rating its streams and rivers from A, or pure, to D, the worst. It rated the Prestile B and used that as a lever to continue cleaning it. The Water Improvement Commission's engineers were diligent and the stream began to improve radically. Then Vahlsing started discharging potato scrap from his plant and the stream's quality collapsed. When the commission took action against him, he built a series of holding ponds which he called lakes and thought would solve the problem. But the stream remained polluted and the commission kept constant pressure on him to improve his treatment of the water.

The commission's weapon was a state law which said that anyone who discharged into a stream had to have a permit which could be withdrawn if the discharge tended to drive the stream's quality below its classification. This had done nothing to improve the sewerlike quality of Maine's principal rivers, however, because the Republican Legislature had exempted from this law all plants built before 1953, which included the entire pulp and paper industry and most of the state's other major plants.

It was to Vahlsing that the now desperate sugar-beet group turned. Why didn't he take over, build the refinery and process sugar beets at Easton, next to his potato plant? Vahlsing liked the idea. He asked for assurances that Maine farmers really would grow the beets and then plunged in. The group had no hesitation in promising him a supply of beets. Despite Great Western's test patch, the University of Maine believed beets could be grown, and after nine consecutive potato disasters, Aroostook farmers were desperate for relief. Vahlsing went to Washington to arrange with the ARA to take Great Western's place in the deal. That was acceptable except for one fundamental problem: Vahlsing's potato plant already was in violation of the classification of the Prestile Stream; if the sugar plant added to the pollution, and there was no way of knowing if it would, the state would be required under the law to shut it down, which obviously would jeopardize the ARA loan. On that basis, the ARA blocked the loan, which in turn blocked the whole deal.

By then the time factor was critical because of the delay caused by Great Western's withdrawal. If it did not have a refinery in operation in twenty months, Maine's sugar allotment would run out, and it normally takes thirty months to construct a refinery. Obviously it was now or never. The solution on which everyone fixed was to lower the classification of the Prestile to D—meaning as a practical matter that anything goes—until it was determined how much pollution the refinery would generate. Again the decision was thoroughly bipartisan. The Legislature of the moment was Democratic—that historic gift of Goldwater to the people of Maine—and the Republican governor, John H. Reed, who was from Aroostook himself, called a joint session to plead for the bill that legitimatized the destruction of the Prestile. Muskie fully favored the bill. "Our decision, which had to be made quickly, hinged on whether we wanted to pursue the sugar-beet allotment," he said in a statement. He said he favored the move for its potential economic benefits and because he knew the "public officials would insure reclassification of the Prestile at its present high level within a reasonable time." He added, "I made my choice in the belief that it is possible in the long run to have *both* the sugar-beet industry and high water quality in the Prestile Stream."

That was the decision from which the criticism of Muskie grows, but first it is worth seeing what happened next. Vahlsing built the plant, investing millions in the process, and met the deadline, December 31, 1966. As he started building, however, the potato market suddenly improved. The boom or bust crop now boomed. The 1964–1965 crop was good and so was the next year. When the spring of 1966 arrived and it was time to plant the beets Vahlsing had been promised, a crop that was still untested and uncertain, not many farmers were interested. At one time there had been predictions of 120,000 acres of sugar beets; in fact, in that first year 3,300 acres were planted. The refinery opened, processed the crop in a few days and shut down. The next year 10,000 acres were planted and in the third year 26,000 acres were planted, but much of it was on marginal land and the yield was low. It was becoming clear that whatever future Aroostook had in sugar beets, the matter was much trickier than anyone had expected. With so little to refine, the refinery was losing money and it stopped paying the farmers, which infuriated them and brought the experiment to an instant halt. The money stopped and the State of Maine began meeting the refinery's mortgage payments. The refinery stands silent today, an extraordinary building with a monumental air looming alone like a giant hangar on a flat plain, filled with motionless machinery, gloomy, and ghostly, a place of defeated hopes.

In the summer of 1968 Vahlsing impulsively bought a huge trainload of potatoes which were about three-quarters rotted and processed them through his potato plant. The rotten part of this trainload of potatoes went down the Prestile. Most potato plants close in the summer: the remnant of the crop is junk, the streams are low and the summer's warmth exacerbates the obvious problems. When Vahlsing's potato slop went down the Prestile, the effects were unbelievable. Piles of filthy gook built up around bridges and coated rocks. Fish leaped out of the water and died. People who lived near the stream vomited in their homes. The paint on their houses turned black and formed bubbles. Where the Prestile crosses into New Brunswick, a group of angry Canadians with bulldozers threw an earthen dam across it, blocking the horrid waters and attracting world-wide publicity. They removed the dam in a few days and erected a marker commemorating it. Conservationists everywhere focused on the rape of the Prestile as symbolic of what a sane society no longer can allow.

The disaster on the stream, the economic debacle of the refinery and Vahlsing's ebullience—he appeared at the 1968 Democratic National Convention and buzzed around the Maine delegation like a fly—brought waves of criticism, most of it aimed at Muskie. But the proper question and the crucial point goes straight back to 1965 when Muskie endorsed the downgrading of the stream. He had to make a quick decision and he fell to the economic side. Given the times and the importance of a second crop to the 100,000 people of Aroostook County, it probably was a decision he made naturally and easily.

But it also is true that at that very time Muskie was working on a bill that had the effect of requiring states to adopt water-quality standards not below a certain minimum, and that minimum was the equivalent of Maine's C classification—better than what Muskie had supported for the Prestile. His friends point out that the downgrading did not actually take effect until the refinery was ready at the end of 1966 and that it remained in effect only ten months. Then Muskie's new federal law forced the state to reclassify its streams, and the Prestile officially was raised to C, the lowest classification, where it remains today.

All this really is an empty argument, however, for Muskie already was a national leader in the fight against pollution and he had to know what really was involved: the effect of the lowering action, even though it did not take place for some time, was to cripple the progress that engineers of the Water Improvement Commission were making in forcing Vahlsing to rescue the stream. The men who were actually involved say unanimously today that the effect was to tie their hands and deliver the Prestile to Vahlsing. The stream is small, and yet if we are to work real change we will have to stand at places like the Prestile as well as the Potomac. On balance, it appears that Muskie acted on the basis of compromise and that the old instinct took him down the wrong path. There have been attempts to impute something more sinister to Muskie's part and to Vahlsing's relations with the Democrats, but this appears to be pure politics and dirty at that. It has all been investigated and reinvestigated, and there is no evidence, nor will any responsible figure say that anything is amiss. The issue is not graft or politics; it is compromise and this time compromise failed Muskie.

The Prestile was a simple matter that turned on a single quick decision. But the same attitudes toward government, though in a different and more complicated form, are at the root of Muskie's position on that immensely complex subject, the war in Vietnam.

When Muskie came to the Senate in 1959, his background was parochial and neither his committee assignments nor his own initiative took him very far into foreign affairs. He accepted a standard view of the cold war, but he was a moderate in that he was not very exercised about it. He disagreed with President Kennedy over the Berlin Wall in 1963 and told a reporter that he felt "We should have acted to prevent its construction. I felt it was an opportunity to take the initiative against the Soviet . . ." In a speech late in 1959 Muskie took what can be seen in retrospect as nearly opposite positions on two of the several parallel thrusts that later seduced us into Vietnam. He subscribed without question to the concept of a monolithic enemy, referring darkly to "those who would destroy us." In the same speech, however, he noted that "our assumption of manifest superiority is no longer valid." Unfortunately, the first view influenced him more than the second.

His first real experience with Vietnam came in late 1965, after American combat troops had been introduced. He was one of four senators whom Mike Mansfield included on a study trip that was known as the Mansfield mission. Mansfield is a foreign affairs expert and in 1963 he had led a similar mission. He had invited Muskie then, too, but schedule conflicts prevented Muskie's going. The 1963 mission's Vietnam report said that "there is no interest of the United States in Vietnam which would justify, *in present circumstances,* the conversion of the war in that country primarily into an American war, to be fought primarily with American lives." It was a strong statement, though it drew specific attention to its italicized caveat.

The 1965 mission produced a devastating commentary on the expansion of the American combat role. In view of its warnings and of Mansfield's standing, that it generally was ignored by the public and the administration illustrates the momentum of the cold war attitude and the bureaucratic investment in Vietnam. The report said:

> The basic concept of American policy . . . casts the United States in the role of support of the Vietnamese Government and people. This concept becomes more difficult to maintain as the military participation of the United States undergoes rapid increase. Yet a change in the basic concept would have a most unfortunate impact upon the Vietnamese people and the world at large. What is involved here is the necessity for the greatest restraint in word and action, lest the concept be eroded and the war drained of a purpose with meaning to the people of Vietnam.

Chances for negotiations seemed slim, the report continued, and a standstill cease-fire would leave most of the country in the hands of the Viet Cong, but

> the visible alternative . . . is the indefinite expansion and intensification of the war which will require the continuous introduction of additional United States forces. The end of that course cannot be foreseen, either, and there are no grounds for optimism that the end is likely to be reached within the confines of South Vietnam or within the very near future . . . The situation . . . offers only the very slim prospect of a just settlement by negotiations or the alternative prospect of a continuance of the conflict in the direction of a general war on the Asian mainland.

Those prophetic lines, "the continuous introduction of additional troops . . . the end cannot be foreseen . . ." surely would have been discouraging had anyone been listening, for as Mansfield said recently, "It warned that the war was open-ended." Muskie's partisans offer his part in the Mansfield mission as evidence of his early awareness of the Vietnam peril. If this was true it would put his later actions in even less flattering light, but it appears that he did not share the clear-cut vigor of Mansfield's view. A Senate committee tends to reflect its chairman's ideas, particularly when he is Majority Leader and an expert in the field. It was Mansfield who reported to President Johnson, met with Rusk and McNamara and wrote the report. Obviously Muskie wouldn't have signed it had he disagreed, but he did not feel the points as strongly as Mansfield did.

In a major foreign policy speech in Philadelphia on February 28, 1966, Muskie said, "Some observers have concluded that the report of the Mansfield mission presents a hopeless predicament. This is not accurate." He said the mission had found that "the presence of U.S. combat forces has acted to arrest the deterioration in general security in government-controlled parts of South Vietnam. The ability of the Vietnamese government to hold Saigon, the strategic heart of the country, the coastal bases and certain other key areas in the country has improved . . . There has been a return of confidence among Vietnamese civilians." And he added, "This balance sheet . . . certainly does not suggest an unmanageable situation. To improve it is within the capabilities of the world's greatest power."

As usual, Muskie analyzed it all and then said he endorsed the administration's policy of "the application of unremitting pressure in a carefully measured response to the aggression of the enemy." He thought debate of the administration's course was one of the costs of freedom, but since "the enemy is closely watching . . . [and] undoubtedly is encouraged" by this division, "let us decide, unite and press forward in a way that will convince the enemy we mean and will support what we say." The enemy was The Enemy, and hardly a mere peasant in pajamas fighting a revolutionary civil war. This was the central theme of the view that even then was taking the administration down the garden path, and toward the end of the speech Muskie could have been cribbing from Rusk himself: "We believe that the right of small nations to work out their own destinies is at stake. We believe that containment of expansionist communism regrettably involves direct confrontation from time to time and that to retreat from it is to undermine the prospects for stability and peace. We believe that the credibility of our word and our purpose as a nation is at stake: and that its loss would be an enormous setback for the forces of freedom."

The certainty of this view, however, began to fade. In the following year Muskie was back in Vietnam as an election observer. He asserted his independence by arranging his own schedule and list of people to see. In his Christmas letter to his constituents in 1967 he reaffirmed his belief that our purpose in Vietnam was to block "aggressive communism" but this time, drawing on an old quote from Benjamin Franklin, he took pains to note that he spoke with "doubt as to my infallibility."

In 1966 and '67 and '68, the country was engaging in a great conversion based on the growing understanding that our course in Vietnam was a disastrous mistake. Eventually nearly everyone could see that the war wasn't working, it wasn't worth the cost in blood or money and that it was time to get out. On one side of this understanding were people who continued to see the matter in political terms and whose central interest was in how we could get out. This could be said to include the administration, which continued to insist its course was righteous while it desperately sought negotiations with North Vietnam. The other side of this understanding saw it as a moral issue—and that made all the difference.

Muskie was among those who saw the matter in political rather than moral terms, and this is what led to most of the controversy around his positions on Vietnam. The focusing issue in late 1967 and through a few days before the 1968 election was the bombing of North Vietnam. The United States was trying to press North Vietnam into negotiations; North Vietnam refused to respond while under attack and the United States refused to stop the attack in the absence of response. In January 1968, shortly before the Tet offensive, which awakened so many more Americans, Muskie wrote President Johnson proposing that he stop the bombing. Muskie opened by saying he would not make his counsel public. He believed the President was being criticized so heavily in the press that to speak publicly would be to join a chorus which the President ignored. He hoped that the privacy of his views, might give them weight. He argued that the bombing of the North was unproductive and urged the President to stop it unilaterally. Then, he argued, the United States would be in a credible position to wait and see what response was forthcoming and thus whether "the other side is really interested and committed to a negotiated settlement in its own interest . . ."

The argument was tactical, not moral. He had lost faith in the administration's course and wanted to change it. He could be effective only in private. Johnson was notorious for refusing to hear those who criticized publicly. Men who went outside—Fulbright, McCarthy, Robert Kennedy and many others—had no effect on the administration short of their contribution to its ultimate destruction.

Mansfield, who said recently that nothing in government had "so distressed and upset me" as the war, also remained within the situation. A man intimately involved in the Senate machinery observed, "Mansfield felt the proper tack was to keep open the lines of communication. That's why when he talked he was listened to. Anyway, in the mid-1960s, the country wasn't ready for open challenge. It was an ineffective way to force change on the President because at the time it was very easy to discredit. Later, of course, it became effective because people were educated by those who went outside and a constituency grew. Johnson knew how Mansfield felt—everyone did—but when he spoke on it, he always opened with praise of Johnson. Then he cut him up in the middle of the speech and then praised him again at the end."

Of Muskie, Mansfield said, "Ed was tortured by Vietnam eventually. He hated to come out against the President. He tried to take a middle course. It's a slow process and each senator has to work out his own position and approach."

It was in Muskie's pattern to stay inside. As early as 1963, speaking of disagreements with President Kennedy, Muskie told a reporter that he preferred to "disagree quietly" with the President, that "I avoid the kind of break that comes when you speak out publicly." Furthermore, by 1968 Muskie had developed prestige and influence in the Senate and with the White House and he was trying to use it for maximum influence on a policy he thought a mistake.

It was from this background that Muskie came to the peace plank at the 1968 Democratic National Convention. Before the convention there had been extensive maneuvering between the peace forces, represented by McCarthy, McGovern and Robert Kennedy's associates, and the administration side, represented ostensibly by Humphrey but actually by Johnson himself. In the natural centering effect of a committee many of the differences between the two had been smoothed out, but both sides held fast on the bombing.

The plank of the peace forces called for "an unconditional end to all bombing of North Vietnam while continuing to provide in the South all necessary air and other support for American troops." The administration plank said, "Stop all bombing of North Vietnam when this action would not endanger the lives of our troops in the field; this action should take into account the response from Hanoi." Literally, the difference between the two was narrow because on March 31, 1968, Johnson had ordered most of the bombing of the North discontinued; North Vietnam had not responded. Actually, however, the issues for which the narrow difference stood were huge: Senator Gale McGee of Wyoming caught them precisely when he was quoted as saying, "Play with the language all you like. Some are saying get out and some are saying stick it out."

Muskie did not see it in such sharp terms. He led the debate for the administration plank without reluctance. Muskie believed the difference between the two planks was essentially emotional and rhetorical and while he made a few barbed remarks, characteristically he directed most of what he said to exploring the planks. Much later he said, "I felt they were not diametrically opposed. I felt that Hubert would act to wind down the war faster than Nixon would, and that he could do so under either policy, the majority plank or the minority plank. My effort actually was to minimize their differences in order that if we were to prevail, the interpretation of our winning would not be a harsh, hawkish position but a rational approach to the problem of winding down the war, one that would enable us to support the cessation of the bombing and the other risks necessary . . . I wanted to see the Democratic Party win and I wanted it to win through a war policy that would permit us to end the war. I thought this debate could serve a very useful purpose, an escape valve that would cast a discussion in such a way as not to destroy whatever hopes the convention had. My effort was simply to do what I could to insure that the difference wasn't so great between the two positions that if my side prevailed it would alienate everyone on the opposite side."

When the story broke in mid-campaign that Muskie had written Johnson in January to oppose what in August he had— in effect—argued for, it cast him in an unhappy light, an implication that he has steadily resisted. Actually, nothing had changed. Muskie's position was still political and tactical, his opponents' still moral and emotional.

After the election, Muskie was, of course, outside the Republican administration and now he saw himself as a national leader in his own right. It had become a political necessity to speak out on Vietnam. Nevertheless, his propensity for thoroughness and his insistence on offering responsible alternative solutions kept him silent for nearly a year. A group of men who once had accepted the administration's policies and had changed, men such as Clark Clifford, Cyrus Vance and Averell Harriman, were advising him. He talked to everyone he could find with ideas on Vietnam and found none of them satisfactory.

On an airplane for Boston one afternoon in late September 1969, Muskie used a man flying with him as a bouncing board for these questions. Setting his companion up, Muskie asked, "What would you do about Vietnam? Given that you were President and had to decide, what would you do?" Predictably the man said, "I'd get out." It was the answer Muskie had sought; he glared and said, "Oh, yes. My, isn't that easy. With just a snap of your fingers, I suppose."

But it was rather different, he thought, if you actually aspired to responsible leadership. Then, in a long monologue, he pursued the complications. It's much easier to make a decision than to unmake one; unmaking a decision has immense consequences, and the longer one delays, the greater the consequences. It may be comfortable to say that nothing matters so much as recognizing the fundamental error of going in and therefore the fundamental solution of getting out, but in fact other things *do* matter. Those commitments that now are so widely dismissed as meaningless were made in good faith with the expectations they would be honored.

Over the years, Muskie continued, our course of action no doubt should have changed, but it didn't. We have to change, should have changed before, but what effect will it have on the people of South Vietnam, on Japan, the Philippines, Thailand? Are there points for staying in another month? Three months? Six months? Is there still a chance for some sort of compromise? If you decide to get out, do you announce it? Do you set a date? Will your last troops have to fight their way to the troopships, and if they do, do you go back in? If you're guilty of fundamental error, does simply reversing it correct it? Perhaps getting out also is fundamental error. It could have untold consequences down the line. Two fundamental errors don't make a right and it's as serious to turn from one error as to make the first. So how do you decide the right course even if you agree you're on the wrong?

Well, his companion interjected sententiously, there comes a time when—at which Muskie, suddenly angry, snapped, "Goddammit, I'm not asking for a lesson in political courage, I'm talking about the realities."

After a long silence, he added, "Sometimes, you know, I set people up in positions I want to take and then I tear the hell out of them."

About three weeks later, on October 15, 1969, Vietnam Moratorium Day, Muskie made his first public break with the administration, present and past, on the war. He raised for the first time in public his doubt of the war's basic premise, that it was fought to resist external aggression instead of to take sides in a civil war. In that speech he said he believed we should disengage our forces in an orderly fashion as soon as possible, and that we should do so in such a way as to promote a negotiated settlement and to give the South Vietnamese time to adjust to our moves. We should, in other words, get out, but not so precipitately as to leave in chaos all the problems our coming had set in motion. He endorsed Clark Clifford's plan for removing U.S. ground combat forces by the end of 1970 and continuing logistical and air support for a somewhat longer period.

Thereafter, Muskie's position moved steadily into what was solidifying as the liberal Democratic posture. In 1970 he co-sponsored the McGovern-Hatfield resolution to end the war. In March he challenged the President in a National Press Club speech to focus on a negotiated rather than a military end to the war. In May he offered a resolution of his own in the Senate calling for the orderly removal of all American forces by the end of 1971. He condemned the Laos and Cambodia actions. In 1971 he co-sponsored McGovern-Hatfield again and was a leader in the Senate Democratic Caucus resolution demanding withdrawal—in effect offering the President bipartisan backing for getting out of Vietnam. Muskie went into the 1972 campaign aligned on the war with other liberals, leaving the date of his conversion the only arguing point.

The key to his change still was factual. Once the premises

of the war failed, all failed. Once one saw internal civil war instead of Korea-like external aggression, once the idea of saving people became preposterous when it was necessary to destroy them to do so, once the concept of the monolithic ideological enemy collapsed, the only valid question left was how and under what circumstances and with what effect do we get out?

In early 1971 Muskie said, "This train of thought began at about the time I wrote that first letter to the President urging the unilateral cessation of bombing. I concluded that continuing military pressure was not the way to resolve it, that the thing was to reduce military pressure in order to induce the other side to negotiation." He said he had no total program then, but "I certainly was clear that it required a change of direction, so I think there's a logical progression in my positions, from unilateral cessation of bombing to the resolve to get out, to the acceptance of a definite date to do so, to publication of that date—I think they were progressive steps."

He has come to see the issue in moral terms. "Well, the morality of it has to do with an unjustified interference in the affairs of a small country that was helpless to avoid our interference once it built up a certain momentum. And that interference has just completely destroyed the indigenous character, society, economy; they can never return to it. That is the morality of the question, whatever the decency of our motives, the effect was wrong."

But, he added, "After you recognize the mistake, does that give you the corrective? It isn't just the question of what happens to those people physically. We've disrupted a whole society, pulled it right out of its track. Would just leaving put that society back on a track that services its people? Maybe there's no way of putting it back. If we did that society a wrong, we have an obligation to do what we can to right it. We're assuming that continued military involvement has nothing to do with righting it for them, but is that a correct judgment? We always assume that helping the South Vietnamese to heal their society means technical assistance and economics; maybe that isn't enough.

"Well, you toss all these things in the air and take your choice as they come down, so I've taken my choice; but can I really be sure I'm right, whether by moral or pragmatic standards, in terms of achieving something that's on the plus side for the South Vietnamese against all the negatives that we helped put into their lives? I don't know, I don't really have a sense of moral well-being. You feel decisive, you decide we ought to be out by the end of this year, you know it's clean and clear; is it right? It may or may not be, but the answer is not so clear-cut as to make me feel that I have suddenly found the fundamental truth about it all. I don't get any more satisfaction from the feeling that I'm right now than I did when I supported the Johnson policies with all the reservations I had. I suppose there are those who feel their souls swept through with a fresh breeze when they take such a decision. I haven't had that feeling. I can't be that sure. I don't think anybody can."

At Portland State University in Portland, Ore., someone asked Muskie in mid-1971 for his position on Vietnam and then asked why he didn't have it in 1968. "Well," Muskie said, "I didn't. And I'm not about to try to rewrite history." He sketched out all those premises that he had once accepted and now rejects. He had had misgivings, he said, but he had not expressed them loud enough; if he had known then what he knows now, he would have. He thinks the position he now holds is the right one, but, "If you want to judge me on the basis of that historical inconsistency, that is your right and I wouldn't quarrel with you."

Muskie's slowness to come to a position on Vietnam was just another point in his reputation for caution and procrastination which has dogged him since he became nationally prominent. He is deliberate and cautious, but the quality is more important for the larger question, which is why he didn't move earlier on great national issues. The answer lies partly in his odd patterns of growth. He was growing steadily in his own arena, which was the internal workings of the Senate. He was from a small state, without the constituency, the staff or the range of interests provided by states like New York and California. He had no call on the great group constituencies like organized labor. He was given uninteresting committees and it was his nature to stay with them.

In the Senate, Muskie once said, "You lead where you have committee responsibilities, and I've got a leadership record in those areas—the urban area, pollution, intergovernmental relations." To lead in other areas is difficult, for senators guard their preserves and one needs committee-staff help to develop expertise. For years Muskie's staff numbered about a dozen and it cared not only for Maine and constituent problems but for much of his committee work. Muskie had asked for Foreign Affairs at the start and again a couple of years later. In the mid-1960s a seat was open, but by then he was deep in other things, which is why he didn't join the committee until 1971.

After the 1968 election there was talk of his challenging Russell B. Long of Louisiana for Majority Whip. It's doubtful that Muskie could have won; he said at the time that he thought it a poor place from which to pursue national ambitions. Done well, Senate leadership ties a man down, as Johnson found in 1960. The incident would have been unnoticed except that Ted Kennedy, whose political weight then was greater than Muskie's, challenged Long and won. That led to talk of Muskie avoiding the fight; but as it happened, Kennedy spent little time on the job and two years later lost ignominiously to Robert Byrd of West Virginia, who is no national leader. As a factor for judging Muskie, the whole affair was insignificant.

Muskie represents a conservative state and this may have been the clearest brake on his national leadership before 1968. He has been working for years to make Maine's public opinion more liberal and bit by bit he has been succeeding. "I guess my first real act in the Senate was when I had been here a couple of months and we wrote a housing bill in Banking and Currency. Eisenhower had vetoed one in the previous Congress and we had another one out the second month I was there. We voted it, the President vetoed it and I voted to override the veto. And I got a hell of a beating editorially in Maine because Maine public opinion just didn't support that kind of program. But now public opinion there has turned around, it is wholly for legislation in this field, Model Cities, Urban Renewal. I changed opinion up there and it was tough to do, too.

"But you know, Maine people have always regarded me as more liberal than they are. Polls in 1970 showed some sixty-five percent of them thought I was more liberal than they, and still they support me. I guess if one hundred percent thought that, I wouldn't be here. And that's my constituency. After all, I was a senator, not a candidate for President, I didn't have any constituency except my own, and I had to move my own people to more liberal views. People criticize me now for compromises, say I've given too much or I could have gotten more. How the hell does anybody know if that's true? But I look back over the last seventeen years and all I can see is that Maine public opinion has moved dramatically."

6

The
Candidate II

In January 1970 Muskie held a crucial meeting. Through 1969 he had tested the water with a tentative air, moving about in frustration, insisting on applying the thoroughness of his narrow Senate years to the broad field now before him, refusing to accept financial backing, being not quite a real candidate. Just before Thanksgiving, 1969, his advisers met and decided that Muskie had to organize a serious bid for the Presidential nomination soon or forget it. He agreed somewhat reluctantly and called the January meeting. It was at Berl Bernhard's house, and it included Clark Clifford, Averell Harriman, Paul Warnke, Jack Valenti, Harry McPherson, David Tillinghast, Don Nicoll and Matt Lifflander, a New York attorney who long had been close to Muskie.

The meeting was curiously formal. Muskie began by saying he was faced with the decision of becoming an undeclared candidate and the question was, was it worthwhile? "The question really was," Lifflander said later, "would they support him? Muskie's beautiful—he doesn't talk politics, he does politics."

Harriman interrupted and after that Muskie hardly spoke. Harriman said he was the one in the room who should worry; he was the oldest and he didn't want to die with Richard Nixon in office. He said he thought Muskie could beat Nixon and that he should; Muskie had his support. They went around the room, each man agreeing. Referring to the early strength Nixon then was showing, Clifford reminded them of Harry Truman's polls in 1948 and said that if Muskie could get the nomination there was no question that it had value. At the end Muskie thanked them and said he would try. He had made the key decision, which separated the past of his life from all that would follow: he agreed to start raising money for the campaign.

This was the turning point because a man cannot function as a Presidential candidate without the staff, the national organization and the communications that are beyond the financing ability of any individual who is not very rich. Once the man takes money he is a candidate with all a candidate's responsibilities; he can quit, but he cannot turn back. And a man who has been a candidate for the Presidency can never again be what he was before.

Once again, Muskie surged from being a senator to a handsome national candidate in a few weeks in the 1968 campaign. For most of 1969, however, he expanded only slightly because he had not determined that the way was open or, more properly, that he intended to force the way open. When he decided, he immediately began to grow again at a pace that suited the opportunity. First there was the Maine campaign to be settled because that was still his constituency and it was a test that professionals all over the country would watch. Afterward there were his staff problems, on which he waited dangerously long but eventually acted effectively.

He became more attuned to the national electorate. He still cared—he will always care—about the commonsense view of Maine, but now he spoke as a national figure. In 1969, for instance, Muskie had allowed the fact that Margaret Chase Smith spoke first against the nomination of Clement Haynsworth to the Supreme Court to deter him from speaking. He doesn't like to follow Mrs. Smith, but obviously at that point he was more aware of Maine than of the nation. Less than a year later, however, he was on a chartered airliner bound for Jackson, Miss., and while it was an unusually vivid move that one may suspect left Muskie not fully comfortable, it certainly was not done with an eye on Maine, where his supporters have been complaining about it ever since.

Muskie did not abandon thoroughness, but he expanded his concept of it. In years past, he personally wrote the legislation he offered. As the pressures grew he let others do the writing, though he attended all the meetings and made the decisions. Gradually he reduced his participation to the basic meetings that determined what the legislation was to accomplish and then he reviewed the finished product. He still controlled the machinery but he let the machinery do the work. His approach to the Senate itself also expanded. He used his new authority and political muscle to pass an abundance of tough new legislation. He involved himself in tax matters, stockbroker responsibility, health affairs, welfare problems. He had been a foot soldier in the 1964 Civil Rights Act but he was a leader in Proxmire's 1970 fight to scuttle the SST. In late 1971, as an alternative to Nixon's plan for stimulating the economy through tax credits for business investment, Muskie developed and presented an ingenious plan for giving consumers tax credits "of up to $100 annually toward the purchase of major consumer durables." Columnist Joseph Kraft described the "striking and manifold" advantages of this plan and pointed out that "since millions of individual taxpayers would be the beneficiaries rather than corporations, it would be less of a giveaway to the rich," and would have a more immediate and direct effect on the economy. In the middle of 1971 Muskie made a radical break with the past: he began ignoring Senate routine. He paid close attention to important legislation, his own and others', but he stopped worrying about his record on roll-call votes and only hurried back to Washington for a vote when he thought the issue worth it. This was a real departure for a man who had always seen his Senate duties as primary and rigid.

Through his new seat on Foreign Relations, he involved himself in international affairs. In early 1971 he made a sweeping visit to Moscow and Bonn and to Tel Aviv and Cairo. After long talks with West German Chancellor Willy Brandt, who was in the midst of his great shift in relations with the East, Muskie changed his position on U.S. troop levels in Germany and later voted against Mansfield's resolution calling for a reduction. As chairman of the Subcommittee on Arms Control and International Organization, Muskie challenged the administration to take new initiatives toward negotiating a comprehensive nuclear test-ban treaty, noting, "Recent progress in seismic means of detection requires a reassessment of the need for on-site inspection, the primary obstacle to such a treaty in the past." After his talks with leaders in Cairo and Tel Aviv, he went on record for maintaining the balance of power in the Middle East through an adequate arms level for Israel. He backed Israel's request for more F-4 Phantom jets and said he feared "the military balance has been shifting in the last year against Israel." He said he believes the security of the United States and of Israel is interrelated and that this should be the foundation of U.S. policy. "A lasting peace will result only from negotiations by the parties directly involved. The United States must do nothing to undermine Israel's bargaining position."

Sometime in mid-1971, Muskie seemed to catch his stride. Men traveling with him after an absence of a few months noticed a somewhat intangible difference. He was more assured, authoritative and relaxed. His schedule was harder but he managed it better and was less exhausted. He was warmer and more intimate with crowds and caught their interest most readily. The old restraint that sometimes produced a counterrestraint in crowds was fading. His organization was far from perfect, but it was professional and extensive. He had representatives in nearly every state, and working staff in the major primary states. In the fall he even

chartered his own airplane, a four-engine turboprop Electra re-
fitted from airliner to campaign plane. He also was lining up
political support—governors, senators, congressmen, mayors,
local leaders. There was little of the threats and pressure associated with John F. Kennedy's moves in 1959, but Muskie did not
hesitate to tell men that his bandwagon was rolling and the first
ones on got the best seats.

As he grew, his tone and the things he said were harder and
more pointed. He flew into Puerto Rico to address the National
Governor's Conference on the day that New York police stormed
the state prison at Attica causing the immediate deaths of twenty-
eight inmates and nine hostages (the final death count was
higher). Muskie had prepared a speech on revenue sharing; he
gathered his staff in a hotel room and they spent most of the
night on a new speech. The next day Muskie told the surprised
governors that we cannot yet judge the events at Attica, "but in
our sorrow we can ponder how and why we have reached the
point where men would rather die than live in America." That
was a stinger that governors had hardly expected from the quiet
man from Maine. Muskie continued, "The Attica tragedy is more
stark proof that something is terribly wrong in America. How
many of us are really ready to face that truth? Not many . . ."
And he added, "The system has not failed—but some of us have
failed the system."

He had come a long way from 1969.

There is an increasing feeling that America, and probably
the world as well, has entered into one of those great historical
transitions in which rapid change is the order and old ideas and
attitudes will not hold. In such a situation, the man who leads had
better be prepared. One cannot discuss literally how a man would
respond to change when its terms are still unknown, but the
threat of change has run through Muskie's career, beginning with
his dragging Maine into modern times by its own bootstraps.
Much of his work in the Senate has focused on change which

begins quietly but is likely to become increasingly startling. The pollution legislation, for instance, introduced the idea of setting standards for the environment which in itself was a huge battle. Great change follows because standards imply policing to maintain them. We have been regulating individuals or individual entities for years, doctors, or utilities or corporations, but this involves restraining masses of people from doing what individually seems merely the exercise of the oldest rights but collectively becomes something like mass suicide. When the day comes, certain in a few years, that Manhattan or Baltimore or Los Angeles must limit the number of cars on its streets to maintain a certain quality of air, we will be in a whole new era of handling massive public problems.

We are simply going to have to change the way we live, Muskie once said. "It may be, for instance, that by 1980 we'll have to prohibit the use of the internal combustion engine or maybe ban it in metropolitan areas. And the pressure will be on to develop new kinds of power plants for individual automobiles, electric or steam or some new form not yet developed . . . We ought to be monitoring the developing of all new consumer products, whether in pesticides or new forms of transportation, so that we have a way to check these products that add to the pollution load. The aluminum beer can is an example, a non-biodegradable product developed because of consumer appetite and the desire for greater profits. That's the toughest part of the problem in a free enterprise society, but we're going to have to do it."

The central thrust of Muskie's revenue-sharing plans, beyond putting money where it is desperately needed, is to change the patterns that have separated cities and suburbs. "The problem of the cities fundamentally," Muskie once said, "is that the resources of these great metropolitan areas are not being adequately applied to the problems of people. And what are the roadblocks? They include the present political subdivisions of these cities which are used to build places of refuge for those who resist change and to imprison those who need change and to hamper the efforts of those who are trying to bring about change in orderly, rational ways." Another time he remarked, "We're going to have to rearrange cities, not just for environment problems but for people problems. We're going to have to restructure cities, break down jurisdictional boundaries that divide the central cities from the suburbs; we're going to have to restructure housing patterns and employment patterns and all the rest of it . . ."

Muskie's refusal to dominate the Democratic Party in Maine dovetails with the reforms dictated nationally since the 1968 convention. At the national level, party reformers fought a hard battle in October 1971 to name Senator Harold E. Hughes chairman of the Credentials Committee at the 1972 Democratic National Convention. The committee, of course, will examine the extent to which state delegations have complied with the new rules. Somewhat uncharacteristically, in that he rarely interferes in Maine political fights, Muskie backed Hughes emphatically. He sent two of his chief political operatives to lobby for Hughes with individual committeemen, which irritated party regulars. When Hughes was soundly beaten by the regulars' candidate, Mrs. Patricia Harris, it appeared to be a defeat for Muskie as well, though he may have earned a claim on Hughes for help in the future. On the other hand, he declared plainly where he stood. It has become a cliché which Muskie finds immensely irritating to accuse him of being unwilling "to break his lance" in a cause; this time he broke his lance.

Another theme that has run through Muskie's career and his legislation is the idea of opening institutions, government and private, to common people. In a period when monopoly, reliance on electronic data processing, sophisticated manipulation of power and plain bigness have closed government and institutions more than ever, this represents real and important change. Many political observers believe this is one of the critical keys for holding the future together. Fred Dutton, in his book *Changing Sources of Power,* notes that "Power is rarely shared willingly, but this country could risk the dangers of instability and repression for a very prolonged period if it does not open up and share much more than presently is the case."

Muskie's campaign in 1954 and his governorship was predicated on bringing people into preserves that had belonged to politicians. His pollution legislation includes provisions to give local people a voice in local decisions. There are elaborate mechanisms for open hearings and appeals. Part of the Nader task force's criticism of his 1967 air bill was that these provisions institutionalized delay, and of course they do; Muskie thinks the virtue worth the delay.

The same concept is basic to his intergovernmental-relations legislation. His original complaint about the Model Cities Bill was the complicated nature of its mechanism for giving the people who lived in the area a voice in how change was to be made. Upon taking over the bill, he immediately rewrote those provisions. He introduced the Corporate Participation Act, which gave minority stockholders a voice in corporate decisions that have social implications; this bill influenced his endorsement of Campaign GM, a movement that most people associated with radicals.

Change relates directly to how we are to function overseas. The effect of bureaucratic and military momentum in Vietnam and the power of the military-industrial complex urges new directions. Muskie believes one of the answers to the problem is in opening the decision-making process. One reason he opposes the all-volunteer army is that he believes the draft acts as a brake on any President's adventurism. Of Vietnam, he once said, "As a people we didn't understand what we were getting involved in, didn't appreciate its consequences and suddenly we were in over our heads." Perhaps it was a lesson we had to learn, he said, but it certainly argues for selectivity in the future. We should have "a more open process of communication about these things. We've tended to regard national security as something that could be understood by only a handful of people at the top of government, decisions to be made in closed rooms. These are delicate questions, but what we've got to understand is that if we want public support for these policies, then we must take people into our confidence..."

Muskie's flow of ideas and his willingness to discuss them freely are basic to the leadership he offers. But offering leadership can be frustrating, for it is always difficult to project across the entire country. Muskie's speech on Attica was an example; he was outraged and he said so, and by chance he was on the platform offered by the Governors Conference and therefore was well-covered by press and television. It was, he said later, "a chance to dramatize a broad question, and I took it."

That too is part of leadership: one must be ready for opportunities. The Election Eve speech was another side of leadership, for it could easily have failed. The mere television time, the guaranteed audience, *mano a mano* with the President, did not assure its success. It could have been a disaster before so huge an audience and could have killed Muskie's hopes in a single stroke. A man who can't seize these opportunities and act on them probably won't be visible enough to be counted a leader. And yet, a leader can't afford a violent tone very often, lest he become strident and wear out what he has to say. One reason that Muskie's speech on Attica drew attention is that he does not often speak in such bitter language. The times are full of bitter rhetoricians and people seem weary of them.

In the end, therefore, one doesn't really seize leadership. Even while taking advantage of the opportunities, the putative leader spends most of his time moving around, talking to small audiences, being seen on local television and written about in local newspapers, taking positions on great issues and trying to be sure that he dominates his own field of expertise. If he has a theme, gradually the sense of what he is or is becoming settles in people's understanding.

The theme that Muskie strikes is simple and natural. He believes that he can bring people together, that he has qualities of mind and nature and attitude and style that are attractive and reassuring to a wide range of different kinds of people, often people who have little use for each other.

For some time, Muskie has been talking about a coalition of interests. It has become popular, he once observed, to believe that the key to political success lies in exploiting the so-called "social issue." Muskie thinks that short-sighted and erroneous. So he has gone about the country talking to blacks about the problems of poor whites, to whites about the torment of blacks, to the old about the ideals of the young, to the young about the fears of the old. On Oct. 6, 1971, Muskie spoke to a Liberal Party dinner meeting in New York City. He talked about "the failure of American liberalism," and in doing so gave a good view of his own political theme.

"The blunt truth is," he said, "that liberals have achieved virtually no fundamental change in our society since the end of the New Deal . . . If the liberal mission has any overriding obligation, it is to enlist enough of our people to make change a reality and not just a rallying cry. And if we truly care about the character of American life, how can we ever find satisfaction in the righteous conviction that everyone else is wrong?

"Never again can we justify teach-ins in which liberals talk to themselves and agree with each other. We should talk to the country—to hard hats and housewives and clerks—to men and women who will support liberal principles if those principles give them programs they can trust. . . .

"Our task . . . is to build a consensus for liberal change in America . . . rooted in the recognition that the hopes of most Americans are liberal hopes—a consensus that can vindicate liberal ideals by appealing to the common interests of different people."

The other side of confrontation and controversy, Muskie believes, is creativity; in a time of ferment we are shaking out our attitudes, reexamining our values, developing new relationships, and how we land will determine our future. Thus the test of a free people: can we survive troubled times and remain free?

People don't trust their leaders but they want to: Muskie believes they are hungry for men in whom they can believe and wary of men who try to divide them. They want to be reassured that values by which they live and which grow from their common past are still relevant. They want to know that change won't destroy them as it reshapes institutions, and until they know that they cannot respond wisely and well. "You cannot expect people to behave always as though they were gods," Muskie once said.

Muskie thinks in terms of programs. He likes them and believes in them. But programs are the mechanics of leadership; the leader's vision is its driving force. Every leader's inspiration is his own, and rarely do his words reproduce satisfactorily on paper. But one night in Hartford in early 1971 Muskie caught extemporaneous fire and said what he is about as well as he ever had or is ever likely to:

"I visited what is called the cradle of civilization, circling what was the Roman world, visiting the ancient places of Israel and Egypt and Moscow and Germany. And I talked with the leaders and what I sensed in these four places which generate some of the most explosive issues of our time is the restlessness of the dreams which are moving people to seek better lives. If governments articulate policies which threaten war, it's because they feel the pressure from their people. If governments articulate positions which seem intransigent, it's because they feel the pressure of their people. If governments change their policies in ways that are incomprehensible to us, it is because they feel the pressures of their people.

"If we seek the pressures which can move mankind toward the uplands of peace and justice, we must find them in the *people* of this planet. They do not want war. They do not want misery. They do not want fear. They do not want hatred and suspicion and distrust. But they do not yet have it within their power to eliminate the conditions which breed such hatred, such instability and such unrest. But they have ways of bringing pressure upon their government and their countries' policies.

"What the leaders—the enlightened leaders—of this planet must somehow identify are the policies, the goals, the ideals which can mobilize the teeming masses of humanity behind the policies of wisdom and restraint and enlightened choice and understanding.

"Impossible? When one looks at the fact that Jesus and Mohammed and the other great religious leaders have not yet persuaded man to commit himself to such ideals, then perhaps political leaders presume too much when they accept the burden of the same responsibility. But it *is* the same responsibility. And if we are to achieve this kind of life, which is the only kind that holds the potential of livability for the earth, then not only God's spokesmen but man's leaders must aspire to the same ideals and objectives.

"And it may be that in this year we finally see mankind moving toward the ultimate crunch when he either chooses that path or the path of total destruction and annihilation. It may be that our human fallibilities and weaknesses and short-comings are too great for us to reach this far. But to reach for them is the most exhilarating experience that can come to a society, to its leaders, to its government. It is this kind of response to the restless urgings of deprived and hungry people—and that includes most of God's children—that can revitalize and reinvigorate the purpose of organized institutions on this planet. That's the nature of our challenge. It's not often well articulated. And it gets lost in the grubby nuts and bolts of government organization, revenue-sharing plans, reforms of the federal structure—and these are all essential chores. But as we apply ourselves to them, let's not lose sight of the ultimate purpose of it all and that is to make life better for God's children on this planet. There is no other challenge. There is no other job.

"Unless we have some sense of the sacredness and the

enormity of that challenge and are willing to gird ourselves for it, we will not meet it. And we will have lost everything. But in striving for it, we can achieve something that we've achieved so many times in this blessed land of America, and that is an awareness from time to time that we've made more progress toward it than man has ever seen before and that the progress we have made in the past is the promise that we can do more in the future.

"That is the task to which I would like to apply myself and intend to for as long as I am given any political responsibility whatsoever."

Pragmatism alone is no virtue; the totally practical man is useless, for he has no concept of sacrifice. At heart, Muskie is just the opposite, an idealist who approaches his ends in practical ways. More than it has for decades, the country needs a warm man in whom it can trust, an idealist who can get things done; the test of Muskie's leadership will be whether he can persuade the American people that he is that man.